Authentication of Hadith
Redefining the Criteria

DEDICATED TO MY WIFE, SHAHNAZ BEGUM

An ideal Muslim woman in my life

AUTHENTICATION OF HADITH

Redefining the Criteria

•

ISRAR AHMAD KHAN

THE INTERNATIONAL INSTITUTE OF ISLAMIC THOUGHT
LONDON • WASHINGTON

THE INTERNATIONAL INSTITUTE OF ISLAMIC THOUGHT
P.O. BOX 669, HERNDON, VA 20172, USA
WWW.IIIT.ORG

LONDON OFFICE
P.O. BOX 126, RICHMOND, SURREY TW9 2UD, UK
WWW.IIITUK.COM

ISBN 978-1-56564-448-9 paperback
ISBN 978-1-56564-449-6 hardback

Typesetting and cover design by Shiraz Khan
Printed by MPG Books Group, UK

ACKNOWLEDGEMENT

All praise is due to Allah alone. It is He alone to Whom I stand indebted for this work. He willed that I should will and by His infinite grace, I willed. Allah, then, helped me to take the task to its completion.

My thanks to The Research Management Centre, International Islamic University Malaysia (IIUM), which sponsored my research projects that now form the 3rd, 4th, 5th, 6th, and 8th chapters of this book. I am deeply grateful to its Dean, Deputy Deans, Directors, Assistant Directors, and other officials for their timely and generous help which I needed for the completion of the research projects.

Associate Professor Dr. Hazizan M. Noon, Dean of the Faculty of Islamic Revealed Knowledge and Human Sciences, IIUM, deserves my thanks first for approval of my research proposal and for inspiring me to continue my research on the subject.

Professor Dr. Muhammad Nejatullah Siddiqi, Professor Dr. Ibrahim M. Zain, Associate Professor Dr. Jamal Basheir Badi, and Dr. Muhammad Tahir Mesawi who encouraged me, advised me, and shared with me their observations on my work. I am extremely grateful to them all.

Dr. Jamal Barzinji, Vice President of the International Institute of Islamic Thought (IIIT USA), greatly inspired me with his willingness to publish the work. May Allah bless him!

My wife, Shahnaz Begum, my four daughters, Mariya Seemin, Juwayriya Naznin, Naeylah Zarrin, Hamnah Sheerin, and my five sons, Muaaz, Muawwiz, Yasir, Samrah, and Owaym. Throughout my difficult task they all supported me in both words and practice, remaining ever patient and encouraging, never putting the slightest burden on me and shielding me from any pressures, adverse or otherwise, that could have impacted on my work. I pray to Allah for their well being in this world and in the hereafter. *Āmīn.*

CONTENTS

Foreword ix
Introduction xiii

[CHAPTER 1] Fabrication in Prophetic Traditions: Causal Factors and Remedial Measures 1

[CHAPTER 2] The Contribution of Muslim Scholars to the Authentication of Hadith 28

[CHAPTER 3] The Qur'an and Authentication of Hadith 46

[CHAPTER 4] Authentication of Hadith Through Rationally Authentic Traditions 72

[CHAPTER 5] Authentication of Hadith Through Sound Reasoning 85

[CHAPTER 6] Authentication of Hadith Through Established History 118

[CHAPTER 7] Moderation in Relation to Authentication of Hadith 127

[CHAPTER 8] Al-Bukhārī's Chapter on Predetermination: An Evaluation and Interpretation 139

Notes 189
Bibliography 205
Index 208

Usage of the Word "Tradition" to Denote Hadith and Sunnah

Readers will note that the author has often used the word "tradition/s" in lieu of the more familiar Arabic terms, Hadith and Sunnah. General readers may feel confused over this usage but this is a convention that has been adopted by both Muslim scholars of Hadith as well as Orientalists. Further, the International Islamic University Malaysia (IIUM), considered a pioneer in introducing many religious disciplines, including Hadith Studies, into English, commonly employs the term to signify Hadith and Sunnah. English dictionaries in addition define the term "tradition" similarly in this context for example, "(in Islam) a saying or act ascribed to the Prophet but not recorded in the Koran. See HADITH" (*The New Oxford Dictionary of English,* Oxford: Clarendon Press, 1998). Finally some English-Arabic dictionaries define "tradition" as *al-Hadīth al-Sharīf* (e.g. Munir Baʿalbaki, *Al-Mawrid*, Beirut: Dār al-ʿIlm li al-Malāyīn, 1998).

FOREWORD

بسم الله الرحمن الرحيم

Of knowledge, we have none, save what
You have taught us. (The Qur'an 2:32)

The International Institute of Islamic Thought (IIIT) presents this scholarly work on the topic of *Authentication of Hadith: Redefining the Criteria* to cast new light on the issue of Hadith fabrication.

Israr Khan addresses the sensitive topic of Hadith authentication, focusing on the criteria adopted by compilers of the major collections to argue that concentration on the continuity and accuracy of the chain of narrators, rather than the textual content of Hadith, has led to certain *aḥādīth* being included which either contradict other *aḥādīth* directly, project the Prophet (ṢAAS)[*] in an uncharacteristic light, or do not reflect and/or conflict with the teachings of the Qur'an. Furthermore, he maintains, given the great mass of traditions which circulated soon after the Prophet passed away, it would be unwise to ignore the fact that many contained targeted forgeries. These not only intended to corrupt the essential message of the Faith but also to bolster political, sectarian, economic, and even theological support. Political as well as religious differences, motivated largely by rivalry towards the fledgling Faith, led to a sustained and well-known campaign of disinformation using the vehicle of Hadith.

Although the misuse and abuse of Hadith is nothing new, in today's complex and volatile world the consequences of relying on fraudulent and counterfeit Hadith to legitimise extremist behavior, justify blatant abuse, particularly of women, and issue disturbing fatwas calling for violent acts, is not only far too easy but in fact very dangerous. In addition, given the widespread anti-Islamic sentiment currently dominating

---

* (ṢAAS) – *Ṣallā Allāhu ʿalayhi wa sallam*. May the peace and blessings of God be upon him. Said whenever the name of Prophet Muhammad is mentioned.

mainstream discourse, it is imperative that the issue of fabricated *aḥādīth*, extensively publicised and ruthlessly exploited to support the thesis of Islamic violence and backwardness, is addressed. It is consequently the responsibility of Muslim scholars well versed in the Islamic sciences, to root out with honesty and courage those *aḥādīth* which have clearly been fabricated, and which not only invite spurious interpretation but also perpetuate ignorance betraying both the Qur'an and the Prophet.

Any serious study of the content and scope of these traditions must necessarily start at the beginning, in this instance after the death of the Prophet Muhammad. The author traces in precise and careful detail the historical development of the oral and written traditions, as well as the many targeted attempts at fabrication that took place, critiquing in methodical detail certain *aḥādīth* which have come to be widely accepted as "authentic." In any matter of dispute concerning the Hadith, the Qur'an must be the final arbiter. As such, notes the author, any hadith which seems to go against the Qur'an must be examined carefully and accurately, and if no interpretation to resolve the contradiction found, it is to be rejected. Further, as Muhammad was the Last Prophet sent to all mankind, interpretations of both the Qur'an and Hadith are not to be fixated in time, but rather to be carefully examined and reinterpreted to give practical guidance meeting the requirements and challenges of a new age, that is taking into account the time-space factor. It is here that the science of *maqāṣid al-sharīʿah*, or the higher intents and purposes of Islamic law, comes into its own as the heart and philosophy of Islamic Law.

So, to answer the difficult question of whether there is any real need for research into Hadith authentication we must realistically, and in the footsteps of Islam's best scholastic tradition, answer yes. The pursuit of greater accuracy is in no way meant to undermine Muslim confidence in Hadith. Far from it. It is from Hadith, maintains the author, that the life of the Prophet Muhammad has been taken from memory and brought to life, the great forms of Islamic worship and prayer codified, and the foundations of the Sunnah laid. Moreover, the prominent collections we have today, were made possible by the development of the science of Hadith criticism, and Muslim scholars deserve deep appreciation not only for their painstaking work, but also their invaluable contribution towards preserving the Hadith literature to the best of their ability. However, insists the author, the process is ongoing, and the closed door policy which currently seems to surround Hadith authentication needs careful and systematic reexamination. It is in this vein that he attempts in *Authentication of Hadith* to redefine the criteria used to check traditions, and to then apply this criteria to certain selected *aḥādīth* recorded. His work has added a valuable and useful contemporary and scholarly dimension to the study of Hadith literature.

This study has been published to widen discourse, invite scholars to respond, and hopefully pave the way for further research. Doubtless readers may agree with some of the issues raised, and also disagree with others, but it is hoped that for the most part both general and specialised readers will benefit from the perspective offered and the overall issues examined in the book.

Since its establishment in 1981, the IIIT has continued to serve as a major center to facilitate sincere and serious scholarly efforts, based on Islamic vision, values and principles. Its programs of research, and seminars and conferences, during the last twenty-eight years, have resulted in the publication of more than four hundred titles in both English, Arabic and other major languages.

We would like to express our thanks to the editorial and production team at the IIIT London Office and all those who were directly or indirectly involved in the completion of this work. We would also like to express our thanks to the author, who, throughout the various stages of production, cooperated closely with the editorial team.

IIIT London Office
Muharram 1431 AH, January 2010

Introduction

The Status and Importance of Hadith in Islam

ISLAM'S SYSTEM OF BELIEF, thought, life activities, social order, economic rules, political regulations, cultural bounds, moral principles, educational norms, intellectual codes, and religious laws are all governed by the Qur'an and the Hadith. The Qur'an represents the precisely revealed words of Allah (SWT)* and the Hadith constitute the practical and methodological dimensions of the Qur'anic commands and instructions.

The Prophet Muhammad, as the Messenger of God, had to carry out a fourfold mission (62:2): (1) to rehearse the messages of the Qur'an to people in general and to his followers in particular, exactly as he received them from God (2) to transform the whole nation of Arabia conceptually as well as behaviorally (3) to unfold the truth revealed in the Qur'an and (4) to demonstrate Qur'anic principles practically in his life the and to teach those who entered the fold of his faith. For these heavy and manifold responsibilities he needed the guidance of God and was vouchsafed two things, the Qur'an and its *Bayān*, that is its explanation or meaning:

> Move not thy tongue in haste, [repeating the words of the revelation:] for, behold, it is for Us to gather it [in thy heart,] and to cause it to be read [as it ought to be read]. Thus, when We recite it, follow thou its wording [with all thy mind]: and then, behold, it will be for Us to make its meaning (*Bayānahu*) clear. (75:16–19)

---

* (SWT) – *Subḥānahu wa Taʿālā*: May He be praised and may His transcendence be affirmed. Said when referring to God.

The Qur'an contains the precisely revealed words of Allah and the *Bayān* is the demonstration of the Qur'an by the Prophet. The *Bayān* of the Qur'an is what is known in Islamic legacy as the Hadith and the Sunnah. The status of the Hadith and the Sunnah in Islamic life is actually the position of the Prophet, meaning that today, when we talk about the Hadith and the Sunnah we actually deal with the Prophet. The Prophet held certain positions such as final judge, guide etc. and since he is no longer with us, his sayings and doings will be looked at from the same angle.

- Blessings of Allah cover those who obey Allah and His Prophet (3:132).
- His obedience is incumbent on his followers (4:59).
- He is a judge in all disputes of life (4:65).
- Deliberate indifference to obedience to Allah and His Prophet forms a serious offence (8:12–25).
- Avoidance of Allah and His Apostle's guidance ultimately leads to failure in life (8:46).
- Disregard of the instructions of Allah and His Apostle causes the deeds of man to become meaningless (47:33).

The Approach of Contemporary Muslims to Hadith

In terms of their approach to Hadith Muslims may be classified into four categories: (1) Those who totally reject the relevance of Hadith in Islamic life. (2) Those who fall blindly into accepting everything that appears to be a hadith regardless of its authenticity. (3) Those who make indiscriminate selection from Hadith for practical purposes. (4) Those who believe in the sanctity of the Prophetic traditions but opt for an extremely careful approach with regard to their logical and practical relevance to Islamic life and civilization.

Of all the categories those in the fourth seem to be the most justly balanced between the extremes. For those in category one, total rejection of Hadith as an important source of Islamic life-values is in sheer conflict with the Qur'an's own statements. In a number of places in the Qur'an Allah commands the believers to: "Obey Allah and obey the Prophet" (e.g. 4:59). Obedience to Allah is to follow the instructions enshrined in the Qur'an; and obedience to the Prophet signifies acting upon the methodological pattern of life available in the authentic traditions of the Prophet. Concurrent mention in the Qur'an of both kinds of obedience – to Allah and the Prophet – can in no way be construed to mean obedience to Allah only, as those who deny the Hadith claim. Total rejection of the Sunnah and the Hadith, can only result in Islam becoming a mere philosophy vulnerable to variations in its interpretation. It is often claimed that the deplorable plight of Muslims today is due to their stereotyped religiosity, however even if this line of argument is given any serious consideration, the Sunnah and the Hadith cannot be held responsible. On the contrary Muslims are not suffering because of some rigid adherence to old traditions of the Prophet, but rather for having strayed far from both the Qur'an and the Sunnah in their thoughts and practices.

Opposed to those who totally deny the validity of Hadith are those whose love for it and the Sunnah is unconditional, being generally semi-literate Muslims who stand misguided and who consequently misguide many, blindly adhering to anything termed a Prophetic tradition regardless of the authenticity of the traditions reported in the sources. Furthermore, if a survey were to be conducted on Prophetic traditions very popular among Muslims today, the findings may be shocking, for in religious circles a great number of such traditions are being narrated, interpreted, and practiced as if genuine when in reality they are little more than the remainders of fabricated Prophetic traditions. As such this is one of the main factors behind Muslim backwardness and decline in virtually every field of life including the religious and spiritual.

People of previous divine Scriptures have been criticized in the Qur'an for their half-hearted treatment of them (2:85) as well as indifference to the commands of their prophets (5:20–24). Even the hypocrites during the time of the Prophet have been rebuked in the Qur'an for their selective approach to the Revelation and the Prophet's exhortations (4:150). In the Muslim world today there are people who select only those Qur'anic *ayāt* and only those Prophetic traditions which benefit in one way or another their vested interests and covert agendas. The Qur'an refers to these Muslims as those in whose hearts is a disease, not sincere to Islam or its cause. A highly balanced approach to the Qur'an as well as the Sunnah and the Hadith seems to be the only viable approach to take, as recommended in the Qur'an (2:143). A balanced approach to the Sunnah and the Hadith denotes a belief in, and practice of, only those traditions of the Prophet that are highly authentic and far beyond any doubt whatsoever.

Authenticity of the Sunnah and the Hadith

Islamic writings both old and modern abound in Sunnah and Hadith literature, testament to the great importance of these subjects. Compilations of Hadith may be classified commonly into four categories according to the rank of their authenticity:

(1) Those collections of Hadith that are claimed to be the most authentic works such as al-Bukhārī's and Muslim's.

(2) Those collections that contain only a few dubious reports such as al-Tirmidhī's, al-Nasā'ī's, and Abū Dāwūd's.

(3) Those collections which comprise many problematic traditions such as Ibn Mājah's and Aḥmad's.

(4) Those collections that have too many weak and fabricated traditions such as al-Ṭabarānī's.

Authenticity of Hadith as claimed by Hadith authorities is entirely dependent on the authenticity of the chain of narrators reporting Hadith. There is hardly any serious attention paid to the authenticity of Hadith by the authentication of the text of Hadith.

Authentication of Hadith Text

Muslim scholars and students believe that if the chain of narrators of a hadith fulfils five criteria – continuity in the chain of narrators (*ittiṣāl al-sanad*), integrity of character (*ʿadālah*), infallible retention (*ḍabṭ*), freedom from any hidden defect (*ghayr al-ʿillah*), and safety from any aberrance (*ʿadm al-shudhūdh*) – the hadith is to be accepted as authentic. The last two criteria are also applicable to the examination of the text of a hadith. In practice, however, this remains confined to only debates and discussion in the works of *ʿUlūm al-Ḥadīth*, and the compilers of Hadith have rarely accommodated them in their examination of Hadith text. Some scholars at a later stage of Islamic history did suggest the examination of Hadith from a textual angle but their call fell on deaf ears.

Is there any real need for Hadith authentication from a textual angle? The answer to this question is both a difficult and an easy one. Difficult because today's Hadith scholars lack the courage required to answer to it, and easy because reasons justifying the examination of Hadith text are numerous.

1–*Controversy over the Position of a Particular Narrator*

It is well-known that Hadith scholars are not all unanimous over the reliability of some narrators and examples of these can be found in the biographical dictionaries. For instance, concerning a particular narrator Muslim's observation differs from that of al-Bukhārī; one biographical expert claims a narrator to be reliable (*thiqah*), whilst another finds him weak (*ḍaʿīf*), with a third authority concluding there is no problem in him (*lā ba'sa bihi*)! How is one to act and react in this situation?

2–*Inability of Some Narrators to Maintain the Preciseness of the Report*

Almost all the Hadith scholars are of the view that most of the Prophetic traditions have not been narrated in the words of the Prophet but in terms of the meaning of the message. Freedom to narrate Prophetic statements in terms of the meaning is not free from problems and, as this work will show, certain reporters could not even maintain this. The following example, as cited by al-Zarkashī in his monumental work *Al-Ijābah*, is illustrative of this concerning two *adhāns* signifying the call for morning prayer (salah) in the month of Ramadan, one pronounced by Bilāl and the other by ʿAbd Allāh ibn Umm Maktūm: ʿAbd Allāh ibn ʿUmar said that the Prophet said: "Bilāl indeed calls for prayer while it is still night; you may continue eating and drinking until ʿAbd Allāh ibn Umm Maktūm comes to call for prayer." ʿĀ'ishah blamed Ibn ʿUmar for reporting the Prophetic statement wrongly. She corrected the statement that the Prophet said: "Ibn Umm Maktūm is blind when he calls for prayer, continue eating and drinking until Bilāl gives the call to prayer." Here one might suggest that al-Bukhārī has recorded two reports on the same subject matter, one on the authority of Ibn ʿUmar and the other on the authority of ʿĀ'ishah; and both the reports are the same hence ʿĀ'ishah's correction of Ibn ʿUmar seems unsubstantiated. It does appear so, but there are other reports on the authority of ʿĀ'ishah and others as recorded in other Hadith works such as Ahmad ibn Ḥanbal's and al-Bayhaqī's, which corroborate the view of al-Zarkashī as mentioned above. It should be born in mind that the reports on the authority of ʿĀ'ishah on this matter as recorded in sources other than al-Bukhārī are equally highly authentic from the angle of the chain (*sanad*). According to al-Zarkashī, ʿĀ'ishah also observed that Bilāl could see well the time for morning prayer and ʿAbd Allāh ibn Umm Maktūm due to his blindness was not in a position to discern the time. This rational justification suggests that a reporter in al-Bukhārī's chain of the report might have erred and inverted the order of the names, Bilāl and Ibn Umm Maktūm.

3–*Textual Conflicts among Reports*

Whether we examine al-Bukhārī's compilation of Hadith or Muslim's there are several instances where certain reports concerning the same matter vary from each other, not only in words but also in meaning. It is generally suggested that such differences in reporting are not due to errors on the part of narrators but because the Prophet himself made the statements differently on different occasions. This principle may be true in some cases but is not relevant everywhere. For example, in his chapter on *al-Musāqāt* (sharecropping) Muslim has recorded fifteen traditions on the spiritual loss that the domestication of dogs may bring, seven on the authority of ʿAbd Allah ibn ʿUmar and the remaining eight on the authority of Abū Hurayrah (Muslim: 3999–4013). Out of seven reports narrated on the authority of Ibn ʿUmar five traditions inform us of the daily deduction of two carats (*Qīrāṭān*) from the deeds of one who keeps a dog as a pet without any genuine purpose, but two of them refer to the deduction of only one single carat (*Qīrāṭ*). Out of eight reports narrated on the authority of Abū Hurayrah only one mentions the deduction of two carats of good deeds, whereas the remaining seven put the deduction to only one carat. How is one to resolve the discrepancy and is there any way to make a compromise between them?

4–'Delusion' of Reliable Narrators
At times the chain of narrators is extremely authentic but there exists some obvious problem in the text of the narration. In this situation instead of examining the issue carefully Hadith commentators immediately put the blame on one or other of the narrators anonymously, observing that he must have had a misunderstanding/misconception (*qad wahima*), leaving the matter at that. They prefer not to examine the text as a possible source of unreliability or defect and why this would be so and the most probable reason they fail to do this is because they do not see any problem in the chain of narrators. In fact, if they find some problem in the text it must be declared as such. If delusion on the part of a narrator is detected, what is the criterion to determine this? There has to be some criteria to identify defect in the text.

5–Practical Correction of Narrations
Even during the time of the Companions the reporting of Prophetic traditions was given serious attention, particularly as to their preciseness. Chapters three and four will illustrate how some statements of the Prophet that were reported incorrectly were then corrected by those who were at the forefront of Islamic knowledge. The following example demonstrates the issue well. Abū Saʿīd al-Khudrī reported from the Prophet that: "The one who is dead will indeed be revived in the dress he put on at the time of death." This was immediately corrected by ʿĀ'ishah stating that the Prophet mentioned deed, instead of dress. She then argued with the help of another tradition of the Prophet that "People will be raised naked, barefooted, and non-circumcised" (*al-Ijābah*: 120). This correction was in the text. Should this state of affairs be allowed to continue given the confusion and problems it creates?

6–Identifying the Contemporary Relevance of Hadith
The Qur'an and Hadith encapsulate the teachings of the Prophet and are meant for practical application in our daily lives, not for mere lip service. As Muhammad was the Last Prophet sent to mankind his comprehensive teachings are relevant for every person, time, place, and situation. Therefore interpretations of both the Qur'an and Hadith are not to be fixated in time, but to be carefully examined and reinterpreted to give practical guidance meeting the requirements and challenges of a

new age, the time-space factor. In the process of doing this one will no doubt come across various interpretations already advanced by Hadith commentators, and these interpretations may, at times, be mutually conflicting. To overcome this and avoid confusion the best way forward would be to re-examine the position of the words used in the text of Prophetic traditions.

7–*Understanding the Methodological Dimension of Hadith*

The Prophetic traditions may be classified into two major categories, legislative and non-legislative, with one of these being binding and the other not. As for the binding traditions, their position must be viewed vis-a-vis the Qur'an, one's reason, and the *Sunnah Mutawātirah* (that is, a hadith which is reported by such a large number of people that they cannot be expected to agree upon a lie, all of them together). There is a possibility that the Hadith and the Qur'an may contrast one another in which case scholars need to place their efforts into affecting a compromise among the conflicting traditions. If this is not possible, traditions lose their eminent status as authentic. Only the authentic text of a tradition can be used as source of guidance, both methodological as well as practical.

8–*Probability of Fabrication in Hadith Text*

There is no denying the fact that around two decades after the Prophet traditions were fabricated and falsely attributed to him. The number of these runs into untold thousands. Undoubtedly, Hadith scholars did their best to identify the genuine from the false but despite great care and effort they could not ensure one hundred percent accuracy. Consequently there remains the possibility that some fabricated traditions are still considered genuine merely because of the authentic chain of narrators behind them. Scholars have already identified, for instance, around ninety traditions in *Sunan Ibn Mājah* as fabricated. Are we to close the door on exposing them forever? In terms of the chain of narrators it might be considered closed but in terms of textual examination the door should remain open. In other words we have no other way to check for fabricated traditions in the most popular sources other than to examine the text of the traditions concerned.

9–Fiqhī Controversy among Fuqahā'

Many controversies exist among Muslim jurists concerning certain issues related to Islamic life. One of the main reasons of this occurrence is that certain texts of a particular tradition are preferred to other texts. Instead of viewing all as authentic it could be that some are authentic from the angle of the chain of narrators, but are not necessarily authentic in terms of the text. The *fiqhī* controversy may be overcome therefore by authentication of Hadith text.

10–Sanctity of Hadith

Aḥmad ibn Ḥanbal was once asked as to why he investigated the life and character of a narrator declaring them to be either reliable, weak, or liars, especially as this would be considered a form of backbiting against people, an unlawful practice in Islam. He confidently observed that he did not care if the people affected complained against him on the Day of Judgment for he could not afford to face a situation in which the Prophet would be a plaintiff against him on the Day of Judgment, complaining that he had not done anything to ensure the authenticity of the Prophetic traditions. The responsibility of scholars is not yet over. They have to continue doing their best to leave no lacuna or gap in the authentication of Hadith. The Hadith hold a very sacred position in Islamic life, but this sanctity is exclusively for the genuine traditions of the Prophet.

History of this Research

Like any concerned Muslim, I felt uncomfortable with the idea of an apparent conflict existing between various texts of Prophetic traditions recorded as ostensibly genuine. On discussing the issue of textual disparity with several scholars I met with one of two reactions, either discouragement from pursuing debate on Hadith further or encouragement to continue discourse. Despite some heated discussions and opposition I persevered and continued deliberation upon traditions recorded in al-Bukhārī and Muslim, reading Hadith commentaries of these two works, and also particularly the works of al-Nawawī, al-ʿAynī, and Ibn Ḥajar. It seemed to me that the Hadith commentators had not used any well-established and universally defined principles of

Hadith commentary, and that they had not been justly balanced in their approach to Hadith, placing main focus on the chain of narrators, and not on the text of the traditions. As I felt somewhat dissatisfied with the interpretations made by the great scholars I began more serious research on the authenticity of Hadith from the point of view of its text. I applied to the International Islamic University Malaysia, obtained sponsorship and ultimately produced a study entitled "Authentication of Hadith: Redefining the Criteria" copies of which were sent to several scholars including Hadith scholars and experts in Islamic law, seeking their comments, observations, and suggestions. The general observations were encouraging and I submitted a small portion of the research to a highly recognized international refereed journal in America, where it was published, after which I decided to have it published as a book, culminating in this work. In order to do this I have had to include two new chapters not originally part of the research.

Contents of the Book

The first chapter focuses on fabrication in the Prophetic tradition from a historical perspective, tracing factors that lead to this as well as the remedial measures taken by distinguished Muslim authorities. The second chapter identifies the contributions of scholars from two perspectives, the chain of narrators and the text.

Chapter three examines the Hadith in the light of Qur'anic principles and instructions. Chapter four is devoted to a textual Hadith examination using highly authentic traditions of the Prophet. Chapter five concerns the checking of the authenticity of Hadith text through reasoning. Chapter six discusses the criterion established in history to authenticate the historical dimensions available in Hadith texts. Chapter seven traces the acceptability of Hadith in line with another criterion e.g. moderation.

The eighth and final chapter is based on discussion and reinterpretation of a particular chapter of al-Bukhārī, *Kitāb al-Qadar* (Chapter on Predetermination). In chapters three, four, five, six, and eight the traditions selected for examination and interpretation are taken from al-Bukhārī and Muslim.

It is my strong personal belief that the discussions undertaken in these chapters are, to a great extent, original. I have tried to do two things in the discussions concerned, firstly, to rationally define the criteria of Hadith text and secondly, to sincerely apply them to selected traditions by using relevant methodology.

Finally, dates cited for the various scholars and individuals listed are mentioned on their first occurrence only.

Translation of the Qur'anic *Āyāt*

The Qur'anic verses cited throughout the work have primarily been taken from the translations of Abdullah Yusuf Ali, Muhammad Asad, and Muhammad Muhsin Khan, with a general preference given to the translation of Muhammad Asad which I believe is based on the concept of thematic unity in the Qur'an. In any case the most appropriate translation for the verse(s) in question has been used throughout.

The Significance of Chapter Eight – Al-Bukhārī's Chapter on Predestination/Predetermination

It may appear to readers that chapter eight is not connected to the theme of this book, and that the traditions discussed could easily be more appropriately rearranged under chapters three, four, five, six and seven where the respective criteria have been applied to ascertain the authenticity of prophetic traditions. However, the twenty-seven traditions of al-Bukhārī's *Kitāb al-Qadar* (chapter on predetermination/ predestination) cannot be easily evaluated under certain particular criteria only. They further needed to be treated separately, practically because these traditions need analysis from several angles and therefore cannot be scattered in various chapters, and psychologically because of the nature of *Kitāb al-Qadar's* subject matter and its deep impact on Muslims' psyche.

An Earnest Appeal

In Muslim, specifically religious, academia those works which appear to differ from established norms and beliefs are forthrightly rejected as nonsense. Established dogma in relation to Hadith consists of two components:

(1) If the chain of narrators is authentic, the hadith is considered authentic regardless of the problem(s) its text may contain.

(2) The traditions selected and recorded by al-Bukhārī and Muslim are regarded as highly authentic. Any apparent discrepancies in the texts of these traditions can be interpreted but to declare any report from these two sources as unreliable is considered an almost unacceptable stance and a virtual offence.

In this study I have done what I sincerely felt compelled to do. My objective has in no wise been to discredit the effort and unparalleled contributions of the great Hadith scholars, but rather to consolidate the position of Hadith further. Yet, I can in no way claim perfection in my work for only Allah is Perfect. Human effort is never free from shortcomings, and if there are any flaws in my presentation I welcome their being pointed out. In possible future editions of the book I will take these suggested changes into serious consideration. I pray to Allah, the Source of all knowledge, to make this humble work useful for all those concerned. *Āmīn!*

ISRAR AHMAD KHAN
15 July 2008

1

Fabrication in Prophetic Traditions: Causal Factors and Remedial Measures

FABRICATION IN PROPHETIC traditions, literally as well as technically, signifies attribution of a statement or practice to the Prophet falsely with or without intention. Reports containing information about the Prophet's sayings or deeds, which he never said or did, are unanimously rejected (*mardūd*) as lies.

Hadith scholars have identified various statements used in the traditions which point to their apocryphal nature, some of these are obviously indicative of fabrication whilst others refer to fabrication metonymically. When authorities refer to some transmitters in a chain of narrators (*sanad*) using expressions which are superlative, exaggerated or simple degree adjectives, these constitute for them obvious terms signaling fabrication. Examples of superlative verbosity include: the greatest fabricator of all (*awḍaʿ al-nās*), the source of the lie (*manbaʿ al-kadhib*), the lie ends with so and so (*al-kidhb yantahī ilayhi*) etc. Examples of exaggerative verbosity include: totally engrossed in fabrication (*waḍḍāʿ*), extremely given to lies (*kadhdhāb*), diehard falsifier (*dajjāl*), fanatically inventing falsehood (*affāk*) etc. Examples of simple degree adjectives include: So and so fabricates traditions (*fulānun yaḍaʿu al-ḥadīth*), so and so coins traditions (*fulānun yakhtaliq al-ḥadīth*), this or that Hadith authority has declared so and so to be a liar (*fulānun kadhdhabahū*) etc. Some metonymical references to reporters also prove the reports concerned to be false such as so and so narrates false reports (*fulānun yuḥaddithu bi al-Abāṭil*), and to his credit there are false reports (*lahū aḥādīth bāṭilah*). Likewise, Hadith authorities use several terms to declare a tradition to be unacceptable. These include *mawḍūʿ* (fabricated), *bāṭil* (false), and *hādhā al-ḥadīth lā aṣla lahu* (this tradition is baseless) etc.

Historical Background of Hadith Fabrication

According to historians, who particularly focus on events during ʿUthmān's (RAA)* Caliphate, it was initially Ibn Saba' who fabricated traditions in the name of the Prophet in a bid to tarnish the image of Islam and cause rift among the Muslims.[1] This would seem to suggest that fabrication in the Prophetic tradition began in the middle of ʿUthmān's Caliphate.

In Akram Diya al-Umri's opinion the first person to fabricate a tradition in the name of the Prophet was Ibn ʿAdīs, one of the opponents of the third Caliph, ʿUthmān ibn ʿAffān. He falsely reported a statement of the Prophet on the authority of ʿAbd Allah ibn Masʿūd containing a condemnation of ʿUthmān.[2] It would appear from this that fabrication in Prophetic traditions began towards the end of ʿUthmān's Caliphate.

Muhammad Abu Zahw and Ahmad Amin on the other hand believe that fabrication in Prophetic traditions begin earlier, and can be traced to the time of the Prophet himself.[3] Their only evidence in support of this is the Prophet's warning: "He who consciously attributes to me some lie deserves to be allotted a place in hellfire."[4] This reasoning is a little strained for the Prophet could easily have made the statement as a precautionary measure to ensure the originality of his sayings and doings (there was a trend in Arab society to attribute statements falsely to anyone) and not necessarily to warn those among his followers who had already begun to start fabricating traditions in his name. In addition, the Prophet's Companions were so sincere in their commitment to him, a loyalty almost legendary in nature, that it is inconceivable to even imagine that they would knowingly fabricate traditions in his name. They loved him more than anyone, including their own selves, and were prepared to lay down their lives for him.

Muhammad Abu Shahbah traces fabrication in the Prophetic traditions to the year 41 AH when the enemies of the third Caliph had

*(RAA) – *Raḍiya Allāhu ʿAnhu*. May Allah be pleased with him. Said whenever a Companion of the Prophet Muhammad is mentioned by name.

succeeded in instigating the people against him. He refers to Ibn Saba' as the originator of fabrication coining and attributing many traditions wrongly to the Prophet. One such fabricated hadith stated that the Prophet declared ʿAlī ibn Abū Ṭālib to be his successor.[5] However, Abu Shahbah seems to have overlooked an important historical fact, the third Caliph was assassinated in 35 AH. If, therefore, Ibn Saba' was indeed the first to have begun the traitorous act of fabricating traditions in the name of the Prophet to instigate Muslims against their faith, one another and their leadership, then this should not have been in the year 41 AH but rather 30 AH.

Subhi al-Salih believes that fabrication first registered an appearance during the beginning of fourth Caliph ʿAlī ibn Abī Ṭālib's rule, that is during a time when the Muslim community had divided into various camps. Each community played a part in inventing traditions attributed to the Prophet to garner support for its stand.[6]

In sum it would appear that fabrication of Prophetic traditions began sometime during the middle of ʿUthmān's Caliphate, climaxed during the time of ʿAlī and Muʿāwiyah, and continued in later years of Muslim history until the Abbasid period.

Causes of Fabrication

It may not be too difficult to trace the main factors which led to fabrication in the Prophetic traditions. Even a cursory examination of fabricated reports yields an indication of what was coined in the name of the Prophet and why. When it comes to intentional fabrication it seems that traditions were invented in the Prophet's name by those who a) were very much interested in convincing the general populace of their respective stands on the Caliphate and its succession, b) wanted to smear the originality of Islamic teachings, c) wanted to promote their respective businesses, d) wanted to overzealously attract people to a religious life, e) desired worldly gain by pleasing people in power, and f) aspired to earn fame as those who were knowledgeable.

1–Political Movements

Certain sections of the expanding Muslim empire were resentful of the way ʿUthmān, the third Caliph, had been tackling administrative matters of the state and this ultimately culminated in his assassination, a terrible event which shocked the general populace and leaders of society. When ʿAlī was instated as the fourth Caliph, a number of leading personalities demanded strict measures against those responsible for plunging the Muslim community into chaos. Since the new Caliph had his own method for resolving the problem, the Muslim community once again became divided, this time into three major political camps, pro Muʿāwiyah, pro ʿĀ'ishah, and pro ʿAlī. Political division led to grim military conflicts between the opponents. These battles not only inflicted serious losses on the warring parties but also created a psychological environment of distrust such that the majority of Muslim society became aghast that such a corrupt state of affairs had come about. Each political faction wanted to win the majority of Muslims over to its own particular side and one of the easiest ways of doing this was to coin traditions in the name of the Prophet to support their respective positions.

Traditions fabricated in this heightened state of affairs were of two categories, one set condemning prominent leaders and the other set commending them. For example, one can trace how the position of Muʿāwiyah became elevated by examining relevant traditions fabricated in the latter category. Narration one mentions that Archangel Gabriel came down to the Prophet with a golden pen. The Prophet was then asked to give the pen, in accordance with Allah's will, to Muʿāwiyah and to advise him to write the *Āyah al-Kursī* (2:255) with it. Using the pen Muʿāwiyah wrote the verse (in very beautiful script), upon which the Prophet informed him that Allah had credited his account with a cumulative reward equivalent to the recitation of that verse by readers until the Day of Judgment.[7] Narration two cites the Prophet as having said: "In the eyes of Allah there are three trustworthy figures, myself, Gabriel, and Muʿāwiyah."[8] A third narration cites the Prophet as saying: "Allah trusted with regard to His revelations Gabriel in the heaven, and Muhammad and Muʿāwiyah ibn Abī Sufyān on the earth."[9] In a fourth narration the Prophet is said to have called for Muʿāwiyah, and when he came commanded those present around him, including Abū Bakr and ʿUmar, to entrust Muʿāwiyah with the leadership of the Muslims because he was the most powerful, and the most trustworthy.[10] A fifth narration cites the Prophet as saying that on the Day of Resurrection Muʿāwiyah would be revived with a cloak made of light on his body.[11]

In stark contrast, condemnation of Muʿāwiyah is also apparent from fabricated reports. In one narration the Prophet is said to have mentioned, "If you see Muʿāwiyah from this particular pulpit, kill him."[12] In a second the Prophet informs Muʿāwiyah that he, "as leader of the Muslims, would make the evil good and the good evil; and that his wrong doings would be enormous."[13] In a third, the Prophet once prays against Muʿāwiyah and ʿAmrū ibn al-ʿĀṣ saying: "O Allah! Put them both in serious chaos; O Allah! Throw them both into hellfire."[14]

Traditions were also fabricated both in favor of and against ʿĀ'ishah. In praise we have the following: The Archangel Gabriel once informed the Prophet that it was Allah's will that he marry one of Abū Bakr's daughters as a result of which the Prophet requested Abū Bakr for the hand of his daughter in marriage. Abū Bakr had three daughters for marriage and showed them all to the Prophet who chose ʿĀ'ishah because Allah had exhorted him to marry her.[15] This is a very clear lie on two counts. First, the Prophet married ʿĀ'ishah in Makkah, and not in Madinah as this tradition reports. Historically, the Prophet married ʿĀ'ishah in Makkah with consummation of the marriage taking place in Madinah. Second, Abū Bakr only had two daughters at the time, Asmā' and ʿĀ'ishah, and not three as the report asserts. In fact Abū Bakr did have a third daughter but she was only born after his death in 13 AH. Her name was Umm Kulthūm.[16]

In terms of condemnation of ʿĀ'ishah, the following tradition was fabricated on the occasion of the battle of the Camel: "The Prophet stated that people who are led by a woman cannot achieve success."[17]

A great number of traditions attributed to the Prophet also surfaced in praise of ʿAlī ibn Abī Ṭālib. A few of these are listed below:

(1) The Prophet said that he, Hārūn ibn ʿImrān, Yaḥyā ibn Zakarīyyā, and ʿAlī ibn Abī Ṭālib were created from one and the same clay.[18]

(2) The Prophet said that ʿAlī ibn Abū Ṭālib was his brother, his minister, and his successor, who would pay off his [the Prophet's] debts and fulfill his promises after him.[19]

(3) The Prophet said that looking at the face of ʿAlī is an act of devotion (*ʿibādah*).[20]

(4) The Prophet said that he who wished to see Adam with his knowledge, Noah with his understanding, Abraham with his wisdom, John with his devotion, and Moses with his grip, should see ʿAlī ibn Abū Ṭālib.[21]

(5) The Prophet said that his name in the Qur'an was *wa al-Shams wa Ḍuḥāhā* (by the sun and its splendor), the name of ʿAlī ibn Abū Ṭālib *wa al-Qamar idhā talāhā* (by the moon as it follows it), the name of al-Ḥasan and al-Ḥusayn *wa al-Nahār idhā jallāhā* (by the day as it shows up the glory), and the name of the Umayyad dynasty *wa al-Layl idhā yaghshāhā* (by the night as it conceals it).[22]

(6) When Abū Bakr and ʿUmar proposed to Fāṭimah, the Prophet said: "O ʿAlī! She is for you, not for the imposters (*dajjāl*)."[23]

In contrast against ʿAlī we have the Prophet saying to him: "Leadership is not for you, nor for any of your descendents."[24] It seems that those hostile to ʿAlī fabricated this tradition in order to prevent people from believing in the eligibility of ʿAlī for the Caliphate.

In 66 AH, al-Mukhtār al-Thaqafī an unprincipled and designing man, rebelled against the establishment and seized power in Kufah. He once requested one of the then authorities on Hadith to fabricate traditions in the name of the Prophet that could validate his stand. In exchange he offered the scholar tens of thousands of dirhams, horses, a retinue of slaves, and precious clothes. The *muḥaddith* refused to do so but, consented instead to fabricate traditions attributed to some of the *Ṣaḥābah*.[25] In fact, many traditions were fabricated out of political motivation as an attempt to discredit those in power by showing them to have been condemned by the Prophet. For example, the Prophet is said to have declared Yazīd ibn Muʿāwiyah as the killer of al-Ḥusayn and cursed him. Likewise, al-Walīd ibn ʿAbd al-Malik was condemned through one such fabricated tradition in the name of the Prophet.[26]

2–Inimical Missions against Islam and Muslims

In Islamic history many hadith were fabricated by a group known as *zanādiqah* (heretics/hypocrites who feigned Islam outwardly but who harbored enmity within, spreading heretical beliefs). They fabricated traditions in almost all matters of Islamic life. ʿAbd al-Karīm ibn Abī al-ʿArjā' was one such heretic who would insert his own concocted traditions in the document of genuine traditions compiled by one of his relatives, Ḥammād ibn Salamah. Before being put to death, he claimed to have fabricated four thousand traditions in the name of the Prophet in a bid to declare the lawful as unlawful and the unlawful as lawful.[27] Al-Mahdī, a great scholar of Hadith is reported to have said that one of the heretics confessed before him to have fabricated four thousand traditions and to have circulated them among the populace.[28]

In addition Madinah was home to a number of Jewish tribes whose various forms of treachery against the Prophet caused their eventual expulsion. With military expeditions and open propaganda not viable options, it seems that the more resentful factions amongst these decided to focus on sabotaging the fundamental teachings of Islam through fabrication of *aḥādīth*. The aim was to create a rift in the unity of the Muslims and a new version of the religion. A case in point is that of Ibn Saba'. A Jew who apparently embraced Islam he traveled widely throughout the Islamic empire in the garb of his new faith managing to dupe unsuspecting believers in the new Muslim territories. He fabricated a number of traditions in the name of the Prophet and circulated them among Muslim society.

Another case is that of Bayān ibn Samʿān al-Nahdī, a heretic who claimed to be an apostle of God. Naturally, he must have come up with some justification through his fabricated traditions in support of this outrageous claim. He was later put to death for blasphemy. Mughīrah ibn Saʿīd, a magician, also played a part in polluting the sacred heritage of Prophetic traditions. He was beheaded for this gross offense.[29]

Some spectacular examples of fabricated traditions manufactured by the opponents of Islam are given below:

(1) In response to a question as to the basic element of God, the Prophet said that it is neither from heaven nor from earth; He rather created a horse and made it run; when it perspired, God created Himself from that perspiration. This was fabricated by a heretic, Muḥammad ibn Shujāʿ al-Balkhī.[30]

(2) A female jinn used to visit the Prophet along with other female jinn. One day she appeared late. When asked by the Prophet she

said: "I went to India to offer condolence to a bereaved family. On the way I saw something very strange." The Prophet then asked her to relate what she saw. She continued: "I saw Satan praying salah on a rock. When I asked him what made him mislead the descendents of Adam, he avoided the answer. When I asked him as to why, he then prayed, and answered that he hoped for the forgiveness of his Lord." Upon this the Prophet laughed like he never laughed again.[31] In all likelihood, this fabrication was aimed at creating some sort of sympathy for Satan in the hearts of Muslims.

(3) The Prophet said: "He from whose hands a non-believer accepts Islam will inherit property from the new Muslim."[32] This is quite obviously an attempt to alter the law of inheritance in Islam.

(4) The Prophet said: "One who did not pay zakah during his life can compensate for the loss by making his bequest in the light of the Qur'an."[33] This fabrication was obviously meant to console those who had avoided paying the zakah.

(5) The Prophet said: "In the year 150 abstain from marriage; he who married in that year, Allah would take away his mind and destroy his religion, and he would be deprived of both this world and the hereafter."[34] It seems that these fabricators wanted to weaken Muslims demographically by discouraging them from marriage.

(6) The Prophet said: "Nothing affects faith negatively just as nothing brings good with polytheism."[35] This was fabricated in order to encourage Muslims to do anything they pleased whether good or bad and to convince them that they could commit sinful acts such as lying, stealing, committing adultery and fornication, killing someone unjustly, taking usury, usurping another's rightful property, etc. without this having any adverse impact on their faith.

(7) The Prophet said: "There will be no prophet after me except if Allah wills otherwise."[36] The first part of this tradition – "There will be no prophet after me" – is a genuine statement of the Prophet recorded in the most authentic works of Hadith including *Ṣaḥīḥ al-Bukhārī* and *Ṣaḥīḥ Muslim*. The last part of the tradition – "except if Allah wills otherwise" – is a later insertion by a well-known heretic, Muḥammad ibn Saʿīd. These enemies of Islam were well aware that the unique basis of the religion rested on the finality of Prophet Muhammad. The obvious aim of fabrications

such as these was therefore to create doubt in people's minds concerning the finality of Prophet Muhammad and to further remove doubt about the position of impostors after him. In addition Muḥammad ibn Saʿīd claimed that whenever he heard an apparently nice statement, he developed for this a chain of narrators linking it to the Prophet![37]

3–Corroboration of Particular Schools of Thought

The expansion of Islamic territory and the extension of its frontiers to as far as Rome and Persia brought about an interaction between Muslim people and those of the new realms. The heritage of the latter passed into the hands of the Muslims and this new knowledge borrowed and learned from others led to the emergence of debate among scholars, which ultimately resulted in the appearance of several conflicting thoughts and views particularly of a philosophical nature. The main subjects of these debates concerned the position of the Qur'an, the concept of preordination of man's destiny, the freedom of man, the nature and consequence of major sin etc. As it was not easy for anyone to convince the public through the simple force of rational argument, debaters and supporters of a particular point of view resorted instead to the fabrication of traditions in the name of the Prophet.

Enthusiasts of the historically well-known theological groups, the Muʿtazilite, Murji'ite, Qadarite, Jabrite, and Ashʿrite, ventured into forbidden territory and dared to fabricate traditions in the name of the Prophet so as to validate their own respective schools of thought. A repentant member of one of these schools divulged what he and others from the same camp had used to do stating: "Whenever we saw an appreciable opinion, we turned it into a prophetic tradition."[38]

For example, one school of thought believed that faith (*īmān*) was not static, but rather increased and decreased. However proponents of the idea remained dissatisfied with their own line of reasoning and began to attribute this statement to the Prophet so as to further strengthen their own approach and convince the people in general of its veracity. Another group who favored the opposite idea, that faith was in fact static, conveniently came up with a contrasting tradition in support of their belief, fabricating the following in the name of the Prophet: "A delegation from Thaqīf asked the Prophet whether faith increases and decreases. The Prophet answered: 'Faith is firm in the hearts like firmly erected mountains on the earth; its increase and decrease constitute blasphemy'." The Murji'ite group coined many other traditions in the name of the Prophet to prove the authenticity of their view. Muḥammad ibn al-Qāsim al-Ṭālkānī, a prominent leader of this group is a case in point. He fabricated many traditions to substantiate the group's view including the following:

> The Prophet said: "Those who have proclaimed increase and decrease in faith should know that its increase is hypocrisy and its decrease is blasphemy. If they repent, leave them; if not, chop their necks with a sword. They are the enemies of the Most Merciful. Remember, their salah, fasting, zakah, hajj, and religion are not acceptable. They are not related to the Prophet."[39]

The Jabarites believed in the fore-written destiny of man. To rebut this the Qadarites fabricated a tradition in the name of the Prophet as follows: "On the Day of Judgment Allah will gather all at the same place; a crier from beneath the Divine throne will proclaim: 'Lo! One who was purified of his sins, let him enter Paradise.'"[40]

Fanatics of these theological schools crossed all bounds, fabricating traditions in the name of the Prophet condemning each other, seemingly oblivious of the gravity of what they were doing. Further examples of such fabricated traditions are given below:

(1) The Prophet said: "Verily, for each community is a magian [fire worshippers]; the magians of this Ummah are the Qadarites. Do not visit them when they fall sick; and do not join their funeral prayer after they die."[41]

(2) Once the Prophet said that Allah had cursed four categories of people through the tongues of seventy prophets. His Companions then asked about their identity. The Prophet answered: "Qadarites, Juhmites, Murji'ites, and Rafizites." When requested to explain their problems, the Prophet said: "Qadarites claim that good is from Allah and evil from Satan: Remember! Good and evil are both from Allah, whoever says other than this is doomed; Juhmites say that the Qur'an is creation: Remember! The Qur'an

is non-creation, whoever says other than this is doomed; Murji'tes believe that faith is mere utterance without action; Rafizites revile Abū Bakr and ʿUmar: Remember! One who angered the two is doomed."[42]

(3) The Prophet said that if the dead body of some Qadarite or Murji'ite were to be excavated three days after burial, his face would be turned toward a direction other than the Kaʿbah.[43]

(4) The Prophet said that Murji'ites, Qadarites, Rafizites, and Kharijites would be stripped of their faith in the unity of God by one fourth and thrown into hellfire as non-believers to abide therein forever.[44]

It is amazing that stalwarts of theological schools of thought went to such terrible lengths misusing the name of the Prophet to simply give legitimacy to and bolster their own opinion.

4–Jurisprudential Rivalry

Islamic law has been interpreted by many jurists. The most prominent among them are Abū Ḥanīfah (d.150 AH), Mālik ibn Anas (d.179 AH), Muḥammad ibn Idrīs al-Shāfiʿī (d.204 AH), and Aḥmad ibn Ḥanbal (d.241 AH). Although differences of opinion existed among them on many issues these great scholars guided people to the best of their ability in interpreting Islamic law based on their own ijtihad. Unfortunately, although these differences were minor in nature, followers of these great scholars and imams considered them to be major and eventually came to believe that their own particular imam's view was the right one and that of the others' wrong. Hence they condemned each other. To this extent, the controversy remained tolerable, but when these followers began to fabricate traditions in the name of the Prophet to not only support their respective schools of jurisprudence, but to also condemn prominent jurists by name, they crossed a limit the seriousness of which they should have been acutely aware. Examples of such fabricated traditions to support a particular view on a given matter are quoted below:

(1) The Prophet said that one who raised his hands in salah, his salah would not be accepted.[45] This tradition was fabricated to rebut what had been reported in authentic traditions that the Prophet and his

Companions raised their hands in salah. This is a striking example of prejudice on the part of the jurists' followers. Astonishingly they show little or no care for the sanctity of the Prophet's own genuine acts and utterances on the matter meaning that they gave greater value to the predominance of their respective school of jurisprudence. In other words if their blind approach cast aspersion on the authenticity of genuine traditions of the Prophet, it did not matter to them.

(2) Archangel Gabriel informed the Prophet that Allah commanded him to pray the salah in the manner of Gabriel and other angels in the seventh heaven: that is to "raise your hands in the beginning of prayer while saying *Allah Akbar*, and do the same while bending, and also while raising your head from a bending state. Verily, for everything there is a ladder; the ladder of salah is raising hands at each proclamation of *Allah Akbar*."[46] The supporters of raising hands in salah did not find the Prophet's and his Companions' practice in this regard sufficient and fabricated a tradition endorsing their view vehemently.

The insolent also boldly fabricated a tradition condemning the great jurist al-Shāfiʿī whilst admiring another Abū Ḥanīfah: "There will be a man namely Muḥammad ibn Idrīs al-Shāfiʿī in my Ummah; he will be more harmful to my Ummah than Satan; and also there will be another man in my Ummah namely Abū Ḥanīfah; he will be the lamp of my Ummah, he will be the lamp of my Ummah."[47]

5–Commercial Propaganda

Man is a material being and needs access to the resources of life. One of the ways to obtain these is to simply purchase them from someone else, and for this there needs to be an act of sale. From time immemorial man has been practicing the art of trade, buying and selling goods to meet the requirements of the market. All businesses, whether big or small, need some form of publicity to promote sales and where in modern times this takes the form of highly attractive and visually stunning advertisements both in electronic and print media, in the old days this system was not available. During the 1st, 2nd, and 3rd centuries after hijrah, when Islamic rule had spread across the major part of the world, shopkeepers and businessmen needed to advertise their commodities and the only method available for commercial publicity was verbal communication. It seems that businessmen resorted to using prophetic traditions for this purpose. Unfortunately, when they failed to find anything in Hadith literature to promote their goods, they dared to fabricate traditions in the name of the Prophet to make their businesses profitable and attract more and more customers. It is apparent in the sources that a number of traditions were fabricated in praise of pomegranates, date fruit, almonds, melons, grapes, bread, milk, vegetables, cucumbers, lentils, salt, dairy products, endives, chickens, egg-plants, woolen cloth etc. It is very likely that businessmen paid those capable of fabricating traditions in favor of their respective commodities. Even physicians followed suit, fabricating Hadith to promote sales of their medicine. Below are a few illustrative examples:

(1) Every pomegranate fruit is injected with a seed of the heavenly pomegranate.
(2) Watermelon is mercy and its sweetness like that of the melon in Paradise.
(3) In the grape are things to eat and drink and to make raisins out of.
(4) O Allah! Make us enjoy with Islam and the bread; if the bread was not there, we would not pray, fast, perform pilgrimage, and participate in war.
(5) O ʿAlī! You must use salt because it serves as a cure for seventy diseases such as leprosy, white spots, and insanity.
(6) After taking curd the Prophet used to utter these words: "O Allah! Grant us blessing in it and increase it for us."
(7) He who takes cucumber with meat is protected from leprosy.
(8) You must use lentils because they soften the heart, increase tears, and seventy prophets blessed them.
(9) Almond and cheese are both maladies, but after reaching the stomach they become a source of cure.
(10) You must serve vegetables on the dining table because they chase Satan away.
(11) On each leaf of endive is a drop of water from Paradise.
(12) The eggplant is a cure for every disease and there is no harm therein.
(13) If people knew the significance of dairy products, they would buy them even in exchange for gold in equal weight.

(14) The Prophet commanded the rich to take the goat and sheep and the poor the chicken.

(15) A man came to the Prophet and complained of a problem concerning his sexual prowess. The Prophet, then, advised him to take eggs and onion.

(16) Give your women during their menstruation period date fruit to eat; it will cause the baby thus born to be kind hearted; Mary took dates when Jesus was born; if Allah knew any other meal better than date fruit, He would have arranged it for her.[48]

(17) You must wear woollen garments; it will give you the sweetness of faith in your hearts. You must wear woollen garments; it will help you feel less hungry. You must use woollen garments; you will realize its significance in the hereafter. The woollen garment causes the heart to think, and thinking leads to wisdom, and wisdom runs in the stomach like blood in the veins...[49]

(18) He who has made a ring of carnelian stone and has engraved thereon – "This is but with the grace of Allah" – Allah will grant him all the good and the two angels who are always with him will love him.[50]

(19) One who has made the stone of his ring out of ruby, Allah would keep the poverty away from him.[51]

(20) The stomach is the cistern of the body and all the veins are connected to it. If the stomach is healthy, the veins will remain healthy; if the stomach becomes sick, the veins will also become sick.[52] This tradition was fabricated by a physician named Ibrāhīm ibn Jurayj. It seems he did so to promote his clinic and his services as a physician.[53]

All these traditions have been fabricated in the name of the Prophet with a view to promoting businesses and attracting more and more customers.

6–Ambition to Earn a Livelihood and Acquire Fame

Some people prefer to earn a living in the easiest manner possible using their intelligence and creativity whilst at the same time seeking to build a reputation for themselves amongst the general populace as being somehow "knowledgeable" (scholars being highly regarded). They are by and large intrinsically lazy, hardly interested in working hard to earn a respectable salary to meet their or their family's daily needs. During the peak of Islamic civilization, people of this nature would enter mosques and invite others to listen to them, relating stories of the past, including legends etc. In order to make the audience marvel at their oration, they would narrate traditions of their own making linked to the Prophet because in doing so they really succeeded in getting both money as well as praise. The Mosque was and still is a public place in Islamic society, in fact even more so during the Umayyad and Abbasid periods when the mosques were far more significant. Story tellers could easily gather a ready audience to listen to them and it was the wonderful nature of the stories and traditions that captured people's attention and gave story tellers an easy target. Islam teaches kindness towards the needy so when story tellers mesmerized audiences with the magic of their oration, people would donate generously. Much as today, people in the Islamic civilization developed a love for certain days and acts; if they came across prophetic traditions reflecting their own wishes and desires they would rejoice and story tellers all too aware of this human psyche exploited it well.

Once on the occasion of 10th of Muharram in the Islamic calendar, a story teller devoted his whole talk to the significance of that particular day. He did so in the name of the Prophet narrating a number of traditions. When asked as to the source of these traditions, he brazenly confessed that he had not learned them from any source but had fabricated them instantly.[54]

One day Aḥmad ibn Ḥanbal and Yaḥyā ibn Maʿīn were praying in a mosque when they saw a story teller narrating a tradition in the name of the Prophet through a chain of narrators in which his direct sources, as he claimed, were themselves, Ibn Ḥanbal and Ibn Maʿīn. The tradition, which was so lengthy that it could cover twenty pages of a book, concerned making the declaration "There is no God but Allah," going on to say that Allah creates out of each word of the utterance a bird whose beak is made of gold and whose wings are made of coral. After he had finished, Ibn Maʿīn asked the story teller as to the source of the tradition he had just narrated. He cited, Aḥmad ibn Ḥanbal and Yaḥyā ibn Maʿīn, not actually knowing that the two were standing before him. Ibn Maʿīn then introduced himself and Ibn Ḥanbal making it very clear that the tradition the story teller had narrated on their authority was unknown to them and hence a lie. The story teller, not prepared to be humiliated, argued that he had learned the traditions of the Prophet from some seventeen other sources with the same names, Aḥmad ibn Ḥanbal and Yaḥyā ibn Maʿīn.[55] What a flagrant disregard for the sanctity of the chain of narrators in prophetic traditions!

In another incident a young man stood in the mosque of a small town with a view to seeking financial help from the people there. He made a statement on the significance of helping the needy Muslim, linking this to the Prophet and using the following chain for his narration: Abū Khalīfah, al-Walīd, Shuʿbah, Qatādah, Anas, the Prophet. He then claimed that his immediate source for the tradition was Abū Khalīfah. When asked by someone whether he had ever met Abū Khalīfah, his answer was in the negative. Upon this he was asked how he could possibly narrate from a source he had never seen. The young man felt humiliated and said: "Argumentation with me is against the normal etiquette; I have memorized this one chain of narrators; whenever I hear a tradition whatsoever, I use the same chain."[56]

Story tellers also used to fabricate traditions in which they exaggerated the position of previous prophets, the Prophet, some of his Companions, and also some prominent personalities in Islamic history. Some examples are given below in illustration:

(1) Anas ibn Mālik reports that he and the Prophet met prophet Ilyās in a mountain pass where the Prophet talked to him for long; there came down, in the meantime, from heaven a tray full of dishes; after they took the food, a cloud appeared and in it went Prophet Ilyās toward Syria. He asked the Prophet whether the same kind of meal came down to him from heaven; he said that Archangel Gabriel brought him such a tray of food once every forty days.[57] Two reporters, Yazīd al-Mūṣalī and Abū Isḥāq al-Jarashī, make this tradition unreliable.

(2) Shaykh ibn Abī Khālid fabricated a tradition in the name of the Prophet stating that on the ring stone of prophet Sulaymān was engraved the phrase: "There is no God but Allah and Muhammad is the Prophet of Allah."[58]

(3) Maysarah ibn Ibrāhīm al-Khāḍim fabricated a tradition in the name of the Prophet that every Friday Allah frees from hellfire one

hundred thousand people minus two persons who are from his Ummah; these two are deprived of their freedom from the fire because they hate Abū Bakr and ʿUmar; they are not Muslims...; and that a curse be on those who hate Abū Bakr, ʿUmar, ʿUthmān, and ʿAlī.[59]

Sources such as Muslim have recorded a Prophetic tradition on the authority of ʿUmar ibn al-Khaṭṭāb that there will be a person in Yemen namely Oways al-Qaranī, and whosoever meets him should request him to ask Allah for his forgiveness.[60] This simple prophesy has been enlarged by the story tellers. The tradition thus fabricated runs at least the length of two pages. The beginning of this tradition as narrated by story tellers commences:

> Once when the Prophet was in the courtyard of the Kaʿbah, Archangel Gabriel descended and informed the Prophet that in the near future there would be a man in his Ummah, who would be empowered by Allah to make intercession for as many people as the cumulative number of people in the tribes, Rabīʿah and Muḍar. When Gabriel advised the Prophet to ask him, in case he met him, to make intercession for his Ummah, the Prophet enquired about his name; the name, as told by Gabriel, was Oways.[61]

7–Overenthusiasm in the "Service" of Islam

Psychologically, religious minded people may be classified into three main categories: (1) those who keep their religiosity to their own selves, unmindful of others, (2) those who try their best to be religious in the real sense of the word and try to convey their religious message properly to others, and (3) those who impose too much religiosity on themselves and feel eager to attract others to opt for the same kind of strict spiritual life. It is the third category of people who go to excessive lengths to bring others into their fold. Muslim history is full of descriptions of such people who were very pious in a religious sense and who tried if they saw a differing level of practice in society to persuade people to be as religious as they were. Unfortunately, although they naturally used the Qur'an and Sunnah for their call, it seems that they considered the exhortations in the Qur'an and Sunnah to be inadequate and hence did not find it wrong to fabricate new traditions in the name of the

Prophet. These were concocted either to frighten people of the dire consequences of their belligerence toward piety (that is piety defined according to their own strict standards), or to lure them to the unexpectedly tremendous reward awaiting them for even minor religious deeds. It never entered their hearts that what they were doing in terms of fabricating prophetic traditions was in effect attributing lies to the Prophet and hence committing a great wrong.

In Baghdad there lived a very famous pious person by the name of Ghulām Khalīl. He was highly respected by both the people and the ruler of Baghdad so much so that upon his death the markets of Baghdad were closed in mourning. Yet, this same man when asked as to the source of his traditions from the Prophet had answered that he and others of his kind had fabricated them in order to soften the hearts of people.[62] He did not even shudder at the warning of the Prophet concerning those who fabricated traditions in his name.

Noah ibn Abī Maryam was a man of knowledge and piety. Deeply concerned by people's indifference to the Qur'an he, in good faith, fabricated traditions in the name of the Prophet on the authority of ʿIkrimah from Ibn ʿAbbās, pointing to the significance and great rewards of reading Qur'anic surahs, from *Sūrah al-Fātiḥah* all the way to *Sūrah al-Nās*. Disturbed by these unheard of traditions scholars of Hadith requested Ibn Abī Maryam to verify the truth of his statements, at which point he categorically stated: "When I saw people turning away from the Qur'an and paying attention to the fiqh of Abū Ḥanīfah and the history of Ibn Isḥāq, I fabricated these traditions in order to do right service to the religion."[63] Needless to say reading any portion of the Qur'an is hugely beneficial for mankind.

Isḥāq ibn Ibrāhīm al-Ṭabarī fabricated a tradition in the name of the Prophet that if one read from dawn to the time of the morning salah, *Subḥān Allah wa bi Ḥamdihi; Subḥān Allah al-ʿAẓīm; Astaghfir Allah,* a hundred times, the world would come to him subservient, and that Allah would create out of each word recited an angel who would pray for him to be rewarded until the Day of Judgment.[64]

Isḥāq ibn Wahb fabricated a tradition in the name of the Prophet that when Allah loves someone, He reserves him for Himself and does not let him become busy with his wife and children."[65] This tradition was coined to advise people to cut their links with worldly affairs and to confine themselves with devotion to Allah.

Ibn al-Jawzī has recorded fabricated traditions in the name of the Prophet which describe the significance and reward of around thirty-six special kinds of Salah such as that on the nights of Friday, Saturday, Sunday, and Monday, *Ṣalāh al-Tasbīḥ*, that in the month of Rajab, that on 10th of Muharram, that in the middle of the month of Shaʿbān etc. He has declared all these traditions fabricated and rejected them as lies.[66] It is very clear that these traditions were fabricated to attract people to act upon them.

Ayyūb ibn Mudrik fabricated a tradition in the name of the Prophet which mentions that Allah and His angels shower their blessings upon those who wear a turban on Friday.[67]

8–Avarice for State Patronage

In every society people vary in their approach to those in power, with some preferring to keep their distance except when unavoidable, and others preferring to keep a close watch on officials to keep them in check and rectify them when in error. There is another type however, who have a cynical approach to power, seeking personal gain through obsequious servility, and groveling flattery. During the Prophet's time and the reign of the four Rightly-Guided Caliphs there was no room for sycophancy. However, under the Umayyad and Abbasid dynasties, sycophants gained the opportunity to flourish and fabricated traditions in the name of the Prophet on subjects that would amuse the rulers and state governors. Amongst the fabricated traditions are those which praise particular acts associated with the ruling dynasty, and admire places related to those in power. In sum it seems that these traditions eulogizing cities and certain acts were fabricated in a bid to please certain rulers and authorities.

Abbasid rulers in general and Hārūn al-Rashīd in particular were very fond of concubines, and it is most likely that traditions concerning the significance of slave girls, such as those fabricated by ʿUthmān ibn ʿAṭā' and Ḥafṣ ibn ʿUmar, were meant to cause delight to those who could afford them. One such fabricated tradition reads: "You must take care of concubines because they have highly blessed wombs and they are excellent in conceiving and giving birth to children."[68]

Many traditions were fabricated in praise of the Abbasid dynasty. It seems the objective behind such fabrications was to seek the pleasure of Abbasid rulers. Some examples are given below.[69]

(1) The Prophet said about his uncle al-ʿAbbās ibn ʿAbd al-Muṭṭalib: "This is my uncle, the father of forty Caliphs such as al-Safāḥ, al-Mansūr, and al-Mahdī."
(2) The Prophet said that the Abbasid dynasty would have a double edge over Umayyad rule in terms of duration.
(3) The Prophet said: "Once Archangel Gabriel came down with a black robe and black turban. I asked as to the wisdom behind that dress. The angel said: 'This is the dress of the rulers from the descendents of your uncle al-ʿAbbās.' I, then, asked him whether they would be right. The angel said: 'Yes.'" The Prophet then prayed in favor of al-ʿAbbās and his descendents.
(4) The Prophet said: "al-ʿAbbās ibn ʿAbd al-Muṭṭalib is my father, my uncle, my guardian, and my successor."

As mentioned, traditions in praise of certain cities seem to have been fabricated in order to please certain sections of society. Some examples are given below:[70]

(1) In praise of Jeddah: "Four gates of Paradise are opened into the world, Alexandria, ʿAsqalān, Quzwayn, and Jeddah; the position of Jeddah is superior to these cities just as the House of God in Makkah is superior to all the other mosques in the world."
(2) In praise of Asqalan: "Allah will raise from the cemetery of Asqalan seventy thousand martyrs who will be empowered to intercede for as many people as the population of Rabīʿah and Muḍar tribes. Asqalan is the bride of Paradise."
(3) In praise of Naṣībayn: "The Prophet was introduced to a city which he liked very much and asked Archangel Gabriel as to the name of the city. When the Archangel referred to its name as Naṣībayn, the Prophet prayed: 'O Allah! Expedite Muslims' victory over it and put therein blessing for the Muslims'."
(4) In praise of Basra: "The Prophet advised Anas ibn Mālik to settle in a city known as Basra and take care of its mosques and markets."

(5) In praise of various cities of Khurasan: Ibn al-Jawzī has recorded a long tradition in praise of various cities of Khurasan such as Merv, Taliqan, Bukhara, and Khwarizm etc. This tradition might have been fabricated to earn the pleasure of any particular ruler of Khurasan or several rulers of that state.

The Contribution of Muslim Scholars in Identifying Fabricated Traditions

Muslim *ʿulamā'* are the heirs of the Prophet and as such they have always been entrusted with the task of continuing his mission. As history bears witness, the knowledgeable in Muslim societies throughout the world have always risen to the occasion and done their best to perform their duty. One of the tasks the Prophet Muhammad carried out in his life was the differentiation between truth and falsehood. His successors have to further this cause, constantly identifying the true from the false. When the practice of fabrication surfaced, the *ʿulamā'* took immediate action and did their utmost to protect the sacred heritage of prophetic traditions from any form of corruption.

Muslim scholars took this attempt at falsification as a challenge, and their services in this regard may be classified into six categories:

(1) development of the *sanad* system in the Prophetic traditions
(2) campaigning for Hadith narration only from the most reliable sources
(3) investigation of the reporters of Hadith
(4) biographical dictionaries about the reporters
(5) compilation of works on genuine traditions of the Prophet, and
(6) compilation of works containing unreliable and fabricated traditions.

1–Development of the Sanad System in Prophetic Traditions

In the beginning Hadith narration was not based on a chain of narrators. Mere reference to the Prophet in a statement was considered sufficient evidence for its genuineness. None questioned the sources of Hadith. However, when narration of Hadith became a virtual fashion with almost everything reasonable or unreasonable being narrated in the name of the Prophet, great figures of the Muslim Ummah immediately proposed a viable solution: each hadith was to be prefaced by a chain of narrators along with the text of the narration. Muḥammad ibn Sīrīn declared this requirement of knowledge, that is provision of a chain of narrators (*sanad*), as *dīn* (Islamic way).[71] ʿAbd Allah ibn al-Mubārak stated that in the narration of Hadith there were pillars (chains of narrators) which stood between scholars and the people in general.[72]

2–Campaign for Hadith Narration to come only from Reliable Sources

Some people asked one of the great sons of ʿUmar, al-Qāsim ibn ʿUbayd Allah ibn ʿAbd Allah ibn ʿUmar concerning a matter. When he expressed his inability to answer the question, Yaḥyā ibn Saʿīd took exception to this coming as it did from a descendent of the family of ʿUmar. Yaḥyā said to al-Qāsim that it was quite strange that he could not answer the question for he was after all the son of two great leaders of knowledge, ʿUmar ibn al-Khaṭṭāb and ʿAbd Allah ibn ʿUmar. Upon this, al-Qāsim said: "The most reprehensible thing in the eyes of the knowledgeable is that I say something without knowledge or that I narrate from those who are unreliable."[73]

The *ʿulamāʾ* stressed in their sermons, private meetings, and public addresses the need to narrate Hadith only from reliable sources. The basis of this campaign was the Prophetic warning, as reported by Abū Hurayrah that: "Sometime later, liars and charlatans will narrate *aḥādīth* which you or your fathers never heard of; so be careful, keep away from them lest they should make you deviate from the right path and put you in trouble."[74]

Bushayr al-ʿAdawiyy went to ʿAbd Allah ibn ʿAbbās and narrated *aḥādīth*. When he noticed indifference on the part of the Companion, he complained to Ibn ʿAbbās about his inattention to his narrations. Upon this Ibn ʿAbbās remarked:

> We narrated Prophetic traditions with conviction that no lie could ever be attributed to the Prophet. But when people began going to anyone and everyone, whether informed or ill informed, we maintained extra care in the narration of Hadith from the Prophet; we did not take Prophetic traditions except from those whom we knew very well.[75]

A document containing ʿAlī's judgments was presented to ʿAbd Allah ibn ʿAbbās; he erased most of the information contained therein because it had nothing to do with ʿAlī.[76] After ʿAlī's death, the *ʿulamāʾ* never accepted any report concerning the fourth Caliph except through the students of ʿAbd Allah ibn Masʿūd.[77]

Although Abū al-Zinād knew around a hundred narrators of Hadith in Madinah, who were all pious, he and others never took Prophetic traditions from them because they were declared as unsuitable sources.[78]

Saʿd ibn Ibrāhīm stated: "It was not appropriate to narrate from the Prophet except through the most reliable sources (*thaqāt*)."[79] Ṭāus ibn Kaysān advised Sulaymān ibn Mūsā to narrate Prophetic traditions only from those who were known to him for a long time.[80]

3–Investigation of Hadith Reporters

Hadith experts launched a movement to establish who exactly the individuals being cited in the multitude chains of narrators in Prophetic traditions actually were. Investigating the life of these narrators was a very delicate task, as was the issue of declaring whether they were authentic, weak, unreliable, or fabricators. Initially, some scholars hesitated to pronounce judgment on anyone's character, especially declaring someone to be a liar. This was due to the Islamic injunction to abstain from backbiting and accusing others of lying. However, they later reasoned that exposing a narrator's identity was necessary for the sake of maintaining the sanctity of *aḥādīth*. For instance, Shuʿbah ibn al-Ḥajjāj often invited his friends to investigate the identity of narrators with this statement: "Let us backbite for the sake of Allah." He was, at times, advised to refrain from doing this, but would reply: "Refraining from inquiry into the identity of narrators is not an option because it is a religious matter."[81]

Al-Jurjānī discussed the issue with Aḥmad ibn Ḥanbal confiding that he found it hard to declare that this or that narrator was weak or a fabricator. Ibn Ḥanbal consoled him with the advice: "If you and I keep silent on this matter, how will people in general know which narration is authentic and which problematic?"[82]

Muslim scholars were of the view that those introducing new and foreign ideas to Islam and fabricating traditions in the name of the

Prophet were more formidable than open opponents because the latter harmed Islam openly whereas the former attempted to corrupt Islam from within.[83]

Quite a considerable number of scholars were engaged in investigating the position of the narrators of Hadith. The most prominent among them were: Shuʿbah ibn al-Ḥajjāj, Sufyān ibn ʿUyaynah, Sufyān al-Thawrī, Wakīʿ ibn al-Jarrāḥ, ʿAbd Allah ibn al-Mubārak, Muḥammad ibn Ismāʿīl al-Bukhārī, Muslim ibn al-Ḥajjāj, Yaḥyā ibn Saʿīd al-Qaṭṭān, Aḥmad ibn Ḥanbal, Muḥammad ibn ʿĪsā al-Tirmidhī, Aḥmad ibn Shuʿayb al-Nasā'ī, Sulaymān ibn al-Ashʿath Abū Dāwūd, Yaḥyā ibn Maʿīn, Murrah al-Hamdānī, Ḥammād ibn Zayd, Ḥammād ibn Salamah, ʿAbd al-Raḥmān ibn Mahdī.

As a result of rigorous investigations into the identity of Ḥadith narrators, a very clear picture emerged of those who were trustworthy and those who were not. So rigorous was this analysis in fact that not a single narrator was left unidentified as to his position, that is of being either authentic, weak or a fabricator. Bearing in mind the variations which existed in the views of investigators concerning narrators (whose number runs into around a million), we can divide their classification into four main categories: (1) those whose authenticity is unanimous, (2) those whose weakness is non-controversial, (3) those concerning whom there exists controversy among scholars, and (4) those who have been unanimously declared as liars and fabricators.

The list of those narrators who have been identified unanimously as fabricators or unreliable is long. Prominent among those declared as liars and fabricators are: Wahb ibn Wahb al-Qāḍī, Muḥammad ibn al-Sā'ib al-Kalbī, Muhammad ibn Marwān al-Suddī, Muḥammad ibn Saʿīd al-Shāmī, Abū Dāwūd al-Nakhaʿī, Isḥaq ibn Najīḥ, Ghayāth ibn Ibrāhīm al-Nakhaʿī, al-Mughīrah ibn Saʿīd al-Kūfī, Aḥmad ibn ʿAbd Allah al-Juwaybārī, Ma'mūn ibn Aḥmad al-Harawī, Muḥammad ibn ʿUkāshah al-Kirmānī, Muḥammad ibn al-Qāsim al-Kānkānī, Muḥammad ibn Tamīm al-Fārābī, Muḥammad ibn Ziyād al-Yashkurī, Noah ibn Abī Maryam, Jābir ibn Yazīd al-Juʿfiyy.

Scholars not only identified the position or the credibility of the reporters but also announced their findings in every academic meeting, relevant forum, and discussion concerning Hadith. They did this to make ordinary people, as well as students of Islamic disciplines, aware of the identity and reliability of Hadith narrators.

4–Biographical Dictionaries of Hadith Narrators

Despite their achievements Muslim scholars nevertheless felt dissatisfied. Their painstaking investigations into exposing the identity of Hadith narrators needed to be consolidated and put into writing for wide dissemination. Rather than leaving information scattered in Hadith collections, as had initially been the case, investigation reports were formally compiled into a huge database composed of proper biographical dictionaries. These collections consist of two types: those on narrators in general, and those specifically on narrators considered to be weak, fabricators or liars.

Among the most remarkable biographical dictionaries to have been compiled on narrators in general were:

(1) *Al-Ṭabaqāt al-Kubrā* by Muḥammad ibn Saʿd (d.230 AH).
(2) *Al-Tārīkh al-Kabīr* by Muḥammad ibn Ismāʿīl al-Bukhārī (d.256 AH).
(3) *Al-Jarḥ wa al-Taʿdīl* by Ibn Abī Ḥātim (d.327 AH).
(4) *Al-Taqrīb* by Yaḥyā ibn Sharf al-Nawawī (d.676 AH).
(5) *Tahdhīb al-Kamāl fī Asmā' al-Rijāl* by Yūsuf ibn ʿAbd al-Raḥmān al-Mizzī (d.742 AH).
(6) *Mīzān al-Iʿtidāl* by Muḥammad ibn Aḥmad al-Dhahbī (d.748 AH).
(7) *Tahdhīb al-Tahdhīb* by Aḥmad ibn ʿAlī ibn Ḥajar al-ʿAsqalānī (d.852 AH).

The most widely respected works on weak reporters and fabricators of Hadith are:

(1) *Kitāb al-Ḍuʿafā'* by ʿAlī ibn ʿAbd Allah ibn al-Madā'inī (d.234 AH).
(2) *Kitāb al-Ḍuʿafā'* by Muḥammad ibn ʿAbd Allah ibn al-Barqī (d.249 AH).
(3) *Kitāb al-Ḍuʿafā'* by Muḥammad ibn Ismāʿīl al-Bukhārī.
(4) *Al-Ḍuʿafā'* by Ibrāhim ibn Yaʿqūb al-Jūzjānī (d.259 AH).
(5) *Al-Ḍuʿafā' wa al-Matrūkūn* by Saʿīd ibn ʿAmr al-Bardhaʿī (d.292 AH).

(6) *Al-Ḍuʿafāʾ* by Abū Aḥmad ibn ʿAlī ibn al-Jārūd (d.299 AH).
(7) *Al-Ḍuʿafāʾ wa al-Matrūkūn* by Aḥmad ibn Shuʿayb al-Nasāʾī (d.303 AH).
(8) *Al-Ḍuʿafāʾ* by Zakariyyā ibn Yaḥyā al-Sājī (d.307 AH).
(9) *Al-Ḍuʿafāʾ* by Muḥammad ibn Aḥmad al-Dūlābī (d.310 AH).
(10) *Kitāb al-Ḍuʿafāʾ* by Muḥammad ibn ʿAmr al-ʿUqaylī (d.322 AH).
(11) *Kitāb al-Ḍuʿafāʾ* by Abū Nuʿaym ʿAbd al-Malik al-Jurjānī (d.323 AH).
(12) *Al-Ḍuʿafāʾ* by Muḥammad ibn Aḥmad al-Tamīmī (d.333 AH).
(13) *Kitāb al-Ḍuʿafāʾ* by Saʿīd ibn ʿUthmān ibn al-Sakan (d.353 AH).
(14) *Kitāb al-Majrūḥīn* by Abū Ḥātim Muḥammad ibn Ḥibbān (d.354 AH).
(15) *Kitāb al-Kāmil fī Ḍuʿafāʾ al-Rijāl* by Abū Aḥmad ʿAbd Allah ibn ʿAdī ibn al-Qaṭṭān (d.365 AH).
(16) *Kitāb al-Ḍuʿafāʾ* by Muḥammad ibn al-Ḥusayn al-Azdī (d.374 AH).
(17) *Kitāb al-Ḍuʿafāʾ wa al-Matrūkūn* by ʿAlī ibn ʿUmar al-Dārquṭnī (d.385 AH).
(18) *Kitāb al-Ḍuʿafāʾ* by ʿUmar ibn Aḥmad ibn Shāhīn (d.385 AH).
(19) *Kitāb al-Ḍuʿafāʾ* by Muḥammad ibn ʿAbd Allah al-Ḥākim (d.405 AH).
(20) *Kitāb al-Ḍuʿafāʾ* by ʿAbd al-Raḥmān ibn al-Jawzī (d.597 AH).

5–Compilations of Genuine Prophetic Traditions

Goldsmiths well know that gold excavated from mines is not fully pure, but rather a coarse mixture of gold elements and non-gold components. They prefer to concentrate on the separation of the gold from the entire mass and sideline the remaining elements. Muslim scholars can be likened to goldsmiths. In much the same way, their approach is to sift through all the traditions attributed to the Prophet and isolate the genuine from the rest. To do so they have developed certain criteria to check the authenticity of reports and to distinguish the original from the fake. Their efforts have resulted in the compilation of authentic Hadith works. However, although great in number not all these compilations are of the same level of authenticity, and the most authentic among them are:

(1) *Al-Jāmiʿ al-Ṣaḥīḥ* by Muḥammad ibn Ismāʿīl al-Bukhārī.
(2) *Al-Musnad al-Ṣaḥīḥ* by Muslim ibn al-Ḥajjāj al-Qushayrī (d.261 AH).
(3) *Sunan* by Sulaymān ibn al-Ashʿath (d.275 AH).
(4) *Sunan* by Muḥammad ibn ʿĪsā al-Tirmidhī (d.279 AH).
(5) *Sunan* by Aḥmad ibn Shuʿayb al-Nasā'ī.
(6) *Al-Muwaṭṭa'* by Mālik ibn Anas.

6–Compilations of Fabricated Traditions

Traditions fabricated in the name of the Prophet should have been discarded centuries ago, yet they were not. Instead and despite labeling them as such, Hadith scholars memorized and transferred them to the next generation with a clear message that they were lies attributed to the Prophet. Later generations of scholars preserved them with a view to reminding future scholars and students of what had been fabricated, how and by whom. These compilations are few in number, with some not surviving the vicissitudes of time. The most famous among existing compilations are:

(1) *Al-Mawḍūʿāt* by Abū Saʿīd Muḥammad ibn ʿAlī al-Aṣfahānī (d.414 AH).
(2) *Tadhkirah al-Mawḍūʿāt* by Muḥammad ibn Ṭāhir al-Maqdisī (d.507 AH).
(3) *Al-Abāṭīl* by Abū ʿAbd Allah al-Ḥusayn ibn Ibrāhīm al-Jūzqānī (d.543 AH).
(4) *Al-Mawḍūʿāt* by ʿAbd al-Raḥmān ibn al-Jawzī.
(5) *Al-Asrār al-Marfūʿah fī al-Aḥādīth al-Mawḍūʿah* by Nūr al-Dīn Mullā ʿAlī al-Qārī (d.1014 AH).
(6) *Al-Fawā'id al-Majmūʿah fī al-Aḥādīth al-Mawḍūʿah* by Muḥammad ibn ʿAlī al-Shawkānī (d.1250 AH).

Each work contains detailed and solid evidence to prove that the traditions recorded therein were apocryphal, and fabricated by liars, paying special attention to the chain of narrators cited in each recorded tradition. They further demonstrate how fabricators used the names of reliable sources in their chains of fabrications.

2

The Contribution of Muslim Scholars to the Authentication of Hadith

The *Sanad* and *Matn* of Hadith

AS DEFINED EARLIER THE HADITH consist of reports containing information about the Prophet Muhammad's sayings, deeds, decisions, and tacit approvals, as well as eyewitness descriptions of his personal features. Another term used as an alternative for Hadith is Sunnah which literally means way, manner, habit, practice, custom etc, and technically denotes the ways and practices of the Prophet. At times, the term Hadith is also used to refer to sayings and doings attributed to the Companions of the Prophet. Technically, each hadith is comprised of two components: a chain of narrators (*sanad*) and content/text (*matn*). The *sanad* or chain refers to the names of the sources through whom the utterances or practices of the Prophet have been reported and this chain can be long or short. The words of the report, which communicate what the Prophet said or did, constitute the *matn* or text. Matn may also be long or short.

Authentication of Hadith: Brief Historical Background

During the time of the Prophet and around three decades after he passed away not a single question was raised concerning the chain of narrators (*sanad*). During this period entire focus was placed on the text of Hadith (*matn*) only. Verification of Hadith can be traced back to the time of the first Muslim Caliph, Abū Bakr (d.13 AH) who refused to accept any hadith narrated by one single Companion unless confirmed by another Companion; this was to safeguard against the possibility of any intentional or unintentional error(s) creeping into a report made by only one source.[1] This approach continued during the Caliphate of ʿUmar ibn al-Khaṭṭāb (13–23 AH) who was more strict than his predecessor in accepting a hadith. For instance, in one particular case Abū Mūsā al-Ashʿarī (d.50 AH) narrated a hadith to ʿUmar stating that "The Prophet said: 'One who asks for permission three times and gets no response should leave'." ʿUmar however refused to accept this without corroboration and requested Abū Mūsā al-Ashʿarī to provide a witness to verify the Prophetic statement, only being satisfied once the witness, Abū Saʿīd al-Khudrī (d.65 AH), had been produced.[2] ʿUmar explained his actions to Abū Mūsā stating that he was extraordinarily careful about narrating Hadith of the Prophet.[3] Scholars from the generation of the Companions hesitated in accepting a hadith without further verification.[4]

ʿAbd Allāh ibn ʿAbbās (d.68 AH) mentions that "in the beginning we used to listen attentively to any hadith narrated to us, no matter by whom, but when people narrated all kinds of things attributing them to the Prophet, we did not accept any report aside from that which we recognized to be authentic."[5] It seems that this careful approach was adopted by the Companions as a result of the explosive situation which developed after the murder of the third Caliph, ʿUthmān ibn ʿAffān (d.35 AH), and the civil war that erupted between factions which supported ʿAlī and those which supported Muʿāwiyah. This situation was in turn exploited by those with vested interests who fabricated *aḥādīth* on the authority of ʿAlī ibn Abī Ṭālib (d.40 AH).[6] The *ʿulamāʾ* were not oblivious to the realities of events occurring around them, and acted swiftly, doing their best to verify traditions attributed to the Prophet. If a report was narrated on the authority of ʿAlī, the knowledgeable (*ahl al-ʿilm*) did not accept it until it had been confirmed by the disciples of ʿAbd Allāh ibn Masʿūd (d.32 AH), one of the most knowledgeable Companions in the field of *tafsīr* and Hadith. Muḥammad ibn Sīrīn (d.110 AH), a highly acclaimed scholar of *tafsīr* and Hadith, mentions very clearly concerning the authentication of Hadith after the civil war that:

> People never asked about the chain of narrators, but after the civil war requested reporters to identify their sources. If the chain consisted of names from the *ahl al-sunnah* [the orthodox], the hadith was accepted as authentic; if the chain comprised people from the *ahl al-bidʿah* [the innovators], it was rejected as unreliable.[7]

Scholars from later generations categorized a hadith as authentic only when they had established that all its narrators were highly authentic. Ṭā'ūs ibn Kaysān (d.106 AH) exhorted his students to accept *aḥādīth* only from those who were reliable.[8] Abū al-Zinād (d.130 AH) mentions that there were around a hundred well-known pious figures in Madinah during his time, but they were not considered reliable in Hadith.[9] From the second half of the first century after hijrah the chain of narrators assumed a significant place in Hadith authentication. It is this significance of the chain that ʿAbd Allāh ibn al-Mubārak (d.181 AH) refers to in his comment: "The chain of narrators holds religious sanctity. Had the chains not existed, anyone would have uttered anything he wished."[10]

Once he rejected a tradition attributed to the Prophet as unreliable merely on the grounds that the last narrator in its chain, al-Ḥajjāj ibn Dīnār (d. uncertain, probably in the 2nd century after hijrah), had not disclosed the sources that lay between him and the Prophet.[11] Towards the end of the first century after hijrah scholars had developed a fully-fledged discipline of knowledge directly related to the study of Hadith, known as the *ʿilm asmā' al-rijāl* (biographical dictionaries). This knowledge of narrators of Hadith was then extensively used to check the authenticity of a chain. If a chain was found to be reliable, the text reported through that chain was identified as authentic. In case of any problem in the chain, the report was classified as weak or unreliable. Hadith authentication remained in verbal form for around 140 years after hijrah. The first works written on authentic traditions were those compiled by Saʿīd ibn Abī ʿArūbah (d.156 AH) and al-Rabīʿ ibn Ṣabīḥ (d.160 AH).[12] These works were followed by a number of compilations of traditions, the most prominent among them being those compiled by Mālik ibn Anas, Ibn Jurayj (d.150 AH), al-Awzāʿī (d.157 AH), Sufyān al-Thawrī (d.161 AH), Ḥammād ibn Salamah (d.167 AH), Aḥmad ibn Ḥanbal, and Isḥāq ibn Rāhwayh (d.238 AH).

By the time we come to the era of al-Bukhārī, innumerable compilations of traditions existed. However, these works were full of problems. Al-Bukhārī embarked upon a mammoth task, to produce a work comprising the most authentic *aḥādīth* available, and for which he had to select traditions from a mass of 600,000 *aḥādīth*.[13] Likewise Muslim selected *aḥādīth* for his *Ṣaḥīḥ* from a bulk of around 300,000 reports.[14] The works of al-Bukhārī and Muslim were followed by many others. All these compilations of Hadith have one feature in common, the authentication of Hadith through authentication of their chain of reporters (*sanad*). However, one cannot identify any work of Hadith in which reports have been recorded based on both verification of text as well as authentication of chain. Scattered comments and observations on certain *aḥādīth*, from a textual perspective, can be attributed to some scholars, but, on the whole, serious efforts are missing from the scholastic legacy.

Evaluation of Chain and Text

Hadith experts developed five universally acceptable criteria to determine the credibility and authenticity of Hadith:

(1) continuity of the chain (*ittiṣāl al-sanad*),
(2) integrity of narrators' character (*al-ʿadālah*),
(3) precision of the report (*al-ḍabṭ*),
(4) non-deficiency (*ghayr al-ʿillah*), and
(5) non-aberrance (*ʿadm al-shudhūdh*).[15]

The first three criteria are exclusively concerned with verifying the chain of a hadith whilst the remaining two are applicable to both the chain and the text. If a hadith fulfils all these five criteria, it is declared authentic. If it contains any defect failing to meet any of these five criteria, it is described as weak. Ibn Kathīr summarises this succinctly when he states that the authentic hadith is the one whose chain of narrators are all continuously connected to each other, possess integrity of character, and demonstrate powerful memory, and one which is free from any aberrance and defect.[16] As for the weak hadith, it is simply one which remains short of fulfilling the conditions of the authentic one.[17]

Given their importance we will now examine these five criteria in a little more detail.

Continuity of the Chain: The chain of transmitters must be unbroken in order for the hadith to be acceptable. That is, none of the transmitters must be missing from the chain of narrators. Furthermore, each transmitter must also have heard the hadith in question directly from the transmitter before him. Each chain must link directly back to the Prophet or any of his Companions.[18] The position of the Companion in the chain is obvious in that he/she would have met the Prophet and learned from him. The only thing to be verified concerning the transmitter reporting from the Prophet is whether he is a Companion or not. Once it is confirmed that he/she is a Companion of the Prophet, nothing further is checked concerning the transmitter. Other narrators after the Companion are thoroughly investigated as to their connection with their respective immediate sources; scholars minutely scrutinize when and where the two narrators met each other, who was born when and died when etc. For example, if we construct a theoretical chain consisting of the letters A-F we see that: A reports from B who reports from C who reports from D who reports from E who reports from F who reports from the Prophet himself. In terms of the criteria, continuity of the chain denotes that A really met and interacted with B who did the same with C who did the same with D who did the same with E who did the same with F who is a Companion of the Prophet. If investigation confirms that, for instance, there is a gap of time or space between E and F, then this means that E is transmitting a lie that he heard from F, at which point the hadith concerned is considered doubtful as to its authenticity.

Integrity of Character (al-ʿAdālah): The narrator in a chain must be a believer in the real sense of the word, a physically and mentally mature person, free from iniquity with no sign of any human indignity in his character or in his practice.[19] The criterion is comprehensive. Disbelief or hypocrisy, as well as insanity and biological immaturity, on the part of any narrator render him unreliable as to integrity of character. The narrator should not have been reported to have done anything wrong to anyone on any occasion. If a narrator does not pray (salah), does not fast, commits some sin, is found to be involved in frivolous acts, or begs from the public, he is immediately disqualified from fulfilling the criterion of integrity of character.

Precision of the Report (al-Ḍabṭ): It must be verified that the narrator is in possession of a strong and sound memory, and not suffering from weakness in this regard. In addition he should not be found making gross mistakes in his delivery but must convey information accurately; he should not be forgetful or unconscious of what he takes from his source; and he should also not have too much illusions.[20] Any kind of defect in the precision and accuracy of the report, whether from memory or documented material, renders the narrator weak and unreliable.

Non-Deficiency (Ghayr al-ʿIllah): For a hadith to be declared authentic there should be no deficiency within it, whether in text, chain of transmission or both. A deficiency or defect (*ʿillah*) in a hadith denotes something obscure, hidden, or reprehensible in either its chain of narrators or in the text of its report, even though the hadith may initially have appeared to be free of any faults. This deficiency might be due to any one of the following or other factors: (1) a particular narrator in the chain is detected to be alone in making the report concerned, (2) the text of a report stands in contrast to others, (3) a *Tābiʿī* narrator reports directly from the Prophet, (4) the report contains sayings or doings of a Companion, and not of the Prophet, and (5) a Hadith enters another Hadith (meaning that two different traditions get mixed with each other or someone else's statement is inserted into that of the Prophet).[21]

Al-Khair Abadi explains that deficiency in the text can be of various kinds: (1) the text of a tradition goes against the Qur'an, (2) the text is in contrast with the very objective of Islam, (3) the text clashes with established history, (4) the text appears to be irrational, (5) the text contradicts general observation, (6) the text contains information about reward and punishment disproportionately, and (7) the text comprises unsound words and meanings.[22]

Non-Aberrance (ʿAdm al-Shudhūdh): Aberrance (*shudhūdh*) in Hadith means non-conformity, that is a report transmitted by an authentic narrator which contains something contrasting with other traditions narrated by contemporaries who are either stronger than, or on a par with him in memory or in the precision of the report.[23]

Obviously, this defect is related to the text of the report. Aberrance can be in five forms: addition (*ziyadah*), inversion (*qalb*), confusion (*iḍṭirāb*), insertion (*idrāj*), and mispronunciation (*taṣḥīf*).

Addition (*ziyādah*) refers to some addition in the original statement of the Hadith because of which the very nature of the Prophetic command changes. For example, ʿAbd Allāh ibn ʿUmar decreed that the Prophet prescribed one standard cup (*ṣāʿ*) of date fruit or barely as *zakāt al-fiṭr* (an obligatory charity at the end of the month of Ramadan) for all people from the Muslim community.[24] But upon investigation it was discovered that the last words "from the Muslim community" were an addition made by some narrator.

Muslim has recorded the same tradition by Ibn ʿUmar through five chains of narrators, three of which contain the addition and two of which do not.[25] With these additional words the nature of the command changes. Without the addition the command of *zakāt al-fiṭr* becomes compulsory for all; with the addition however, it remains confined to only Muslims. Such a defect in the text renders the hadith unreliable.[26]

Inversion (*qalb*) signifies change in the word order of a Hadith. For example, on the authority of Abū Hurayrah Muslim has recorded a tradition of the Prophet concerning the divine protection of seven categories of people on the Day of Judgment. The sixth category mentioned states: "The one who did charity work and concealed it to the extent that his right hand did not know what his left hand spent in charity." According to known practice, the right hand was used to give charity, but this tradition also mentions the left hand as a giver of charity. A narrator has changed the word order in the report. The original statement might have been: "...that his left hand did not know what his right hand spent in charity."[27]

Confusion (*iḍtirāb*) can be defined as variations in reports on the same matter through the same source. For instance, al-Khair Abadi gives five traditions on the authority of ʿAbd Allāh ibn ʿAbbās which he believes refer to the same case but because the reports vary from each other have led to the occurrence of confusion. All five traditions are quoted below:

(1) A man checked with the Prophet whether he should do compensatory fasting on behalf of his mother who had passed away. The Prophet's answer was in the affirmative.
(2) A woman consulted the Prophet on whether she should do compensatory fasting on behalf of her dead sister. The Prophet allowed her to do so.
(3) A woman asked the Prophet whether she could observe fasting on behalf of her mother who was dead. The Prophet permitted her to do this.
(4) Saʿd ibn ʿUbādah enquired of the Prophet whether he could fulfill the vow his mother could not fulfill before her death. The Prophet gave him permission.
(5) Saʿd asked the Prophet as to what kind of charity work he should do on behalf of his dead mother. The Prophet advised him to build a source of water for public consumption.[28]

Insertion (*idrāj*) can be defined as the inclusion of a non-Prophetic statement into a hadith. For example, the Prophet taught ʿAbd Allāh ibn Masʿūd *al-Tashahhud* for salah and said: "after reciting *al-Tashahhud*, you may remain seated if you wish; you may also leave if you wish to do so."[29] Al-Nawawī claims that the last part "after reciting *al-Tashahhud*, you may remain seated if you wish; you may also leave if you wish to do so" is Ibn Masʿūd's statement, which became inserted in the text as a statement of the Prophet.[30]

Mispronunciation (*taṣḥīf*) refers to the misunderstanding of a word or words in a hadith. For example, the Prophet prohibited people from gathering in circles (*ḥilaq*) before Friday prayer. But the word *ḥilaq* is pronounced by many reporters and *muḥaddithūn* as *al-ḥalq* (shaving of the hair).[31] Obviously, due to the change of pronunciation the word changed in form as well as meaning.

The Role of al-Bukhārī and Muslim

Any history of Hadith compilation remains incomplete without mention of al-Bukhārī (194 AH–256 AH) and Muslim (204 AH–261 AH). Although other scholars of Hadith such as al-Tirmidhī, Abū Dāwūd, al-Nasā'ī, and Aḥmad ibn Ḥanbal are given great recognition for their contributions to the preservation of Hadith, al-Bukhārī and Muslim are held in special regard. Ranked as two of the most eminent and respected Hadith scholars of all time, their method of classification and examination, based on well-defined criteria, laid the foundation of Hadith authentication and methodology as we know it today and as followed by others who came after them. It is little wonder therefore that al-Bukhārī and Muslim hold the status of teachers and pioneers in the field of Hadith authentication.

Imam al-Bukhārī

Al-Bukhārī was born in the city of al-Bukhara (in what is today known as Uzbekistan). His great grandfather al-Mughīrah was originally a Magian (fire worshipper) by religion but became the first person in the lineage of al-Bukhārī to become a Muslim when he converted to Islam at the hands of the governor of Bukhara. His father, who was also a student of Hadith, had the privilege to meet and hear from Mālik ibn Anas. Al-Bukhārī began to acquire knowledge at a very tender age memorizing both the Qur'an and the Hadith in addition to investigating the latter. By the time he was sixteen, he had not only memorized the books of ʿAbd Allāh ibn al-Mubārak and Wakīʿ ibn al-Jarrāḥ but also developed a true understanding of their content. His in depth study of Hadith began in Makkah at the age of sixteen where, within a year or two of his stay, he commenced compiling the verdicts and statements of the Companions and their disciples. It was in Makkah that al-Bukhārī composed his work "*al-Tārīkh*." Once someone suggested to al-Bukhārī's teacher, Isḥāque ibn Rāhwayh, to compile a book containing the traditions of the Prophet. Al-Bukhārī was inspired by this request and decided to embark on the project himself. He recorded nine thousand and eighty two traditions of the Prophet in a masterpiece entitled, *al-Jāmiʿ al-Ṣaḥīḥ*. This selection was in itself distilled from a colossal six hundred thousand *aḥādīth* he had memorized, a staggering feat by any standard. In fact, the actual number of traditions cited in the book is two thousand six hundred and two, but as he repeats his traditions, the total number swells to almost four times higher. The work contains ninety-seven chapters arranged along *fiqhī* themes. Before including any Prophetic traditions in his work al-Bukhārī subjected each and every tradition to the strictest possible scrutiny in terms of its chain of narrators. It is for this reason that his work of Hadith is taken as the most authentic compiled on the Prophetic traditions. Despite this rigor, some Hadith experts such as al-Dārquṭnī challenged the position of around seventy of the traditions recorded by al-Bukhārī. Ibn Ḥajar has proved al-Dārquṭnī's criticism untenable.

Imam Muslim
Muslim was born in Nīsāpur, a city in the Razavi Khorasan province in northeastern Iran. He began studying Hadith at the age of twelve, learning from such eminent scholars as Yaḥyā ibn Yaḥyā and Isḥāque ibn Rāhwayh. His ardent study of Hadith led him to travel widely and considerably to such places as Makkah, Madinah, Kufah, Basrah, Baghdad, Syria, Balkh, Egypt, and Rayy etc. Out of the many works he authored, the most important is indisputably *al-Musnad al-Ṣaḥīḥ* containing a collection of around four thousand traditions. Imam Muslim followed the same rigorous and painstaking methodology of Hadith examination as al-Bukhārī, the only difference being in their grading of some reporters; al-Bukhārī felt that some of Muslim's chains of narrators were not perfectly safe from criticism. In addition Hadith critics suggest there are more problems in Muslim's work than those in al-Bukhārī's. Nevertheless, the beauty of Muslim's work lies in its particular arrangement of traditions, recording as it does all authentic reports on the same subject in one place, and not scattering them in different areas as al-Bukhārī had done.

Authentication of Hadith from a Textual Perspective

It cannot be claimed in any manner possible that al-Bukḥārī and Muslim, and other Hadith authorities, ever examined the texts of *aḥādīth* against certain universally established criteria. Convinced that establishing the authenticity of a hadith's chain of narrators ensured authenticity of its text, their major focus was therefore squarely on authentication of Hadith through a rigorous examination of the chain of narrators. Even when Hadith works have been criticized, particularly those believed authentic, this has been carried out from the perspective and analysis of the chain only. This is not to say that scholars of *ʿUlūm al-Hadīth* have paid no attention to content. References to problems contained in the texts of some of the traditions recorded in authentic Hadith works, including al-Bukhārī and Muslim, have been made in places. Yet a truly serious attempt is largely absent. There exist at least three, to an extent, serious contributions towards the authentication of Hadith through examination of text: (1) Ibn al-Jawzī's *al-Mawḍūʿāt*, (2) Ibn al-Qayyim's *al-Manār al-Munīf fī al-Ṣaḥīḥ wa al-Ḍaʿīf*, and (3) al-Dumaynī's *Maqāyīs Naqd Mutūn al-Sunnah*.

Al-Mawḍūʿāt by Ibn al-Jawzī

Ibn al-Jawzī's work, *al-Mawḍūʿāt* is a compilation of fabricated traditions spread over fifty themes. Once again, his classification of recorded traditions as fabricated has been based not on analysis of text but examination of chain only, although all the traditions compiled in this work could easily have been rejected merely on the basis of text alone, without having to look at the position of the chain. Despite this, the book's headings speak volumes of Ibn al-Jawzī's inclination towards authentication of tradition from a textual angle, although he remains short of declaring any tradition in his work to be fabricated in terms of textual analysis. In terms of the latter he does, at times, interestingly state: "The hearts' aversion to the liars' fabrication constitutes sufficient criterion for the rejection of fabricated traditions."[32] Ibn al-Jawzī has classified the traditions mentioned in the authentic collections of Hadith, including al-Bukhārī and Muslim, into six categories: (1) Those traditions, which are unanimously authentic. (2) Those traditions which are authentic but have only been recorded by al-Bukhārī or Muslim. (3) Those traditions which are claimed to be authentic but neither al-Bukhārī nor Muslim have recorded them. (4) Those traditions which are weak in nature. (5) Those traditions which are extremely weak. (6) And those traditions which are nothing but lies fabricated in the name of the Prophet.[33]

Al-Manār al-Munīf fī al-Ṣaḥīḥ wa al-Ḍaʿīf by Ibn al-Qayyim

Ibn al-Qayyim (d.751 AH) was the first to categorically construct some level of criteria for authenticating Hadith through analysis of text. Those criteria developed by him are: (1) the hadith must not contradict the Qur'an, (2) the hadith should not go against highly authentic *aḥādīth*, (3) the hadith should not negate true observation, (4) the hadith should not describe reward and punishment in a disproportionate manner, (5) the hadith should not contain an unsound statement, and (6) the hadith should not praise or condemn illogically any place, person, profession, or thing. Ibn al-Qayyim's book *al-Manār al-Munīf fī al-Ṣaḥīḥ wa al-Ḍaʿīf*, contains fifty sections under each of which he records traditions declaring them to be unreliable in terms of both the chain and the text. The total number of traditions recorded is three hundred and forty seven.

Maqāyīs Naqd Mutūn al-Sunnah by al-Dumayni

Misfir Gurm Allah al-Dumayni is the first scholar to have written a comprehensive book on the importance of Hadith analysis from a textual perspective. His work was originally a doctorate thesis submitted to and approved by Umm al-Qurā University, Makkah. It is comprised of an Introduction and three chapters. The three chapters, briefly outlined below, are entitled (1) "Criteria of Textual Examination of the Sunnah by the Companions," (2) "Criteria of Textual Examination of the Sunnah by Hadith Scholars," and (3) "Criteria of Textual Examination of the Sunnah by Jurists."

Criteria of Textual Examination of the Sunnah by the Companions

This chapter discusses three criteria for textual examination of the Sunnah: the Qur'an, the highly authentic traditions, and reason. Al-Dumayni emphasizes that the Companions used these criteria to further authenticate traditions reported in the name of the Prophet, although they did not doubt the integrity of their colleagues.[34] The Companions were acutely aware that any statement made by the Prophet could not oppose the Qur'an because they believed that both the Qur'an and the Sunnah were from God; if this occurred they would reject it. Al-Dumayni has advanced eight concrete examples to illustrate the Companions' practice of examining Hadith with reference to the Qur'an. For instance, ʿAlī heard the following tradition reported by Miʿqal ibn Sinān al-Ashjaʿī in the name of the Prophet: "The Prophet decided in the case of Barwaʿ bint Wāshiq who became a widow before her husband could consummate the marriage with her, stating: 'She is entitled to the dower and the inheritance from the deceased's property, and also she has to observe a waiting period (*ʿiddah*)'." ʿAlī rejected the report as the narration of a Bedouin because it had contradicted the Qur'anic statement: "And unto those with whom you desire to enjoy marriage, you shall give the dowers due to them..." (4:24). ʿAlī was of the view that this *āyah* (4:24) makes the dower due by the husband applicable only after the marriage has been consummated.[35] The Companions also exercised the practice of comparing an unknown tradition with a known one, not because they wanted to reject the Prophetic tradition but because they guessed that there existed some problem on the part of the reporter. Under this section al-Dumayni has given eleven examples of this type. For example, a tradition in the name of the Prophet was read before ʿĀ'ishah mentioning that the dog, the donkey, and the woman make the prayer invalid. ʿĀ'ishah forthrightly disapproved this report referring to her own proximity to the Prophet at times whilst he prayed, i.e. occasionally while he prayed she would be lying on the bed in front of him, and if answering the call of nature would gently pull away from very close to his leg.[36] Under the criterion of "reason" to verify the authenticity of a hadith text al-Dumayni gives twelve examples. For instance, he mentions that once Abū Hurayrah reported from the Prophet that ablution should be repeated after eating anything cooked with fire. Ibn ʿAbbās did not accept the genuineness of this tradition and objected on the ground that several things can come into contact with fire such as oil and hot water. He did not think that if hot water was taken or oil used, ablution would have to be repeated.[37]

Criteria of Textual Examination of the Sunnah by Hadith Scholars

Under this chapter al-Dumayni has traced the criteria employed by the *muḥaddithūn* in identifying problems in Hadith. He mentions seven criteria that Hadith scholars used in verifying the genuineness of Prophetic traditions: (1) the Qur'an, (2) non-aberrance (*ʿadm al-shudhūdh*), (3) relatively authentic traditions, (4) established history, (5) freedom from unsound words and meanings, (6) fundamental rules and principles of Islamic law, and (7) freedom from abomination and impossibility.

For the application of the first criterion, the Qur'an, al-Dumayni advances thirteen examples. For instance, Ibn Kathīr has shown how Hadith scholars rejected the tradition – "One who eats with someone already blessed with divine forgiveness is also forgiven" – on the basis of *āyah* 66:10 of the Qur'an which reads: "Allah sets forth an example for the non-believers, the wife of Noah and the wife of Lot: they were respectively under two of Our righteous servants but they betrayed their husbands, and they profited nothing before Allah on their account, but they were told: 'Enter the fire along with others'."[38]

For the criterion of "non-aberrance" the author gives twenty examples. Incidentally al-Dumayni has not used the term "non-aberrance" for the criterion but rather the words "comparison among solitary traditions," although the examples he advances are all of "non-aberrance." Under this principle he puts forward examples of insertion (*idrāj*), confusion (*iḍṭirāb*), inversion (*qalb*), mispronunciation (*taṣḥīf*), and addition (*ziyādah*) categorising all these as under "aberrance" (*shudhūdh*). He cites the following in illustration:

Insertion (idrāj) – According to al-Suyūṭī, the tradition "For the slave is a double reward; by the One in Whose Hand is my soul, if it were not for jihad in the cause of Allah, pilgrimage, and taking care of my mother, I would prefer to die the death of a slave" is problematic in terms of insertion. The first part, "For the slave is a double reward," seems to be a hadith, but the later part represents Abū Hurayrah's own wish, later taken to be the genuine statement of the Prophet.[39]

Confusion (iḍṭirāb) – Al-Tirmidhī has recorded a Prophetic tradition on the authority of Fāṭimah bint Qays which states that "In wealth there is indeed the right besides zakah"; Ibn Mājah has recorded the same tradition differently: "In wealth there is not any right except zakah." Due to the obvious contradiction both reports are rendered weak and hence unreliable.[40]

Inversion (qalb) – Al-Bukhārī has recorded a Prophetic tradition on the authority of Abū Hurayrah which states: "As for the fire, Allah increases it for whomever He wills; and with regard to Paradise, Allah will not do anything wrong to anyone." Al-Ṣanʿānī identifies a change of word order therein and suggests that the tradition should in fact have read like this: "As for Paradise, He increases it for whomever He wills; as regards the fire, Allah will not do anything wrong to anyone."[41]

Mispronounciation (taṣḥīf) – Anas ibn Mālik reports from the Prophet that "And whoever said, 'None has the right to be worshipped but Allah' and has in his heart good [faith] equal to the weight of an atom (*dharrah*) will be taken out of Hell." Shuʿbah ibn al-Ḥajjāj says that the word is not *dharrah* (atom) but rather *dhurah* (maize).[42]

Addition (ziyādah) – The same example as that for Mispronunciation is applied.[43]

For the criterion of "relatively authentic tradition" al-Dumaynī has not given any concrete example but has rather noted twenty-two principles outlining how the Prophetic traditions can be checked as to their authenticity.[44]

Under the criterion "established history," he has given nine examples including the following. According to al-Tirmidhī, when the Prophet entered Makkah in victory, ʿAbd Allāh ibn Rawāḥah was present with him. Ibn al-Qayyim rejects this report on the ground that Ibn Rawāḥah had been martyred in the battle of Mu'tah, four months before the victory of Makkah.[45]

Under the criterion "freedom from unsound words and meanings," al-Dumaynī has quoted seventeen traditions in illustration including one "Looking at a beautiful face is a devotional act (*ʿibādah*)" which Ibn al-Qayyim rejects, on the basis that the content of the report is unsound.[46]

Under the criterion "fundamental rules and principles of Islamic law," al-Dumayni cites twenty traditions as illustration. In one particular example Nāṣir al-Dīn al-Albānī is shown to have considered the tradition, "Due to a person's addiction to adultery his wife will be afflicted with the same habit," as absolute rubbish based on the Islamic principle cited in *āyah* 53:39 of the Qur'an: "And for man is nothing but what he strives for."[47]

Under the criterion "freedom from abomination and impossibility" he has given nineteen examples. One such example is the tradition: "Nine angels are entrusted to the sun, [they] throw snow on it every day, otherwise the sun would have burnt everything which came into contact with it." Al-Albānī brushes this aside considering it something akin to a Judeo-Christian tradition and against the principles of astronomy according to which earth's 150 million kilometer distance from the sun prevents it from being burnt.[48]

Criteria of Textual Examination of the Sunnah by Jurists

When exploring the approach of Muslim jurists to Hadith texts, al-Dumayni identifies seven criteria: (1) the Qur'an, (2) the Sunnah, (3) consensus of the Ummah, (4) practice of the Companions, (5) logical analogy, (6) general principles, and (7) the impact of solitary tradition.

Under the criteria of the Qur'an twenty-one examples have been discussed including the following: "Along with a woman as wife her paternal or maternal aunt cannot be taken by the husband as wife at the same time." The Ḥanafites and other jurists do not find the tradition of Muslim to be against *āyah* 4:23–24 of the Qur'an:

> Prohibited to you (For marriage) are: Your mothers, daughters, sisters; father's sisters, Mother's sisters; brother's daughters, sister's daughters; foster-mothers (Who gave you suck), foster-sisters; your wives' mothers; your step-daughters under your guardianship, born of your wives to whom ye have gone in, – no prohibition if ye have not gone in; (Those who have been) wives of your sons proceeding from your loins; and two sisters in wedlock at one and the same time, except for what is past; for Allah is Oft-Forgiving, Most Merciful; Also (prohibited are) women already married, except those whom your right hands possess: Thus hath Allah ordained (Prohibitions) against you: Except for these, all others are lawful...

Jurists are of the view that the tradition specifies the limits placed by the Qur'an.[49]

Under the criterion of Sunnah only four examples have been mentioned. For instance Ḥanafites do not find the tradition "the Prophet decided a case on the basis of a witness and an oath" practically valid because they find this clashes with a more authentic and famous tradition that "the evidence is due on the petitioner and the oath is due on the defendant."[50]

Under the criterion "consensus of the Ummah," nine traditions are given. For example, Mālik ibn Anas recorded a report which stated that al-Qāsim ibn Muḥammad used to sell all the date fruits grown in his garden with the exception of some weight of fruit. Mālik ibn Anas concluded that the practice of al-Qāsim ibn Muḥammad was in line with the consensus of the Ummah.[51]

Under the criterion the "practice of the Companions," al-Dumayni gives ten traditions. For example, Ibn ʿUmar reported that the Prophet used to raise his hands before and after bowing (*rukūʿ*) in prayer (salah). A *Tābiʿī*, Mujāhid reports: "I prayed behind Ibn ʿUmar, he did not raise his hands in the prayer except at its beginning." According to al-Ṭaḥāwī, the practice of Ibn ʿUmar is a valid reason to consider the tradition of the Prophet abrogated.[52]

Under the criterion "logical analogy," we have nine examples i.e. Abū Dāwūd has recorded a tradition which states that "If a person forced his wife's slave girl to have sex with him, the slave would be freed and he would give her replacement to his wife; if the slave girl herself solicited him for sex, she would fall under his possession and he would give her replacement to his wife." Ibn Taymiyyah claims that logical analogy favors the authenticity of this tradition.[53]

Under the criterion of "general rules," we are given six examples of traditions i.e. Mālik ibn Anas rejects the tradition, "If a dog inserts its mouth inside a ware, it is to be washed seven times," on the basis of a general principle in the Qur'an: "...And as for those hunting animals which you train by imparting to them something of the knowledge that God has imparted to yourselves – eat of what they seize for you, but mention God's name over it and remain conscious of God: verily, God is swift in reckoning." (5:4)[54]

Under the criterion "the impact of solitary tradition," al-Dumayni has given in illustration four traditions. In one of these Abū Mūsā reports that once many people laughed whilst in prayer (salah) behind the Prophet; after the prayer he commanded them to make fresh ablution and repeat the prayer. Ḥanafites reject this tradition on the basis of it being a solitary one which if taken as authentic would put the people in difficulty.[55]

Conclusion

Right from the time of the Companions, Muslim scholars have paid special attention to the preservation as well as authentication of Prophet Muhammad's traditions. Initially, *aḥādīth* were examined from both the angles of their chain of narrators as well as the text of hadith. In the 2nd and 3rd centuries when great Hadith works were compiled Hadith scholars developed some criteria in which the examination of the chain remained the focal point. It was scholars of *ʿulūm al-ḥadīth* who also talked in principle about textual examination of Hadith. As for the textual examination of Hadith, the most prominent works are Ibn al-Jawzī's, Ibn al-Qayyim's, and al-Dumaynī's.

3

The Qur'an and Authentication of Hadith

THE MOST FAMOUS AND WIDELY acclaimed collections of traditions considered to be authentic include the *Muwaṭṭa'* of Mālik ibn Anas, the *Ṣaḥīḥ* of Muḥammad ibn Ismāʿīl al-Bukhārī, the *Ṣaḥīḥ* of Muslim ibn al-Hajjāj al-Qushayrī, the *Sunan* of Abū Dāwūd (d.275 AH), the *Sunan* of Muḥammad ibn ʿĪsā al-Tirmidhī, and the *Sunan* of Aḥmad ibn Shuʿayb al-Nasā'ī. Notably, these and other compilations adopted a chain-of-narrators level of critical authentication of Hadith with no Hadith collection ever being compiled on the basis of both authentication of the chain of narrators and content (text of reports) together. This is not to say that content was altogether ignored, some Muslim scholars like Abū Ḥanīfah, al-Shāfiʿī, Ibn al-Jawzī (d.751 AH), and Ibn al-Qayyim did suggest textual examination of Hadith by applying certain universally established criteria, including (as proposed) the Qur'an. Muslim scholars are almost unanimous concerning the position of the Qur'an in relation to the Hadith. According to them, in a situation of uncompromising conflict between a tradition recorded in the name of the Prophet and the Qur'an, the tradition is to be rejected as unacceptable.

Understanding the Position of the Qur'an in Relation to the Hadith

As people hold varying opinions, perspectives, and ideas, they need to refer to some form of a universally established standard under which differences can be settled and a compromise reached. When making judgment concerning the nature of *aḥādith* scholars may reach a point in which they differ from one another and in such situations the first criterion to refer to and apply is the Qur'an. Being the revealed speech of Allah the Qur'an does not represent the human mind and in its own words is to be seen as "the criterion" (*al-Furqān*):

> It was the month of Ramadan in which the Qur'an was bestowed from on high as a guidance unto man, and a self-evident proof of that guidance, and as the criterion by which to discern the true from the false. (2:185)

> And it is He who has bestowed from on high the criterion by which to discern the true from the false. (3:4)

> Hallowed is He who from on high, step by step, has bestowed upon His servant the criterion by which to discern the true from the false. (25:1)

The Qur'an therefore is a God-given criterion, which spells out what is right and what is wrong, distinguishing truth from falsehood. It states that Allah revealed to the Prophet two things, the Qur'an and its *bayān* (interpretation): "Thus, when We recite it, follow its wording: and then, behold, its *bayān* [interpretation] will be upon Us" (75:18–19).

Undoubtedly the role of the Hadith and the Sunnah is to serve as the interpretation of the Qur'an. Thus as the Prophet's utterances and practices symbolize the *bayān*, both the Qur'an and *bayān* should complement each other. There should be perfect harmony between the two. If any component of the *bayān* i.e. hadith contrasts with the Qur'an, the tradition attributed to the Prophet may be forthrightly rejected as unacceptable. The Book of Allah exists not only to serve as a guide but also as a mediator in a situation of dispute. *Sūrah al-Nisā'*: 59 reads:

> O you who have attained to faith! Pay heed unto Allah, and unto the Apostle, and unto those from among you who have been entrusted with authority; and if you are at variance over any matter, refer it to unto Allah and the Apostle.

This *āyah* exhorts the believers to make Allah and His Prophet as the judge in any disputed matter. Compilations of Hadith are not free from controversies in terms of content, therefore the Qur'an as representing Allah's authority can be used as a means to verify the contents of *aḥādith*. If no conflict exists between the two, then the hadith should be declared as authentic. In cases of apparent conflict, traditions should be categorized as unreliable.

ʿĀ'ishah's Approach

The Prophet's wife ʿĀ'ishah (d.57 AH) was a repository of vast knowledge and she was consulted time and again by Muslims concerning Qur'anic revelations, the statements and practices of the Prophet, and Islamic law. She was also regarded as a religions scholar serving as teacher to the knowledgeable, to students, the young and old, senior and junior Companions, women and men etc. ʿĀ'ishah was also often approached to resolve various problems not only after the Prophet's demise but also during his lifetime. Abū Mūsā al-Ashʿarī observes, concerning the position of ʿĀ'ishah among the Companions of the Prophet that: "Whenever we faced a problem concerning a Prophetic tradition, we approached ʿĀ'ishah and found the academic (intellectually satisfactory) solution with her."[1] After the demise of the Prophet she commanded the respect of the Muslims not only as the mother of believers but also for her extensive knowledge. Her approach to Hadith in relation to the Qur'an is apparent from the following examples:

The Prophet once stated: "One, who was called to account [on the Day of Judgment], was punished."[2] ʿĀ'ishah found this contrary to the Qur'anic statement (84:7–8): "As for him whose record shall be placed in his right hand, he will in time be called to account with an easy accounting." She shared her concern with the Prophet who satisfied her by saying: "That is the easy reckoning; but he who was questioned is bound to be doomed."[3] This account of ʿĀ'ishah's concern illustrates the point that a hadith should not contradict the Qur'an.

ʿĀ'ishah was once asked whether Ibn ʿUmar's report that "the Prophet said: 'They [the dead] hear what I say'," was true? She denied the authenticity of the report, presenting what the Prophet had actually said, namely, "They know what I say is true," and ended by reciting the two *āyāt*: 1) "Verily, you cannot make the dead hear" (27:80), and 2) "thou canst not make hear such as are [dead of heart like the dead] in their graves" (35:22).[4] Once again by quoting the Qur'an she wanted to make it clear that the Prophet could not say anything that went against the Qur'an.

When ʿUmar was wounded seriously, Ṣuhayb started crying. Upon this, ʿUmar said: "Why are you crying for me? I heard the Prophet saying: Verily, the dead [person] is punished due to some wailing/mourning its people make [over it]." After the death of ʿUmar, this tradition was brought to the notice of ʿĀ'ishah. She said that the Prophet had not said this, but rather what he did say in this regard was: "Verily, Allah increases the torment of the non-believer due to the cries of his relatives for him." She further said: "The Qur'an should be enough for you in this matter. It says: 'And no bearer of burdens shall be made to bear another's burden'" (6:164; 17:15; 35:18; 39:7; 53:38).[5]

ʿAbd Allāh ibn ʿAbbās is reported to have mentioned that the Prophet saw Allah twice. When this was brought to ʿĀ'ishah's attention, she directly rejected the opinion and recited an *āyah* from the Qur'an: "No human vision can encompass Him, whereas He encompasses all human vision: for He alone is unfathomable, all-Aware" (6:103).[6]

Abū Hurayrah's report of a Prophetic tradition was quoted to ʿĀ'ishah: "Evil portents are in the woman, the animal, and the house." She immediately corrected this saying: "The Prophet said that people of the period of ignorance used to say that evil omens are in the woman, the animal, and the house." She, then, quoted a verse from the Qur'an to further confirm her stand: "No calamity can ever befall the earth and neither your own selves, unless it be in Our decree before We bring it into being" (57:22).[7]

The issue of temporary marriage (*mutʿah*) caused controversy among Muslims, with some wanting to retain it and others considering it to have been prohibited forever. When the matter was presented to ʿĀ'ishah, she stated: "Between me and you is the Book of Allah; it says: 'And who safeguard their chastity, except with those joined to them in marriage bond or whom their right hands possess: for they are free from blame' (23:5–6); hence one who desires other than whom Allah has granted him in marriage or whom Allah has given him as his possession has transgressed."[8]

ʿUmar's Position

ʿUmar ibn al-Khaṭṭāb (d.23 AH) once immediately rejected a statement attributed to the Prophet by Fāṭimah bint Qays, a female Companion, as unacceptable on the grounds that it went against the Qur'an. Fāṭimah claimed that after she had been divorced three times by her husband, the Prophet judged that she had no right to alimony and lodging.[9] ʿUmar's rejection of this hadith was based on the Qur'anic statement (65:1): "Do not expel them [divorcees] from their homes; and neither shall they [be made to] leave unless they become openly guilty of immoral conduct."[10]

ʿAbd Allāh ibn ʿAbbās's Perspective

A statement of the Prophet purporting to put a ban on the meat of domestic donkeys was reported. ʿAbd Allāh ibn ʿAbbās rejected the authenticity of the report on the basis of the Qur'anic *āyah*: "Say: I find not in the message revealed to me any meat forbidden for one who wishes to eat it, unless it be dead meat, or blood poured forth. Or the flesh of swine – for it is an abomination – or what is impious on which a name other than Allah has been invoked" (6:145).[11]

Abū Ḥanīfah's Comment

Nuʿmān ibn Thābit Abū Ḥanīfah remarked in his treatise, *al-ʿĀlim wa al-Mutaʿallim* that one must believe that the Prophet never said anything unjust, or ever uttered, or did anything, that went against the Qur'an. In his opinion any tradition in the name of the Prophet which clashed with the Qur'an was to be rejected as false. Clarifying this further he emphasized that by rejection of a tradition he did not mean rejection of the Prophet's statement but rather one or other of the narrator's lie attributed to the Prophet.[12]

Al-Shāfiʿī's Observation

Muḥammad ibn Idrīs al-Shāfiʿī observed in his masterpiece, *al-Umm* that if a hadith contrasted with the Qur'an, it could not be accepted as having legitimately come from the Prophet, even if its transmitters were authentic. In fact he quotes a hadith of the Prophet himself to support this position: "Hadith will, indeed, spread far and wide in my name; whatever thereof is in conformity with the Qur'an is genuinely mine; and whatever thereof clashes with the Qur'an is certainly not from me."[13]

Ibn Qayyim al-Jawzīyyah's Comment

In response to a tradition attributed to the Prophet that "the life of the world is seven thousand years and we are in the 7th millennium" Muḥammad ibn Abī Bakr ibn Qayyim al-Jawzīyyah read an *āyah* from the Qur'an:

> They will ask thee [O Prophet] about the Last Hour: "When will it come to pass?" Say: "Verily, knowledge thereof rests with my Sustainer alone. None but He will reveal it in its time. Heavily will it weigh on the heavens and the earth; [and] it will not fall upon you otherwise than of a sudden." They will ask thee – as if thou couldst gain insight into this [mystery] by dint of persistent inquiry! Say: "Knowledge thereof rests with my Sustainer alone; but [of this] most people are unaware." (7:187)[14]

Relevant Examples

Further examples are given below of *aḥādīth* whose contents conflict with the Qur'an:

1–Lies Attributed to Prophet Ibrāhīm

Al-Bukhāri, Muslim and others have recorded a hadith on the authority of Abū Hurayrah which mentions that "The Prophet said: 'Ibrāhīm never spoke lies except three lies.'"[15]

This tradition comprises an allegation against prophet Ibrāhīm whereas the Qur'an exonerates him of these kinds of allegations saying: "And call to mind, through this divine writ, Ibrāhīm. Behold, he was a man of truth, a prophet" (19:41). The Qur'an describes prophet Ibrāhīm as a paragon of truth (*ṣiddīq*), whereas the hadith quotes some exceptions to this quality. The Qur'anic word *ṣiddīq* used to glorify Ibrāhīm means "perfectly truthful."[16] Al-Rāghib al-Asfahānī (d.502 AH) mentions four views concerning the meaning of *ṣiddīq*: 1) one in whose life the truth dominates, 2) one who never speaks a lie, 3) one who is so much given to the truth that the occurrence of lie is impossible, and 4) one whose deeds correspond to his assertions.[17] In fact, prophet Ibrāhīm was a man of truth in all these four senses. In Arabic this form (e.g. *siddīq*) of any word (such as *ᶜalīm, khabīr, matīn, karīm, ḥasīn* etc) signifies perfection.

If this hadith is considered authentic, then the Qur'anic statement proves meaningless. If the sanctity of the Qur'an is maintained, then the tradition will have to be classified as unreliable. Ibn Ḥajar al-ᶜAsqalānī, one of the most highly recognized commentators of al-Bukhāri's Hadith work, *Ṣaḥīḥ*, seems to be inclined towards maintaining the authenticity of the tradition. He quotes Ibn ᶜAqīl (d.513 AH) as having stated that the situation faced by Ibrāhīm was such that he was forced to resort to making false statements, which according to him was quite logical.[18] Al-Qāḍī Abū Bakr ibn al-ᶜArabī (d.543 AH) also approves this hadith stating that the position of Ibrāhīm as a prophet and friend of Allah required him to be open with the truth but that he was allowed a concession to lie which he accepted.[19] Al-Qurṭubī (d.671 AH) tries to justify the hadith by using the same argument that Ibn al-ᶜArabī developed.[20] Ibn al-Jawzī rejects as unfounded the allegation that prophet Ibrāhīm lied, stating that what have been attributed to Ibrāhīm as lies are not lies but equivocations (*maᶜārīḍ*). In order to prove his point he advances several examples from Islamic history itself.[21] Yet, he remains short of declaring the hadith as unacceptable. Al-Ālūsī (d.1270 AH) does not find any problem in the authenticity of the report stating that the mention of lies attributed to prophet Ibrāhīm is metaphorical (*majāz*), and not in its actual sense.[22] However, the metaphorical application of the word "lie" may not generally be considered a problem, but to apply it to a prophet is certainly undesirable. Moreover it is inconceivable that Prophet Muhammad would apply the word *kadhib* (lie) even metaphorically to a prophet whom the Qur'an honors with the eminent title of *ṣiddīq* (meaning the most truthful). Amin Ahsan Islahi (d.1997 AC) also seems to justify the authenticity of the hadith. He states that the word *kadhib* has three connotations, lie, mistake, and double entendre, and that in the hadith it has been used in the sense of a double entendre. He further argues that the word *kadhib* was used by Arab poets in this sense and therefore there may not be any intrinsic problem with the report.[23]

Nevertheless even though Arab poets and orators have used the word *kadhib* in the sense of a double entendre, it is hard to imagine that the Prophet would use a word which had the potential to mislead people, particularly when the Qur'an takes a very clear stand on the position of this great prophet, Ibrāhīm.

Al-Fakhr al-Rāzī (d.606 AH) on the other hand, categorically declares the hadith to be a lie suggesting that it is more appropriate to accuse the narrators of fabricating the lie than to attribute any lie to the prophet himself.[24] Syed Mawdudi (d.1979 AC) criticizes the approach of those who consider the hadith to be authentic stating that those who do so care more for the truthfulness of al-Bukhārī's and Muslim's sources of information than they do for a prophet standing accused of having lied. It is not reasonable he contends to attribute to Prophet Muhammad such a gross statement merely on the grounds that its chain of narrators is not defective.[25] Finally in Sayyid Qutb's opinion there is no need to refer to prophet Ibrāhīm's statements, as mentioned in the Qur'an – "Nay, this was done by this the biggest one" (21:63); "I am sick" (37:89) – as lies. These are not lies he argues but satirical answers meant for the general public.[26]

2–Predetermination of Human Destiny

In their works on Hadith, al-Bukhārī, Muslim and others have included a chapter on predestination (*Kitāb al-Qadar*). All the reports recorded therein conform to the idea that everything in life is predetermined. The first hadith quoted in these sources is on the authority of ʿAbd Allāh ibn Masʿūd. According to this tradition the Prophet said:

> Verily, the first structural form of everyone of you is gathered in his mother's womb for forty days, then it turns into a clot of blood (*ʿalaqah*) and remains like this for the same period, then it turns into a lump of flesh (*muḍghah*) and remains like this for the same period whereupon the angel is sent who breaths into it life, and is commanded to write its sustenance (*rizq*), life-span (*ajal*), whole life activities (*ʿamal*), and its end either as a condemned one (*shaqiyy*) or as a rewarded one (*saʿīd*). By the One except whom there is no deity but He! One of you indeed performs the deeds of the people deserving Paradise until there is almost no distance between him and Paradise, he is then over-

> taken by destiny (*al-kitāb*); he consequently does the deeds of those to be condemned to Hell, and he enters it. And one of you performs the deeds of the condemned until there is very little distance between him and Hell, he is then overtaken by destiny and he starts doing good deeds, as a result of which he enters Paradise.[27]

According to this tradition, man is not free to think, choose and act, but bound only to do that which has already been fixed by the Creator. This concept of predetermination stands in stark contrast to the "theory of examination" mentioned in the Qur'an. On around twenty-two occasions, the Qur'an reiterates the fact that man is being tested in various ways. For example:

> Behold, We have willed that all beauty on earth be a means by which We put men to a test, to see as to which of them are best in conduct. (18:7)

> He Who created Death and Life, that He might test you, as to which of you is best in deed. (67:2)

These Qur'anic statements are crystal clear concerning the position of man on earth. Man lives and acts in this life as an examinee and the concept of examination entails freedom of will to think, decide, choose and act. The Qur'an mentions that man is, to the extent of his needs, free, whereas the hadith quoted denies him this privilege binding him to a predestined plan.

This tradition also contrasts with the concept of the malleability of man. The Qur'an has used three phrases, "they might" (*la ʿallahum*), "you might" (*la ʿallakum*), and "he might" (*la ʿallahu*) around 44, 68 and 3 times respectively (three of which are quoted below). These phrases indicate that man is able to change if he so wishes.

> And We tried them with blessings as well as afflictions, so that "they might" mend their ways. (7:168)

> In this way God makes clear His messages unto you, so that "you might" find guidance. (3:103)

> But speak unto him in a mild manner, so that "he might" bethink himself or [at least] be filled with apprehension. (20:44)

These assertions refer to man as a malleable creature. The feature of malleability does not allow one to think of man as bound and coerced by destiny.

Nevertheless one might on the other hand object and point to the meaning of those verses in the Qur'an which apparently do support the idea of predestination. However, it should be born in mind that these verses have been interpreted in a way that allows them to appear to be in favor of a fore-written destiny for man. As debate on this issue is beyond the scope of this work, suffice it to say that no verse of the Qur'an contradicts another verse, there being complete harmony among all the statements made in the Qur'an. An interpretation of a verse which goes against another verse is not acceptable and the duty of a *mufassir* is to interpret the Qur'an in such a way that the entire Qur'an appears as an integral whole. Since a number of *āyāt* very clearly mention the idea of man's examination on earth, no *āyah* can ever be construed as speaking in favor of a predetermination theory.[28]

Most of the traditions recorded by al-Bukhārī and Muslim in their *Kitāb al-Qadar* may not withstand any Qur'anic scrutiny in light of its theory on man's malleability and his existence on earth being an examination. In fact, what the above tradition declares and what the Qur'an explains are poles apart, and there may hardly be any way to effect a compromise between them. This is why only one of them can be accepted as right. Naturally, the judgment will go in favor of the Qur'an.

Apart from this the tradition itself contains an intrinsic discrepancy. There are obviously two sections to the tradition, one informing about the process of predetermination, the other referring to the impact of predetermination on man's life and the end-result. In the first section, there is reference to only one book (*kitāb*) according to which man's life will be patterned. But in the second section there is reference to one more book according to which man is to some extent independent to decide and act. The book of destiny overtakes man only after he enjoys his freedom for a certain period of time. This discrepancy alone may suffice to render the hadith unreliable.

3–Man's Deeds Irrelevant for Entry into Paradise

Al-Bukhārī, Muslim and others have recorded this hadith on the authority of various authorities including Abū Hurayrah: "The Prophet said: 'None of you shall ever enter Paradise due to his deed'. Someone asked: 'Even you, O Prophet of Allah?' The Prophet answered: 'Yes, even I, except that my Lord covers me with His mercy'."[29]

This statement seems to contradict the glad tidings given in the Qur'an that the good deeds of sincere believers will lead them to Paradise (7:43; 16:32; 52:19; 77:43). In both the Makkī and Madnī periods of the Prophet, revelations were received assuring the believers and informing the non-believers, that success in this life and the hereafter depended on sincere faith and good deeds (2:25, 82, 277; 3:57; 4:57, 122, 173; 11:23; 14:23; 18:107; 22:14, 23, 50, 56; 29:58; 31:8; 32:19; 42:22; 47:12; 85:11 etc).

The Qur'an uses the term *jazā'* (reward and recompense), when referring to believers' entry into Paradise (16:30–31). In verses 23:1–11 it clearly states that entry into Paradise is the real success (*fālāḥ*) guaranteed for those who do good deeds. *Āyah* 10:4 spells out that the promise of Allah is genuine, and the promise that He will reward justly in the hereafter those with sincere faith and good deeds. Even the mercy (*raḥmah*) of Allah is conditioned to faith and good deeds (45:30). *Āyah* 9:111 announces that there is an agreement between the believers and Allah according to which the believers will sacrifice their wealth and lay down their lives in the path of Allah, and Allah will grant them entry into Paradise. In short, the Qur'an recognizes the significance of good deeds, whereas the hadith denies their impact.

Ibn Baṭṭāl (d.449 AH), a commentator of al-Bukhāri, does not find any contradiction between this tradition and the Qur'anic statements concerning the significance of good deeds. He states that the hadith refers to man's entry into Paradise and everlasting comforts therein, and that the Qur'an (16:30 and 43:72) informs us concerning the role of good deeds in determining the status of man therein.[30] This is mere conjecture. It would appear that whilst Ibn Baṭṭāl is aware of the conflict between the Qur'an and this tradition, his explanation, which is untenable, is more a result of his enthusiasm to maintain the sanctity of the tradition.

Al-Kirmānī (d.786 AH), another commentator of al-Bukhārī, tries to justify the tradition in a different manner. He claims that mere good deeds will not cause one to enter Paradise but rather mercy which will be required, for Paradise is not the recompense of deeds.[31] This opinion is inherently problematic on two counts: First, the Qur'an itself declares unequivocally that Allah has bought from believers their lives and wealth and in return has reserved their places in Paradise (9:111). Second, whilst it is true that Allah's mercy plays a role in this regard, the role of man's deeds cannot be ignored. It is man's good deeds, which make him deserving of Allah's mercy (45:30). If Allah's mercy is conditioned with good deeds, how can one then deny the contribution of man's deeds?

Al-Ālūsī advances yet another argument to forge a compromise between the tradition and Qur'anic statements on the matter. In his view the Qur'an refers to a general reason whilst the tradition discloses the real reason for entry into Paradise.[32] However, this is not satisfactory for it seems oblivious of the fact that the tradition does not give any credit to good deeds at all.

In fact there is the possibility that the tradition could have been developed to silence Muʿtazilite scholars for it is forcefully used to condemn their stand that man will enter Paradise due to his deeds, even though the Muʿtazilites advance the Qur'an to support their view.[33]

Finally, the second part of the tradition, which indicates that even the Prophet himself will not be eligible for entry into Paradise without the mercy of Allah, seems to degrade the position of the Messenger. The Prophet's position is sacrosanct. His name is mentioned beside Allah in the Qur'an. Actually the question itself ("even you, O Prophet of Allah?") is suspect. It may not have been raised by any of his Companions who were well aware that the Prophet was already a sign of Allah's mercy (21:107).

4–Coercion in Conversion to Islam

Al-Bukhārī, Muslim and others have recorded this hadith on the authority of ʿUmar, Ibn ʿUmar and Abū Hurayrah etc: "The Prophet said: 'I have been commanded to wage war (*qitāl*) against mankind (*al-nās*) until they acknowledge (*shahādah*) that there is no deity but Allah; one who professes it (*lā ilāha illā Allah*), his life and property are safe from me, except for the sake of justice, and his reckoning is with Allah'."[34]

This tradition seems to legitimize the use of force to spread Islam across the world. Although Ibn Ḥajar finds a problem in the report, he tries to interpret it in such a way as to fend off accusations of coercion in the faith. He contends that the word 'war' (*qitāl*) may also mean something else that can prevent war, such as imposition of a levy (*jizyah*) on non-Muslims, and in addition that the word *shahādah* signifies both an acceptance of Islam or an enemy's subjugation, which could be achieved by either killing them, drafting a treaty, or by imposing a levy.[35] This interpretation may not be tenable. The tradition as quoted declares in an unambiguous manner that the Prophet was bound to fight people to force them to accept Islam, and in the case of people's rejection of the new faith to wage war against them until they totally submitted to Allah. Al-Samʿānī (d.489 AH) views in this tradition, among other things, an obligation to engage in war against the non-believers.[36] He has rightly understood the import of the hadith. What is absolutely clear is that the hadith stands in marked contrast to certain Qur'anic injunctions:

> There shall be no coercion in matters of faith. Distinct has now become the right way from [the way of] error. (2:256)

> If they turn away, We have not sent you as a guard over them: you are not bound to do more than deliver the message. (42:48)

> And so, [O Prophet,] exhort them; your task is only to exhort: you cannot compel them [to believe]. (88:21–22)

These *āyāt* obviously prohibit the use of force in conversion to Islam. All Islamic jurists hold the position that forcible conversion is, under all circumstances, null and void, and that any attempt to coerce a non-believer to accept Islam is a grievous sin: a verdict, which disposes of the widespread fallacy that Islam places before the unbelievers the close-ended choice of either "conversion or the sword."[37] This verdict of Muslim scholars is without doubt based on the Qur'anic precepts mentioned above.

One might incidentally refer to certain Qur'anic *āyāt*, which exhort believers to fight against non-believers until chaos/oppression (*fitnah*) comes to an end and all worship is devoted to Allah (2:193 and 8:39). It should be born in mind that these *āyāt* categorically refer to a situation where an enemy initiates war against the believers and they have to fight back in self-defense. The backdrop of the two *āyāt* relates to the battles in which Madinah was embroiled concerning invasion by the Quraysh. If these *āyāt* are read along with other *āyāt* preceding and succeeding, there arises no confusion whatsoever. It may be suggested that the tradition is rooted in historical context confining therefore the concept of fighting to be waged only against the non-believers of Makkah. This however, gives rise to another problem. According to the tradition, the Prophet then had to continue the war until the enemy accepted Islam. Historically, no enemies in any war were forced to enter the new faith.

In contrast Islam contains the principle of co-existence between believers and non-believers. The agreement between the Prophet and the Jewish tribes stands witness to this. The Qur'an commands believers to interact justly and generously with non-believers who have no conflict with them (60:8). Although war is allowed against an enemy in certain circumstances in the case of an Islamic victory the use of force to convert the enemy/non-believers is in no way justified.

5–Moses's Power to Delay His Death

Al-Bukhārī, Muslim and others have recorded this tradition on the authority of Abū Hurayrah:

> The Prophet said: "The angel of death went to Moses and asked him to respond to his Lord's call to die. Moses, then, hit the angel's eye and knocked it out. The angel returned to Allah and complained: 'You sent me to such a servant of yours who does not want death; he gouged my eye out.' Allah, then, returned to him his eye and asked him to check with Moses whether he wanted life..."[38]

Even a cursory examination of this tradition seems to indicate that it has probably been sourced from Judeo-Christian traditions (*Isrā'ilī-yyāt*) reminiscent as it is of other similar stories found in the latter, particularly Old Testament, sources. For example, there exists an account of Yahweh (God of the Old Testament) wrestling with prophet Jacob, according to which Jacob defeats God.[39] Some scholars have denied the authenticity of this tradition simply on the grounds that it would have been impossible for Moses, a mortal being, to harm an angel. Ibn Khuzaymah (d.311 AH) calls these scholars heresiarchs (*al-Mubtadiʿah*).[40] He argues that the angel entered Moses's residence in the form of a human being and that Moses, considering him an intruder, and not knowing that he was an angel, hit him in the eye causing injury. Had Moses, he maintains, recognized the identity of the angel, he would not have attacked him thus.[41] This line of argument is mere conjecture and speculation. In fact it is immaterial in what form the angel appeared to Moses, human or not, for it is not possible for a human being to harm an angel.

It is interesting to note that al-Bukhārī has recorded this report as a story related by Abū Hurayrah. Only at the end of the report does he observe that another chain of narrators consisting of, among others, Maʿmar and Hammām, transmits it from Abū Hurayrah as the statement of the Prophet. Even Muslim has quoted it first of all as a story related by Abū Hurayrah himself.[42] So, it seems more reasonable to consider this tradition as a story related by someone other than the Prophet.

However, even if the tradition were to be considered a statement of the Prophet, there may still exist a reason not to justify it. Significantly the tradition goes against the Qur'an concerning the issue of death. The angel of death reported in the tradition only approaches human beings at the time of their death, a time which the Qur'an reiterates, is divinely appointed, so when it comes, it is impossible for anyone to postpone it:

> When death approaches one of you, Our angels take his soul, and they never fail in their duty. (6:61)

> To every people is a term appointed: when their term is reached, not an hour can they cause delay, nor can they advance it. (7:34; 10:49)

> When their term expires, they will not be able to delay for a single hour, just as they will not be able to anticipate it. (16:61)

> And to no soul will Allah grant respite, when the time appointed has come. (63:11)

In the tradition Moses manages to do what the Qur'an maintains cannot be done, that is to postpone his death. It is inconceivable therefore that Moses did so. In a bid to prove the authenticity of the tradition al-Nawawī advances the idea that the angel of death did not first approach Moses to cause him to die but that rather it was the will of Allah to test the angel as to whether he was able to carry out his duty.[43] This is far-fetched reasoning, which cannot be proven either rationally or Qur'anically. Sadly it would appear that *ahl al-ḥadīth* do not hesitate to use even unfounded arguments based on mere speculation (*ẓann*) to bolster their opinion forgetting that mere speculation cannot be substituted for the truth (10:36); truth being that which is contained in the Qur'an.

6–Moses's Condemnation of Adam's Error

Al-Bukhārī, Muslim and others have recorded this hadith on the authority of Abū Hurayrah:

> The Prophet said: "Adam and Moses argued. Moses said: 'O Adam! You are our father; you frustrated our hope and caused our expulsion from Paradise.' Adam said: 'You are Moses; Allah privileged you with His word and wrote for you with His own hand. Do you blame me for something Allah had predetermined for me forty years before my creation?'"[44]

This report is inherently objectionable on several counts. First, it is not befitting that a prophet address his father by his name as Moses addresses Adam. This runs counter to the principle of *iḥsān* (that is, excellent behavior) bestowed on all the prophets including Moses (2:83). Second, the son is not supposed to condemn the father for his error. If bound to refer to his father's mistake, Moses would have had to again apply the principle of *iḥsān* which he clearly does not for Moses's words are very harsh and unbecoming of a pious son for a pious father. Third, why would Moses condemn Adam in the first place for something which Allah had forgiven him? It is a well-known maxim that after repentance the person concerned should not be reminded of his past errors. Fourth, why did Moses blame Adam? Did he not know that Satan had lured Adam into making a mistake? Allah has categorically mentioned that it was Satan who caused Adam to be expelled from Paradise. The Qur'an says: "O children of Adam! Do not allow Satan to seduce you in the same way as he caused your parents to be driven out of Paradise" (7:27).

To reiterate, since Moses received revelation, he must have been aware of Satan's role in causing Adam's expulsion from the Garden. According to Allah, Satan is to be blamed for this, and not Adam, yet nevertheless Moses blames Adam. The whole story is therefore rather strange and unbelievable.

In defense al-Māzarī (d.536 AH), a commentator of Muslim's work, refers to various interpretations.[45] First, he claims that a son may be allowed on certain occasions to condemn his father, in response to which it could be argued that whilst possibly true in certain circumstances, what was the actual necessity of Moses condemning Adam in the first place? In any case the matter is above speculation. The second point in defense of the hadith accounts for the act of the son blaming the father by pointing to the law (shariʿah) of Adam and Moses as differing from each other. In response it could be argued that the parent-child relationship is a timeless phenomenon, meaning that Allah must have revealed to all His prophets the principles governing this relationship. Moreover and as we saw earlier, in Moses's law the concept of *iḥsān* already existed governing the relationship of the two parties. Thirdly, in defense of the hadith al-Māzarī stresses that Moses's blame of Adam was above earthly principles because Adam was already removed from the world of responsibility and in an other-worldly life where blame is ineffective; the issue of blame therefore is not seen as problematic. Ibn ʿAbd al-Barr (d.463 AH) is of the opinion that Moses's blaming of Adam was an exception to the rule that "none should be blamed for something against which he has already repented."[46] This is an oft-applied argument in a situation where no rational or moral arguments exist. It seems that both al-Māzarī and Ibn ʿAbd al-Barr are oblivious of the fact that in the hereafter no one will ever blame the other for anything because this is a frivolous act (*laghwa*), which is impossible in the hereafter:

> They will not hear in Paradise any vain discourse, but only salutations of peace. (19:62)
>
> They shall there exchange with one another a cup free of frivolity, free of sin. (52:23)
>
> No frivolity will they hear therein, nor any mischief. (56:25)
>
> No vanity shall they hear therein, nor untruth. (78:35)
>
> In a Garden on high, Where they shall hear no (word) of vanity. (88:10–11)

Al-Ṭībī (d.743 AH) uses the tradition to reject the views of the Jabarite school of thought, on the one hand, and to condemn the Muʿtazilite scholars, on the other.[47] This creates suspicion about the genuineness of the tradition and it is not unlikely that the tradition was fabricated in a bid to criticize and strike at others.

7–Time Taken for the Entire Process of Creation

Muslim has recorded a hadith on the authority of Abū Hurayrah which states that "The Prophet took hold of my hand and said: 'Allah created on Saturday the earth, on Sunday the mountains therein, on Monday the trees, on Tuesday misfortune, on Wednesday the light, on Thursday spread in it animals, and on Friday in the late afternoon He created Adam....'"[48]

This report runs counter to the Qur'anic statement. The hadith informs us that the entire process of creation was accomplished in seven days, whereas the Qur'an refers to everything in the universe being created in a six-day process: "Verily, your Lord is Allah, who has created the heavens and the earth in six days" (7:54); and "We have indeed created the heavens and the earth and all that is between them in six days..." (50:38). This information is available in many other verses in the Qur'an such as 10:3; 11:7; 25:59; 32:4; 57:4. There is no way to effect compromise between the tradition and the Qur'an. It is strange that Muslim's commentator, al-Nawawī has ignored this contradiction and passed it by without any comment. Was he unaware of the Qur'anic time-schedule for creation? If on the other hand he was aware, why did he keep silent concerning it? It would appear that he demonstrated his prejudice in favor of what seems to be a statement of the Prophet reported through reliable reporters. If a hadith appears to contradict a Qur'anic statement with no possibility of compromise between them, then the tradition should be rejected as baseless.

8–Transfer to Jews and Christians the Sins of Muslims

Only Muslim has recorded on the authority of Abū Mūsā al-Ashʿarī the following three traditions all on the same theme:

(1) "The Prophet said: 'On the Day of Judgment Allah will present to every Muslim, a Jew or a Christian, and say: This is your ransom.'"[49]

(2) "The Prophet said: 'No Muslim dies but Allah consigns a Jew or a Christian to Hell in his place.'"[50]

(3) "The Prophet said: 'On the Day of Judgment many Muslims will appear [carrying] the burden of sins as [big as] mountains. Allah will forgive them for their sins, which He will place on Jews and Christians'."[51]

Al-Nawawī, Muslim's commentator, seems unable to advance any rationale for these traditions and, therefore, unsuccessfully tries to interpret them in a bid to maintain their sanctity. He believes that what Abū Hurayrah has reported from the Prophet, namely that: "For everyone there are two places reserved, one in Hell and the other in Paradise. If a believer enters Paradise, his place in Hell will be taken over by a disbeliever due to his disbelief,"[52] explains the *aḥādīth*. By this he means to say that Jews and Christians will enter Hell owing to their own sins and not because of the sins of Muslims. In order to strengthen his stand he derives an argument from another hadith – "He who introduces an evil act will have to bear the sin of everyone who does it"[53] – and extrapolates that the non-believers will bear the sins of Muslims due to their having introduced evil acts.[54] Al-Nawawī's arguments can hardly stand up to scrutiny. The traditions clearly mention that Allah will transfer the sins of Muslims onto Jews and Christians. The second tradition, which he quotes to explain the matter, does not indicate what he derives from it; he takes only one part and leaves the other. According to this hadith, the introducer of a sin will be burdened not only with his own sin but also with the sin committed by others, whilst the sin of others will not be commuted. The three *aḥādīth* are categorical in the transfer of the sins of Muslims to Jews and Christians, who will then be burdened with two categories of sins: 1) their own, and 2) those of the Muslims.

These three *aḥādīth* as recorded by Muslim alone, are in gross contrast with the Qur'an: "And whatever any human being commits rests upon himself alone; and no bearer of burdens shall be made to bear another's burden" (6:164).

The Qur'an rejects the idea of the transfer of one's sin onto others, whereas the traditions spell out a completely different message. Al-Nawawī does feel very strongly about this contradiction but suggests that we interpret the traditions so as to remove the conflict. As shown earlier, his attempt to effect a compromise between the two apparently contradictory ideas fails entirely, making it crystal clear that there exists an uncompromising conflict between what the Qur'an states and what the traditions convey. It is interesting to note that when Abū Burdah (d.104 AH) quoted the tradition concerning the transfer of sin onto others, on the authority of his father, Abū Mūsā al-Ashʿarī, the Umayyad Caliph ʿUmar ibn ʿAbd al-ʿAzīz (d.101 AH) was surprised and asked Abū Burdah three times, "Did your father really narrate it from the Prophet?" finally asking him to take an oath to that effect.[55] The fifth Caliph was a pious man and seems to have asked a genuine question whose impact is such that it automatically creates doubt concerning the authenticity of the traditions concerned. Although Abū Burdah ultimately took the oath and confirmed that he had heard the tradition from his father, doubt of its authenticity, which had been sown in the mind of ʿUmar ibn ʿAbd al-ʿAzīz, remains in place.

9–Reference to Eve as the Root Cause of Women's Infidelity to their Husbands

Al-Bukhārī and Muslim have both recorded a tradition on the authority of Abū Hurayrah that the Prophet said: "Were it not for the children of Israel, food would never become rotten and meat would never putrefy; were it not for Eve, no woman would ever become unfaithful to her husband."[56]

This tradition traces the cause of two things, decay of food items and the infidelity of women, to the children of Israel and to the mother of mankind respectively. In other words food decay is blamed on the children of Israel and women's unfaithfulness on Eve. If this is the case can one logically surmise that food items did not rot prior to the time of the children of Israel! Al-Nawawī quotes some anonymous scholars as stating that when the children of Israel stored these special food items, *al-mann* (a type of sweet gum) and *al-salwā* (quails), defying an instruction not to do so, these foods became rotten and the decay of food items in general has continued since this time.[57] This line of argument raises several questions. First, was the storing of food items so serious an offense that the whole of humanity had to pay the price? Second, why would the whole of mankind be punished for the belligerency of a section? Third, why was the punishment widened in scope to include all food items aside from *al-mann wa al-salwā*? Fourth, were those elements in food items that are vulnerable to decay non-existent in food items before the children of Israel's actions? There seems to be no easy answer to these logical questions.

The Qur'an has mentioned the blessings of Allah upon the followers of Moses. One such blessing appeared in the form of certain special food items known as, *al-mann wa al-salwā*. We find mention of these in three places, 2:57; 7:160; and 20:80. Here and in other places where the case of the children of Israel has been mentioned, one may also find mention of various offenses which the children of Israel committed and also the punishment commensurate with those sins. None of these descriptions contain any reference to Israelite defiance concerning storage of these food items sent by God. The Qur'an reiterates time and again that it is the major sins which earn the displeasure of Allah, and the storage of food items does not constitute from any perspective a major crime. Aside from this, there is no mention in the genuine sources (the

Qur'an and Hadith literature) that the children of Israel had ever been forbidden to store this or any other food.

The Qur'an also makes clear that punishment is reserved only for those who have committed sin and not for those who have not: "And if anyone earns sin, he earns it against his own soul: for Allah is full of knowledge and wisdom" (4:111). According to the Qur'an, the burden of one person will not be placed on another: "And whatever [wrong] any human being commits rests upon himself alone; and no bearer of burdens shall be made to bear another's burden"(6:164). These are eternal principles of justice as decreed by Allah. There is no way therefore that the burden of the children of Israel would fall onto the whole of mankind. If they had done wrong then only they alone would deserve to be chastised.

Furthermore, the decay of food items is a natural process. If such items were free from putrefaction before the children of Israel's involvement, then they would not have been alterable even in the stomach, in which case, the digestion system of man must have been different! As a matter of fact, man is created with certain elements in his body. In order to maintain physical health man needs water, carbohydrates, vitamins, proteins, minerals, iron etc. These nutrients are supplied by consumption of vegetables, fruit, water, lentils and so on, which in turn are vulnerable to decay because this is the nature of nutritious elements such as these. Man's digestion system demands that items consumed are of a putrid nature otherwise nothing would be digested and man would never be able to consume anything. There might be no evidence to prove that before the children of Israel dead animals did not putrefy but if this were the case man would not have been able to consume meat or digest it. The concept of death is a timeless reality and this together with the decay of edible items must be something which has always existed from the time Adam and Eve stepped onto the earth.

The second element of the tradition concerns Eve. Eve it is said was responsible for man's expulsion from Paradise because she duped Adam into eating the forbidden fruit. This cannot be true. The Qur'an presents the case of Eve in a different manner: "Then did Satan make them slip from the [garden], and get them out of the state [of felicity] in which they had been" (2:36). It is obvious from this verse that

Satan in fact tricked both Adam and Eve into taking the forbidden fruit contrary to the case as claimed by al-Nawawī. He advances the interpretation presented by al-Qāḍī that Satan persuaded Eve to eat the forbidden fruit, and Eve, then, did the same to Adam who took the fruit against the instruction of Allah.[58] The report goes against the Qur'anic statement and is hence unacceptable.

Al-ʿAynī's understanding of the statement concerning the role of Eve as reported in the tradition is that "she invited Adam to eat the fruit of that tree."[59] Ibn Ḥajar explains the role of Eve as "in this statement there is a reference to Eve's persuasion of Adam due to which Adam took from the forbidden tree. *Khiyānah* (dishonesty, violation of rules, infidelity) on the part of Eve means that she accepted what was presented to her by Satan in a beautiful manner; and she presented that idea to Adam in an attractive way."[60] Both these comments by al-ʿAynī and Ibn Ḥajar are classic examples of the Qur'an being sidelined in favor of authenticating a tradition recorded by al-Bukhārī. Had they even given the Qur'anic statement (2:36) a cursory examination, they would not have believed what they did. Once again, the Qur'an mentions clearly, that it was not Eve who forced Adam to do wrong but Satan who persuaded them both. Eve therefore is innocent of the charge leveled against her and should not be blamed for an action she did not commit.

It could be that the statement reported in the tradition was initially made by someone attempting to interpret verse 2:36 of the Qur'an, and later mistakenly reported as that of the Prophet. It was impossible for the Prophet to say anything that would be in contrast with the Qur'an, and in actual fact, it is the Bible which blames Eve for causing Adam to deviate from God's command. This is not to give credence to anyone's position concerning Eve because the original biblical revelation has been lost and its contents corrupted. In this situation, the truth lies with the Qur'an, and not with the Bible.

Finally, the report itself is a source of humiliation for women. Is it only the wife who commits infidelity? Are husbands not also unfaithful to their wives? Why point the finger of blame at women only? In reality infidelity whether on the part of the man or the woman, is not the result of Eve or Adam's error, but rather because Allah has created man with this capacity. The Qur'an says: "By the Soul, and the proportion and order given to it, And its enlightenment as to its wrong and its right"

(91:7–8). If a woman and man commit sin against each other, it is because they have the innate capability to do so. It is mankind's freedom of thought, choice and action that govern whether he does right or wrong.

10–Women, Houses, and Animals as Sources of Bad Omen

Al-Bukhārī, Muslim and others have recorded a tradition on the authority of ʿAbd Allāh ibn ʿUmar which confirms that in women, animals, and houses are bad omens. The tradition in the words of Muslim is: "The Prophet said: 'If bad luck were true, it would be in the horse, the woman, and the house.'"[61]

Al-Khaṭṭābī tries to interpret this report by saying that "evil portent in terms of houses means insufficient space to live in and bad neighbors; in terms of women her impudent tongue and inability to conceive and give birth; and in terms of horses meaning those unfit for war."[62] Although this seems rather neatly put the wording of the tradition does not allow for this kind of interpretation. It is quite clear from al-Khaṭṭābī's interpretation that he does see a problem in the statement reported in the tradition but wanted to remove doubt concerning the authenticity of al-Bukhārī's recorded tradition. Ibn Ḥajar adopts the same approach. Although he quotes various views which reinforce the idea of the position of women being a source of bad omen, he himself is of the view expressed by al-Khaṭṭābī.[63]

For al-Khaṭṭābī and Ibn Ḥajar the bad omen aspect of woman signifies her abusive language and inability to conceive. If the two scholars really maintain this position then one can counter, why confine the issue of evil omen to women only? Do not the same problems also exist in men? Abusive and offensive language and infertilility/sterility are not the domain of women only. Although both sexes are involved men are somehow absolved according to the tradition. Why?

Can one honestly imagine the Prophet condemning women as bad omens? Of course not. The Qur'an was revealed to the Prophet and he was fully aware of the position of evil portents/omens. The Qur'an says: "But whenever good fortune alighted upon them, they would say, 'This is [but] our due'; and whenever affliction befell them, they would blame their evil fortune on Moses and those who followed him. Oh, verily, their [evil] fortune had been decreed by God – but most of them knew it not" (7:131). This verse maintains clearly that the idea of evil omen is nothing but people's own superstition. Actually, when people are afflicted, they immediately try to identify the cause of their pain and generally put the blame on something or someone or some place as a source of bad luck. They forget that suffering is not due to any sort of bad luck on earth but an aspect of the divine law according to which both the states of happiness and distress befall man. It is this message which has been conveyed in verse (7:131).

At another place the Qur'an reads:

> They said: "We see evil omen from you: if you cease not, we will surely stone you, and a painful torment will touch you from us." The Messengers said: "Your evil omens be with you! [Do you call it evil omen] because you are admonished? Nay, but you are a people transgressing all bounds." (36:18–19)

In this verse we find repudiation of the idea of an evil omen. It is simply non-existent and in fact people's suffering, and their ignorance concerning the cause, actually causes development of such concepts of superstition and evil omen.

When this tradition was brought to the notice of ʿĀ'ishah, she corrected the report stating that the Prophet had actually said :"Arabs of the period of ignorance and the Jews used to say that the woman, the house, and the animal were the source of bad luck." ʿĀ'ishah even made the observation that the reporter of the tradition had not heard the first part of the Prophetic statement.[64] Ibn Ḥajar finds the report narrating ʿĀ'ishah's comment defective due to some defect in the chain of narrators. But when he finds himself facing some authentic reports narrating ʿĀ'ishah's observation, he concludes that ʿĀ'ishah's interpretation is too far-fetched in relation to so highly authentic a tradition as that recorded by al-Bukhārī. While negating the approach of ʿĀ'ishah, Ibn Ḥajar says that the Prophet should not have made it (the idea of bad omen) as an information related to superstitious belief of the people of Arabia before Islam.[65]

It seems that the only concern of some of these Hadith commentators has been to insist upon and maintain the authenticity of traditions recorded in this or that collection at any cost. Ibn Ḥajar should not have been so bold as to denounce ʿĀ'ishah's comment. If ʿĀ'ishah's observation is taken into consideration, the problem in the tradition is resolved with great ease.

4

Authentication of Hadith Through Rationally Authentic Traditions

THE POSITION OF THE PROPHET for believers is that of a judge (4:65). His verdicts are final (33:36) and none but the Prophet himself was authorized to review his own utterances. His authority represents the authority of Allah (4:80). As emphasized earlier, under the first criterion, the Qur'an, disputed matters are to be referred to Allah and the Last Prophet.[1]

The Prophet carried out his mission for a period of over two decades before its eventual accomplishment. During this time he explained the Qur'an, taught how to translate Allah's commands into day to day practical life, guided his followers in everything, made judgments in disputed cases, admonished people for wrongdoing, counseled them in their problems, and patterned their life along Islamic principles (62:2). All these constitute an Islamic legacy that was meant to continue, leading people in general and believers in particular, throughout every age, time and place. Although adhered to, it was also unfortunately betrayed by those who sought to gain for themselves many known and unknown advantages. Consequently, people's own desires and whims began to circulate in the name of the Prophet.

In this situation well-known Sunnah and Hadith, as well as the Qur'an, could be used to determine the nature of other traditions supposedly related by the Prophet. The Prophet had said: "If an act done by someone is not approved by us, it is to be rejected as unacceptable."[2] It seems fairly obvious that this advice indicates reference to a criterion for accepting or rejecting a tradition as hadith. In other words, what is in conformity with the known traditions of the Prophet is to be accepted as an authentic report; and what appears in stark contrast with highly authentic Sunnah and Hadith is to be rejected as non-hadith.

ʿĀ'ishah's Approach

ʿĀ'ishah is reported to have rejected certain sayings attributed to the Prophet in the light of her own experiences and knowledge on the matters concerned. Muslim and others, for example, have recorded a hadith on the authority of Abū Dharr and Abū Hurayrah which states that "the Prophet said: 'The woman, the donkey, and the dog break the salah'."[3] When this tradition was mentioned to ʿĀ'ishah, she reacted sharply by saying: "You have likened us [women] to donkeys and dogs. By God, I used to lie in front of the Prophet while he was praying."[4] Another known example of her rejection of a hadith by reference to another is available in Muslim: "Abū Mūsā al-Ashʿarī once asked her about what makes a bath obligatory. She answered, 'the Prophet said: "When someone sat in front of the four organs of the woman, and the two genitals touched each other, the bath became obligatory"'."[5] This response of ʿĀ'ishah is quite in contrast with a hadith recorded by both al-Bukhārī and Muslim. The hadith has been narrated on the authority of Abū Saʿīd al-Khudrī who says: "The Prophet went to a person from Anṣār and called him. When he came water drops were falling from his head. The Prophet said: 'Probably, we caused you to hurry'. He said: 'Yes, O Prophet of Allah!' Upon this the Prophet said: 'If you were made to hurry without ejaculation, a bath was not obligatory upon you but only ablution'."[6]

It is claimed the second hadith, as mentioned above, was abrogated by the first one.[7] If abrogation theory was applied, ʿĀ'ishah would surely have commented as such. However, apparent from her response to the problem concerned, she merely quotes the Prophet's statement on the matter.

ʿĀ'ishah was once approached by ʿAbd Allāh ibn ʿAbbās who asked her whether the report of ʿAbd Allāh ibn ʿUmar from the Prophet "Verily, the one who is dead tastes suffering as a result of people's wailing over his death" was correct. She brushed the report aside, saying: "Once when a funeral procession... passed by the Prophet, in which the deceased's mourners were wailing, the Prophet said: 'They are wailing, whereas the deceased is experiencing painful suffering.'" She also added that Ibn ʿUmar failed to maintain the accuracy of the statement he had heard.[8] She also corrected, on another occasion, Ibn ʿUmar's report attributed to the Prophet stating that "The Prophet did not utter: 'They [the dead] are hearing what I say', what he said was 'they know what I say is true'."[9]

ʿUmar said: "After the throwing of the stones and the shaving of the head in hajj, everything is lawful for you except perfume and women." ʿĀ'ishah denied the validity of ʿUmar's advice, saying that exception was applicable only to women and not to perfume because she herself had applied perfume to the Prophet even in pilgrimage dress.[10]

When certain people mentioned to ʿĀ'ishah that ʿAlī was the executor (*waṣiyy*) of the Prophet, she objected to this saying: "when did the Prophet leave this will; I was with him when he died." She is also reported to have said: "The Prophet did not leave any bequest."[11]

Ziyād ibn Abū Sufyān wrote to ʿĀ'ishah that he had sent two sacrificial animals for the hajj, seeking her advice concerning the decree of ʿAbd Allāh ibn ʿAbbās that "one who offered a sacrificial animal for hajj was just like the pilgrim as to the regulations of pilgrimage." She wrote back: "What Ibn Abbās says is not correct. I myself prepared the collar for the sacrificial animal of the Prophet and the Prophet sent it with Abū Bakr; the Prophet did not make anything unlawful for himself during the pilgrimage season." Muḥammad ibn Shahāb al-Zuhrī shows his appreciation of ʿĀ'ishah with the words: "The first person who removed people's confusion on this matter was ʿĀ'ishah."[12]

Once when ʿAbd Allāh ibn al-Zubayr prayed two extra cycles of prayer (salah) after the ʿ*Aṣr* salah, Muʿāwiyah disapproved the act. The issue was referred to ʿĀ'ishah who maintained that the Prophet once had not been able perform the two cycles of supererogatory prayer connected to *Ẓuhr* prayer due to his meetings with certain visiting delegations, so he prayed the missed two cycles after ʿ*Aṣr* prayer.[13]

ʿAbd Allāh ibn ʿUmar disliked sweating perfume in pilgrimage dress (that is he disliked that the good smell of perfume emanated from his perspiration in pilgrimage dress) and when this was mentioned to

ʿĀ'ishah, she responded: "I applied perfume to the Prophet, and he visited all his wives and the following morning he put on the pilgrimage dress."[14]

Once, ʿAbd Allāh ibn ʿUmar mentioned in response to a question on the number of minor pilgrimages the Prophet had performed, that the Prophet had performed four minor pilgrimages, three in the month of Dhu al-Qaʿdah and the fourth one in the month of Rajab. ʿĀ'ishah corrected Ibn ʿUmar's statement saying that all the minor pilgrimages of the Prophet had been performed in the month of Dhu al-Qaʿdah.[15]

When ʿĀ'ishah heard ʿAbd Allāh ibn ʿUmar's statement that "sudden death is indeed an exasperation for the believers" she corrected this stating that what the Prophet had actually said was "sudden death is mitigation for the believers, whereas it is exasperation for the non-believers."[16]

ʿAbd Allāh ibn ʿUmar mentioned that the Prophet had said: "Bilāl indeed calls for prayer (salah) while it is still night; you may continue eating and drinking until ʿAbd Allāh ibn Umm Maktūm comes to call for prayer." ʿĀ'ishah blamed Ibn ʿUmar for reporting this Prophetic statement incorrectly stating that what the Prophet had actually said was: "Ibn Umm Maktūm is blind when he calls for prayer, continue eating and drinking until Bilāl gives the call to prayer."[17] (The Prophet meant to say that due to his blindness Ibn Umm Maktum was unable to precisely discern the time for Morning prayer call; and he would generally call to prayer before the actual time drew in).

ʿAbd Allāh ibn ʿUmar reported that the Prophet said: "The month is indeed [composed] of twenty-nine days." ʿĀ'ishah said: "May Allah bless Ibn ʿUmar! The Prophet did not say this, what he said was that the month might also be of twenty-nine days."[18]

The decree of ʿAbd Allāh ibn ʿAmrū ibn al-ʿĀṣ that "Women must unravel their hair while taking a bath" reached ʿĀ'ishah. She commented: "How strange! Why did he not ask the women to shave their heads? I used to take a bath along with the Prophet in one and the same ware; I never poured more than three pots of water on my head; and I did not unravel my hair."[19]

Abū Hurayrah reported that the Prophet had said: "One who does not include the *Witr* salah in his prayer, his salah will not be accepted." ʿĀ'ishah reacted to this report saying:

Who heard this from the Prophet? The time of the Prophet is not far from us. We have not forgotten what he said: "One who comes on the Day of Judgment with five times a day prayer [salah] excellently performed in terms of ablution, timing, and the proper state of bending and prostrating with no deficiency in the prayer at all, Allah would never punish him according to His promise. One who came with deficient prayers, it is up to Allah whether to punish him or pardon him."[20]

Abū Hurayrah decreed: "One who has washed the dead body [as part of the funeral rites] must take a bath, and one who has carried the dead must perform ablution." ʿĀ'ishah reacted sharply: "Are the dead of Muslim society impure? What happens if a person carries the pyre of the dead body?"[21] ʿĀ'ishah's questions represented her disapproval of such kinds of decree.

Abū Hurayrah's Attitude

Once Abū Hurayrah decreed that someone who gets up in the morning requiring an obligatory bath should not fast. When they heard this, ʿĀ'ishah and Umm Salamah stated that the Prophet would quite often rise in the morning requiring an obligatory bath and begin his fasting without purifying himself. Dejected by the error he had made Abū Hurayrah retracted his previous narration referring to the source from whom he had heard it.[22]

Al-Khair Abadi's Example: A Critique

Al-Khair Abadi has advanced one such example of two traditions, which appear to be in conflict with each other.

"It is reported on the authority of ʿAbd Allāh ibn ʿAbbās that the Prophet decided a case on the basis of an oath and a witness."[23]

On the authority of ʿAbd Allāh ibn Masʿūd it has been reported: "Al-Ashʿath ibn Qays states: 'There was a dispute over a well between myself and another person [Rabīʿah ibn ʿIbdān]; we took the case to the Prophet who said: "Two witnesses [from the plaintiff] or an oath from the defendant."'"[24]

These two traditions appear to contradict one other, although it may not be difficult to effect a compromise between them. It seems that what Ibn ʿAbbās reports is related to a case different from the one that is mentioned in Ibn Masʿūd's report. It may, then, be presumed that the judge can demand from the plaintiff and the defendant to produce any number of witnesses, sometimes only one and, at times, two or even more; he can also decide the case only on the basis of an oath from the litigants. It all depends upon the nature of case. When the Prophet ordered certain litigants to produce a witness and take an oath, he must have taken into consideration the situation concerning the disputed matter. And when he demanded from the petitioner to either produce two witnesses or let the defendant take an oath, he must have weighed the case in view. We can therefore postulate that the two reports represent two different cases, each of a different nature and concerning different situations.

Comparison of Traditions: A Delicate Task

To compare various *aḥādīth* which concern the same subject matter but yet contradict one another is an extremely difficult and extraordinarily delicate task. If a hadith is rejected as unreliable simply for containing content contrary to another, there must exist some strong reasons for doing so. In a situation where contradiction occurs the first task is to develop a rationally acceptable interpretation, which may remove the nature of the conflict. Where this proves impossible and any compromise between the two conflicting reports can in no way be effected then a very careful selection of which of the two is to be considered unacceptable is highly advisable. For this to happen reason must play a great role. It is this idea that the author has captioned "rationally authentic traditions" and which for him form the second criterion. Some examples are given below.

1–An Eternally Prefixed Amount of Sustenance and One's Life Span

Muslim has recorded on the authority of ʿAbd Allāh ibn Masʿūd the tradition that:

> Umm Ḥabībah, one of the Prophet's wives prayed: "O Allah! Enable me to enjoy company with my husband, the Prophet, my father, Abū Sufyān, and my brother, Muʿāwiyah." The Prophet said to her: "You are asking Allah something related to a fixed life-span, a limited number of days, and an already distributed amount of sustenance. Nothing will occur before its appointed time, and also nothing will take place after its scheduled plan..."[25]

According to this tradition nothing will ever occur but in accordance with a pre-ordained plan; therefore there is no way to increase the amount of one's sustenance and the number of days of one's life. This is why the Prophet is reported to have advised not to pray for longevity of life and increase in income. This report however, is in contrast with another hadith on the authority of Anas ibn Mālik which states:

> My mother committed me to the Prophet as a servant and requested him to pray for me. The Prophet prayed: "O Allah! Increase the amount of his wealth and the number of his children, and also bless him with an increase in what You have granted him [that is, age]."[26]

A compromise between these two traditions seems to be impossible. The tradition related to Umm Ḥabībah may be categorized as doubtful on two grounds. First, it is a mere statement (hadith) attributed to the Prophet, whereas the tradition narrated by Anas ibn Mālik is the Prophet's own practice (sunnah). It may be concluded here that in case of a conflict between a hadith and a sunnah, the latter is to be preferred. Second, there exist traditions which relate the Prophet's invocations, one of which includes "safety from the evil impact of too much wealth and too much poverty."[27]

2–The Prophet's Advice to Drink Camel-Urine for Cure

Al-Bukhārī, Muslim and others have recorded on the authority of Anas ibn Mālik a hadith: "Some people from the tribe of ʿUraynah came to Madinah and due to non-suitability of the climate they fell ill. The Prophet advised them to drink milk and urine of the camels of charity. They did so and were cured."[28]

This tradition suggests that there is cure for certain diseases in the milk as well as the urine of camel. The question here is not whether the camel-urine is efficacious or not. The issue is whether it was advised by the Prophet to the people concerned to drink it. The urine is forbidden. Psychologically, it is disdainful to even imagine and mention of drinking urine. As al-Bukhārī and Muslim have both, on the authority of Abū Hurayrah and Anas ibn Mālik respectively, reported, once a man urinated in the mosque, the Prophet asked people to wash it away with water.[29] According to another hadith, on the authority of ʿAbd Allāh ibn ʿAbbas, the Prophet said that a man was subjected to suffering in the other world because he did not keep himself clean of urine.[30] Another hadith on the authority of Abū Hurayrah advises believers not to urinate in the source of stagnant water and then take a bath in it.[31]

From these *aḥādīth* it becomes clear that urine is impurity; anything affected by it is to be washed and cleaned by water. Is it therefore conceivable that the Prophet advised some Muslims to drink the urine of camels, even though for a medical purpose? Followers of Mālik ibn Anas and those of Ahmad ibn Ḥanbal, on the basis of Prophet's alleged advice to drink urine, consider the urine and excrement of *ḥalāl* animals as pure and *ḥalāl*.[32] This is a blind approach. Urine is not from *ṭayyibāt* (good and pure) but from the category of *khabā'ith* (bad and impure). The Prophet made lawful only what is good and pure, and made unlawful what is bad and impure.[33] Merely the existence of a hadith does not suffice for it to be deemed as an original statement of the Prophet. There is a possibility that someone advertently or inadvertently inserted the word "urine" (*Abwālihā*) beside the word "milk" (*Albānihā*). The report comprising the Prophet's advice to drink urine in addition to milk seems to be disgusting.

It may be suggested here that the Prophet advised ʿUraynans to drink camel-urine due to its highly therapeutic efficacy. Some might even refer to some modern researches on camel-urine which proves its medical benefits in some skin problems such as sores, boils, and some kind of cancers. The authenticity of such researches are yet to be proved scientifically. It is well known that the urine contains chemical constituents that are toxic. Toxic elements are rather more harmful. If the disadvantages of urine outstrip its advantages, it can in no way be declared beneficial.

The Qur'an declares in no uncertain terms: "Those who follow the Messenger, the unlettered Prophet, who they find mentioned in their own Scriptures – in the Torah and the Gospel – for he commands them what is just and forbids them what is evil; he allows them as lawful the things pure (*ṭayyibāt*) and prohibits them from the things impure (*khabā'ith*): he releases them from their heavy burdens and from the yokes that are upon them. So it is those who believe in him, honor him, help him, and follow the light, which is sent down with him; it is they who will prosper" (7:157). *Sūrah al-Aʿrāf* (7) is a Makkan revelation in which the position of the Prophet has been made crystal clear. And the above quoted tradition belongs to the Madinan period of the Prophet. According to the above quoted *āyah* (7:157), the Prophet had to prohibit the people from all that were impure and bad. He had to make them aware of what was pure and good. It is to be determined whether urine of camel is pure and good. It has been seen above that urine is from the category of bad and impure items. Hence it was not imaginable that the Prophet advised some people to drink what was bad and impure. Muslim scholars who consider the camel-urine pure and good have actually developed this idea on the basis of this tradition as quoted above. Scholars should also take into consideration the position of urine in general and also the duty of the Prophet as mentioned in the Qur'an.

It could well be that the ʿUraynans were advised by the Prophet to drink camel-milk only, but the patients chose also to drink camel-urine along with the milk. On their being cured, news about the efficacy of the camel-urine could then have circulated, which is why the narration would include the element of urine in the advice of the Prophet. Strangely enough, throughout the history of the Companions, there is no reference to the use of camel-urine for therapeutic purposes. If camel-urine really had formed a part of the Prophet's advice, surely it would have been utilised in some form or other in the medical system developed and practiced by Muslims. Total reticence on the part of medical practitioners in the Muslim world concerning the therapeutic significance of camel-urine speaks volumes of its insignificance.

3–No Indictment for Slandering the Slave for Adultery

Al-Bukhārī, Muslim and others have recorded on the authority of

Abū Hurayrah this hadith: "He who slandered his slave for adultery wrongly will be punished in accordance with *Ḥudūd* laws on the Day of Judgment, except that what he said was true."[34]

Al-Muhallab (d.82 AH) is of the view that there is a consensus among scholars that a free man is free from punishment for slandering his slave (male or female) wrongly with adultery; and that this opinion is based on the above tradition, which mentions about the punishment of the slanderer only in the hereafter. The punishment, he argues, was postponed to the other world with a view to making distinction between the master and the slave.[35] Slander is a cognizable offense. The offender is to be punished, no matter who the person is. It is not fair to let an offender go free merely because the victim is his slave. Al-Muhallab is satisfied with this discriminative provision hence he refers to it as distinction between the master and the slave. Ibn Ḥajar disagrees with his claim of consensus. He refers to al-Ḥasan al-Baṣrī (d.110 AH) and others as having favored enforcement of the law of slander (80 lashes) if the accused is other than the master here in this world itself. The basis of this decree is the view of ʿAbd Allāh ibn ʿUmar narrated on the authority of Nāfiʿ(d.117 AH): "When asked about his view on the one who slandered someone else's slave-girl for an affair with someone else, Ibn ʿUmar said: The law will be enforced on him as a humiliation."[36] Here arises a question as to why the offender other than the master will be brought to the book, but the master himself will be freed for the same offense. The effected person or the victim is in both the cases is a slave. Al-Nawawī also concludes that the Ummah has consensus on freeing the master for slandering his slave. He suggests that the slanderer of the slave is to be punished but not as per *Ḥudūd* laws but in accordance with the prevalent penal code (*taʿzīr*).[37] In the stand of al-Nawawī there are two problems. First, if the above tradition frees the guilty of slander in this world, there is no way to suggest to punish him, as he is destined to be punished only in the hereafter. Second, if the penal code (*taʿzīr*) applies to the person concerned, what is, then, the problem in applying *Ḥudūd* code to him in this world? If the tradition in view is taken as authentic, no authority can prescribe any punishment to the culprit. In order to bring the slanderer to justice, the tradition will have to be rejected as unreliable.

If the master is accused of an affair out of wedlock by his slave, the law prescribes punishment for the slave. But if the master blames his slave, he is left scot-free. It is discrimination between man and man. It is dishonor to humanity. Slaves are also human beings; they do possess self-dignity. There are *aḥādīth* putting the slaves at par with free men in terms of humanity. Al-Bukhārī, Muslim and others have recorded that the Prophet advised Abū Dharr:

> They [slaves] are your brothers. Allah has placed them under you. Feed them what you eat; clothe them with what you wear; do not burden them beyond their capacity; and if you assign them a heavy task, help them in it.[38]

In this hadith the Prophet has described the slaves as brethren of their masters, and advised them to treat their slaves equally. There should not be, then, any discrimination between the slave and the free man when it comes to the enforcement of criminal law *(Ḥudūd)*. Muslim has quoted a hadith on the authority of ʿAbd Allāh ibn ʿUmar: "The Prophet said: If one slapped his slave or hit him, his expiation is that he should free the slave."[39]

Here in accordance with this tradition, the master is obliged to liberate his slave merely due to causing physical injury. Liberation of a slave means fiscal loss. The master who slanders his slave with adultery is not required to do anything. Is it justice? Slap causes only physical injury, whereas slandering causes psychological injury. At times the latter is more offending and painful, and it may last long.

The above hadith, which frees the master for slandering his slave, says that the criminal law (*Ḥudūd*) will be applied only on the Day of Judgment. *Ḥudūd* laws are for this life, they have nothing to do with the hereafter, where there will be enforced another set of laws prescribed by Allah. The master has a way out to escape from the punishment in the hereafter. He can repent for his error sincerely in this world before his death. Thus, the hadith freed him from the earthly punishment and his repentance made him eligible for concession in the hereafter. It is an established fact that repentance cannot fend off the enforcement of *Ḥudūd* laws. Gḥāmidiyyah had sincerely repented for her sin, yet she was not spared from a death sentence.[40]

4–Condemnation of the Profession of Cupping

Muslim and others (not al-Bukhārī) have recorded on the authority of Rāfiᶜ ibn Khadīj the hadith that "The Prophet said: 'The most evil incomes are from prostitution, the sale of dogs, and the fee of the cupper."[41]

This tradition prohibits, among other things, monetary gain through the profession of cupping (*ḥijāmah*). As al-Nawawī says, scholars are divided into two groups over this matter. One of them does not consider it prohibited, and the other finds it, on the basis of the above tradition, prohibited for the free man but not for the slave.[42] It is very clear that the controversy around this issue is due to an enthusiasm to consider every report which stands authentic in terms of its chain, as reliable and genuine. Al-Khaṭṭābī (d.388 AH) and Ibn ᶜAbd al-Barr have both declared this tradition to be weak even from the point of its *sanad*.[43]

The following hadith, recorded by al-Bukhārī, Muslim and others, recognizes the profession of cupping: "Anas ibn Mālik states that the Prophet hired Abū Ṭaybah for a cupping service, paid him two bowls of food grain, and said: 'Cupping is the best treatment'."[44]

In light of such an authentic practice of the Prophet the report prohibiting the profession of cupping may be considered unreliable. Had there been anything wrong in the practice of cupping and earning an income by it, the Prophet would never have paid for it. Acceptance of both the traditions as authentic causes an unnecessary rift among the Ummah. What causes disunity may not be attributed to the Prophet.

5–Condemnation of Poetry

Muslim mentions a tradition (also recorded by al-Bukhārī, and others) on the authority of Abū Hurayrah and others that the Prophet said: "It is better that man's stomach is filled with vomited out stuffs and blood than that it is filled with poetry."[45]

This tradition goes against the relatively authentic tradition reported by ᶜĀ'ishah. She remarked that the tradition was not taken properly from the Prophet who actually said that, "It is better for someone's stomach to be filled with vomited out stuffs and blood than to be filled with the poem in which I have been defamed and ridiculed."[46]

Notice how the text of the Prophet's statement has been deficiently narrated. Although the tradition as recorded by al-Bukhārī and Muslim is not defective in terms of its chain of narrators, there is a problem in the text. Had it not been corrected, the Ummah would have been under the impression that the Prophet hated poetry and advised his followers to keep away from it. There are other traditions regarding the virtuous position of Ḥassān ibn Thābit, the poet of the Prophet, recorded by al-Bukhārī and Muslim. These traditions describe the significance of Ḥassān in the eyes of the Prophet who used to encourage the poet to compose and read poems in praise of the Prophet and in condemnation of the enemies.[47]

5

Authentication of Hadith Through Sound Reasoning

REASON PLAYS A VITAL ROLE in man's existence (2:170). It is a power that elevates humankind to the highest position on earth (2:30–38) and through proper application helps maintain his humanity (21:10). Its misuse, abuse or non-use snatches away man's superiority over most other creatures (8:22) whilst total suspension of independent reasoning reduces him to the state of animals (7:179). The Qur'an lays great emphasis on the intellectual power of man, such that true faith and good deeds seem to be impossible without the guidance of reason (67:10).

Indeed every single one of God's prophets have invited their respective people to the divine message, appealing to their faculty of reason (2:44; 3:65; 7:169; 21:67). One of the most appreciable traits of the followers of the Last Prophet is that they do not treat Revelation with disregard, turning a blind eye or deaf ear to it (25:73). In his explanation of verse 25:73 al-Zamakhsharī (d.538 AH) states that believers maintain a state of extreme mental alertness when listening to the Revelation, keeping their eyes and ears wide open.[1] This state denotes a critical use of faculties, to gain as true an understanding of the message as possible. When the Qur'an invites people to reflect (*tadabbur*) upon its verses: "Do they not ponder over the Qur'an, or are there locks over their hearts?" (47:24), what it actually asks them to do is to use their minds to grasp the true purport of the Revelation. *Āyah* 47:24 refers to the human heart (*qalb*) as the tool for learning, understanding, analyzing, criticizing, and deliberating over a matter. In other words, to attain the true message of Allah one has to use one's mind. It follows therefore, that if intellectual reasoning is a means to understanding the Qur'an, it should also be an apparatus to understand the substance of hadith literature.

Definition of Sound Reasoning

The use of intellectual faculties does not imply giving free reign to the mind, applying thought processes free of all bounds and limits. Absolute freedom ruins the mind for there are limitations and thresholds beyond which it cannot go and which if crossed can cause it to become imbalanced. The mind, or reason, accordingly needs to work within fixed parameters and this is especially so when analyzing or attempting to understand the nature of hadith texts. A mind that is not governed by Islamic faith, knowledge, wisdom, and sincerity towards Allah and the Last Prophet is immediately to be disqualified for the purpose, and indeed any form of prejudice cannot be accepted as a criterion. For instance, someone harboring an antagonistic approach to the Qur'an or the Sunnah cannot be expected to do justice to their elucidation, despite any intellectual ability. This is precisely why the criteria of reason cannot be defined as simple intellectual capacity but is more comprehensive. It requires a 'sound mind' or 'sound reason', defined as the ability to speculate governed by the Islamic principles of God-consciousness (*al-taqwā*), justice (*al-ʿadl*), honesty (*al-amānah*), truthfulness (*al-ṣidq*), moderation (*al-wasaṭ*), and sincerity (*al-ikhlāṣ*). Cited below are a few examples to illustrate cases where sound reason has been used as a criterion to judge the nature of the traditions expounded.

1– Breast-feeding of an Adult Male

Muslim and others (although not al-Bukhārī) have recorded a tradition on the authority of ʿĀ'ishah stating that:

> Sālim *mawlā* [patron, protector] Abī Ḥudhayfah lived with Abū Ḥudhayfah and his family. One day, Sahlah bint Suhayl, the wife of Abū Hudhayfah, came to the Prophet and said: "Sālim has reached the

age of puberty. He visits us. In his presence, I guess, there is a sign of disapproval in Abū Ḥudhayfah's eyes." Upon this the Prophet advised: "Breast-feed him so that you become prohibited (*ḥarām*) for him, and what is in the heart of Abū Ḥudhayfah disappears." She, then, returned. As she herself stated, she breast-fed Sālim and Abū Ḥudhyfah no longer became uncomfortable.[2]

Commenting on this report, al-Nawawī mentions that the consensus reached by all scholars from the generations of the *Saḥābah*, the *Tābiʿūn*, and across the Muslim world is that the age at which a foster relationship can be established through breast-feeding is less than two. He refers to three exceptions, Abū Ḥanīfah who stated two and a half years, Zufar (one of Abū Ḥanīfah's students) who stated three years, and Mālik ibn Anas, who mentioned two years and a few days. As for the hadith regarding Sālim, al-Nawawī claims that it was an exceptional provision meant for Sālim only.[3] This learned commentator of Muslim seems to have ignored the tradition in which ʿĀ'ishah is reported to have advised Umm Salamah, another wife of the Prophet, to breast-feed her adult slave, Ayfaʿ on the grounds that the Prophet had advised Sahlah to do the same.[4] If Sālim's case had indeed been a special one, why would ʿĀ'ishah whose intelligence and knowledge made her superior to the other wives of the Prophet, then have advanced it as a precedent for Umm Salamah? Nevertheless, al-Nawawī preferred the view of the other wives of the Prophet. In actual fact the whole issue of Sālim's breast-feeding appears to be a controversial one.

Instead of insisting on one or other ruling to be derived from the tradition, it is first necessary to establish whether the information contained therein is rationally acceptable. The first question which immediately comes to mind is whether Sahlah bint Suhayl, who reportedly breast-fed Sālim, had breast milk at the time? If the answer is no, then the sanctity of the tradition can in no way be maintained. According to history she could not have been lactating. Sahlah bint Suhayl only had one child with Abū Ḥudhayfah, born during their stay in Abyssinia after migration in the 5th year after Prophethood. After the family returned to Makkah around a month later the same year, they remained there until the Prophet's emigration to Madinah eight years later. The occurrence of the breast-feeding event as reported in the tradition took place in Madinah, which means that there existed a gap of around 8–10 years between the birth of Sahlah's child and her breast-feeding of Sālim.[5] Normally, a woman may continue secreting milk for around three years after childbirth, and this being so it would be impossible for Sahlah to have been lactating at the time that she is supposed to have breast-fed Sālim. Physiologically, a white substance may secrete from a woman's dry breast, if the nipple is sucked for several days in a regular manner. If this were the case, we would have the bizarre situation of Sālim having had to act this out for several days continuously to enable Sahlah to secret a milk like substance, which still may not be classified as milk. According to the known ruling of scholars, it is breast milk which establishes a foster relationship (*riḍā ʿah*), and not any other substance whether that appear to be similar to milk or not.

Furthermore, in order to breast-feed Sālim, Sahlah would have had to expose her breast, in other words to uncover her *ʿawrah*, something which Islam forbids (24:31; 33:59). Scholars generally agree that a woman's *ʿawrah* includes every part of the body from head to toe excluding the face, the hands up to the wrist, and the feet up to the ankles. There is some disagreement over whether a woman's face, hands, and feet are also to be covered, but other than this there is no other disagreement as to what designates a woman's *ʿawrah*. The Qur'an makes it compulsory for women to cover the alluring parts of their body including the chest. (24:31). Moreover, breast-feeding involves physical contact between two persons, the woman and the child. If Sālim had been breast-fed, physical contact would have had to take place between him and Sahlah breaking yet another of Islam's strict rulings, that a woman and a man unrelated to each other, cannot have physical contact except in certain exceptional circumstances such as medical assessments by a physician. The Prophet never allowed any Muslim woman to make a pledge by putting her hand on his hand, unlike for men.[6] Nevertheless, al-Qāḍī Ḥasan (d.592 AH) suggests another possibility by way of explanation. He conjectures that Sahlah might have extracted her milk in a container and given this to Sālim to drink instead of uncovering her *ʿawrah*, this way no physical contact would have taken place.[7] This is a far-fetched idea and implausible because foster relationships are to be established through contact, that is breast-feeding directly[8] and not simply by drinking breast milk from a place other than a woman's breast.

Biologically, the woman's breasts are among the most sexually sensitive organs of her body, and any physical contact involving this area would easily arouse carnal passion in both adults. Islam forbids men and women even from prolonging and deepening their gaze upon the opposite sex (24:29–30) and exhorts its adherents not only to keep away from adultery but indeed any act which might lead to it (17:32). Once again this particular tradition seems to go against well established Islamic norms.

Then there is the question of why Abū Ḥudhayfah would feel uncomfortable by Sālim's presence in front of his mother, for psychologically a father would naturally never be affected, and Sālim was the adopted son of Abū Ḥudhayfah. According to age-old Arab (before Islam) tradition, the adopted son was considered the real son. People's attitude towards others is governed not only by hereditary traits of behavior but also by cultural traits and since Arabs looked upon their adopted children as their biological children, it is hard to imagine that Abū Ḥudhayfah would look suspiciously at his adopted son Sālim when he saw him near Sahlah. This leads to another obvious discrepancy. If Abū Ḥud-hayfah had been sensitive to Sālim's presence in front of his wife, how could he possibly have allowed Sahlah to have physical contact with him and through such a method? A normal man would never tolerate any adult male touching his wife and in such a compromising manner, and this is even more so the case with Arabs who are deeply sensitive to principles of personal honor an integral part of which is represented by the wife. All these issues throw very serious doubt on the authenticity of this tradition.

2–The Self-Indictment of Four Prophets on the Day of Judgment

Al-Bukhārī, Muslim and others have recorded a long tradition generally known as *Ḥadīth al-Shafāʿah*, the gist of which is that:

> On the Day of Judgment all mankind will be gathered together at one place. They will be in a state of deep sorrow and pain. They will decide to approach Adam for help. When they approach him and draw his

> attention to their plight, he will express his helplessness due to his sin of eating the fruit of the prohibited tree. The people will, then, seek Noah for help. He will also be unable to help them because he will be empty-handed, having been granted a supplication, which he had used against his people. They will thereafter visit Abraham who will extend the excuse, referring to the three lies he had spoken. They will [then] meet Moses who will express his inability to help them due to his killing a person without reason. They will, then, go to Jesus who will send them to Prophet Muhammad. In the end they will reach Prophet Muhammad who will try to help them...[9]

The central element and underlying message is that only Prophet Muhammad will have the power and honor to intercede on behalf of mankind on the Day of Judgment. The hadith may seem acceptable until more attention is paid to the objectionable way in which four prominent prophets, Adam, Noah, Abraham, and Moses, have been described as not daring to beseech Allah for help due to having committed sins in the past.

Adam who refers to his sin of eating the forbidden fruit should not have done so because he had repented and Allah had forgiven him. As repentance and forgiveness make a person innocent of their error, it does not befit a personality like Adam to mention what had been erased from his account as he was well aware of the divine pardon he had received from Allah.

Noah mentions the mistake of having prayed against his own people. This in fact is not a sin. The prophet spent almost a thousand years calling his people to the message of God, yet aside from a small number they refused to listen to him. The situation was such that he felt if the rebels were allowed to continue living on earth, human life would sink into chaos warranting the prayer he made to Allah to punish the culprits. In reality Noah did not pray against his people but tried to save humanity by praying that Allah help him to establish peace and justice on the earth, the first step of which was the annihilation of the anti-social elements existing among society. What he did was just and right. It was not a sin. His prayer in fact saved humanity. Conversely the tradition seems to be describing him as feeling guilty for having made the prayer, but if he had not done anything wrong, why would he feel guilty? Noah was a prophet and knew better than anyone what was wrong and what was right.

As for the self-indictment of Abraham, the issue of Abraham's alleged 'lies' has already been discussed in an earlier chapter. Suffice it to say that as Allah Himself describes Abraham as "*ṣiddīq*, a man of truth" (19:41) it is inconceivable that the Prophet would use a humiliating and derogatory remark against him.

Moses's reference to his sin of manslaughter, committed before his apostleship, does not seem to be justified. Moses had not killed the person concerned intentionally but accidentally, and furthermore, after being appointed as a prophet, was no longer to be blamed for the killing. Moses prayed throughout his life for the sake of his people, and his prayers were all granted. It is strange to suppose that he would fail to mention his sin while praying to Allah but then fear to talk to Allah on the Day of Judgment because of it. If the tradition is true, then it simply demonstrates Moses's ignorance of the nature of his relationship with Allah, and of course no prophet can ever be guilty of this.

Finally we come to prophet Jesus. Although the tradition does not refer to any sin on the part of this great prophet, it still astonishingly deprives him of the right to help people. According to the tradition, Jesus will say to those who ask him for help: "Go to Muhammad because Allah has forgiven all his sins." This implies that Prophet Muhammad is only able to help people because Allah has forgiven him. Is Allah's forgiveness the privilege of the Last Prophet only or an honor granted to all His prophets? Allah's forgiveness is conditional upon true faith and sincere deeds and whoever fulfils the condition deserves His forgiveness (3:31). Furthermore, does not this general rule apply to all Allah's Prophets who were protected throughout their lives from committing sinful deeds? All the prophets carry the great honor of having been forgiven by Allah and if this is the case, it is wrong to claim that Prophet Muhammad's privileged role of intercessor is due to his having been forgiven by Allah. The tradition in fact contradicts the Prophet's advice to his followers: "It is not appropriate for anyone to say that I (Muhammad) am better than Jonah son of Mathew."[10] This tradition concerning intercession is a clear example of extolling the Prophet at the expense of the honor accorded to the other great prophets of Allah. Ostensibly the main theme of the tradition is simply to establish the inability of other prophets to help human beings.

3–Moses Running Naked in Public

Al-Bukhārī, Muslim and others have recorded on the authority of Abū Hurayrah a tradition which states that,

> The children of Israel used to bathe naked, exposing their genitals to one another. Since Moses used to take a bath alone, they commented: "By God, nothing prevents Moses to bathe with us except that he suffers from hydrosol." One day, Moses went to take a bath and the moment he placed his clothes on a rock, the rock flew off with them. Moses ran after the rock desperately trying to stop it until he reached an inhabited area where the people saw Moses's genitalia and stated: "Nothing is wrong with Moses." After this, the rock stopped and Moses took his clothes and started hitting the rock with them.[11]

This tradition seems to come perilously close to undermining the respectable position of a prophet. Muslim has recorded it under the title "Praise of Moses" which is rather inexplicable for how can public humiliation be considered a virtue? Needless to say running around naked in public is an utterly shameful act and if Moses's clothes had somehow been taken away by the rock surely he would not have lost his sense of modesty and run after them. This does him great disservice. Furthermore, by first extolling the modesty of Moses by referring to his abstinence from taking a public bath, the tradition seems to undermine itself by then pointing immediately to his immodesty.

What are we being told exactly by this entire event? The tradition seems to suggest that the entire incident occurred to clear Moses of the accusation of being physically impaired. In other words since Moses did not care for people's comments it implies that Allah had him run naked so that people could see his private parts and become convinced that he did not harbor any disease. It is repulsive to think this or to imagine that nature would somehow plan to disrupt Moses's natural inclination toward modesty. Al-Nawawī suggests that the rock flying away with Moses's clothes was a miracle.[12] Miracles were given to prophets either to prove their authenticity as Allah's representatives or to help their followers to overcome certain unusual problems and Moses was in fact given many miracles, which fall into either of these two categories. A miracle is not a circus act, and for it to take place, the need has to be very pressing. In this particular incident however the need seems negligible (even if we are to accept the 'clearing of an accusation' hypothesis) or nonexistent. If anything the 'miracle' undermines Moses dignity and standard of morality, putting him through a humiliating experience and Allah never lets his chosen servants be humiliated. Because of this issue Ibn al-Jawzī refers to the probability of Moses having worn an undergarment at the time of running after the rock.[13]

Given its many serious difficulties one could surmise that this tradition is not a story related by the Prophet but most probably by someone from among the narrators who possibly picked it up from Judeo-Christian sources and attributed it to the Prophet to assign it credibility and sanctity.

4–The Prophet's Supposed Order to Kill the Innocent

Only Muslim has recorded this tradition on the authority of Anas ibn Mālik:

> A man was accused of having an affair with the Prophet's servant girl (Māriyyah). The Prophet, then, ordered ʿAlī to behead him. ʿAlī went to him, found him in a pond, and asked him to come out. When he came out, ʿAlī found him without male genitalia. ʿAlī did not carry out the execution, and informed the Prophet about it.[14]

The man who was accused of the affair was a eunuch named Maʿbūr presented to the Prophet by the Egyptian ruler, Muqawqis. The Prophet's servant girl referred to was Māriyyah who had also been sent to the Prophet by the same ruler.[15] The narration raises many questions. Had ʿAlī carried out the Prophet's command the innocent eunuch would have been put to death for no fault of his own. ʿAlī however refrains from killing him once he realizes that the affair could not have been possible. This would mean that the Prophet passed judgment against an individual without establishing the truth of the matter and failing to call any witnesses. The case, as reported in the tradition, was that of adultery for which there should either have been four witnesses or a confession by the accused or any other certain evidence of sexual involvement. Although Maᶜbūr's case contained no witnesses let alone four, no self-confession, and no other irrefutable evidence, the Prophet is reported to have issued the order for his execution. It is unimaginable that the Prophet who refrained from sentencing a woman accused of adultery mainly because there was no evidence against her,[16] would order a man to be killed simply on the grounds that he had been accused of adultery.

According to established history, Maᶜbūr had actually been presented to the Prophet as a eunuch, so it cannot be claimed that no one knew of this. Furthermore, eunuchs have certain recognizable effeminate mannerisms, which naturally alert others to their state. Thus, Maᶜbūr's being accused of adultery should have raised some doubt.

Then there is the question of who actually accused the eunuch of having an affair with someone in the Prophet's family, for this was a serious thing to do. It was not possible for Muslims to smear the Prophet's own household, they loved and respected him far too much. One could speculate that the accusation had been made by certain hypocrites, however, the time scale involved does not allow for this. Muqawqis had sent Māriyyah, Maᶜbūr and others to the Prophet in the year 8 AH.[17] During this period we do not find any hypocrites in the Islamic society of Madinah.

Finally, the story leaves us with one final unanswered question. Did the Prophet eventually identify the accusers and subject them to the stipulated punishment of slander (*qadhaf*) once it had been proven that Maᶜbūr was innocent? It would have been the responsibility of the society to bring the culprits to justice but we do not find any reference of this. Historical non-availability of such information denotes the non-existence of such slanderers. And non-availability of slanderers signifies that the story has been fabricated.

5–The Prophet's Wish to Burn People Due to their not Joining the Salah

Al-Bukhārī, Muslim and others have recorded on the authority of Abū Hurayrah a tradition which states that "The Prophet said, 'No prayer is harder for the hypocrites than the Fajr and the ᶜIsha prayers and if they knew the reward for these prayers at their respective times, they would certainly present themselves [in the mosques] even if they had to crawl.' The Prophet added, 'Certainly I decided to order the *Mu'adhdhin* to pronounce *Iqāmah* and order a man to lead the prayer and then take a fire flame to burn all those who had not left their houses so far for the prayer along with their houses."[18]

This tradition conveys two messages. First, that the Prophet was a harsh and hard-hearted man. Second, that being absent from the congregational prayers in the mosque is cognizable. The first message contrasts with the great mercy and gentleness of the Prophet as described in the Qur'an as well as the highly authentic *aḥādīth*. The Qur'an says: "It was by Allah's grace that you deal gently with your followers: for if you had been harsh and hard-hearted, they would indeed have broken away from you" (3:159). In a hadith the Prophet describes his disposition and demeanor in the following words: "I am Muhammad, Ahmad, the final Prophet, leader of the people on the Day of Judgment, an apostle of repentance, and an apostle of mercy."[19] The Prophet was very gentle in his dealings, kindhearted towards people, and a paragon of mercy, therefore it is inconceivable that he would wish to burn his followers alive.

Skipping salah in the mosque is obviously not a desirable action, however the offense is not so terrible that it would warrant the death penalty, and that by fire. Furthermore, no offense or crime in Islam, no matter how serious, carries with it the punishment of being burnt alive. It could be argued that the Prophet did not enforce this punishment on any one but simply wanted to make the people realize the significance of prayer in congregation. It is possible that the Prophet wanted to send a message, yet once again it is inconceivable that he would do so by frightening people in this way. It was also not possible for a man of mercy to even imagine burning his own followers.

How can one possibly attribute these words to the Prophet, when he had prevented his followers from using fire in torture? The Prophet said: "None can be punished with fire except with the fire of the Lord."[20] It is clear from this tradition that the punishment of fire is not allowed; it is the prerogative of Allah alone. Therefore, the Prophet would not have intended to punish these people with fire, for it would have contradicted his own ruling.

It is obvious from a report that the Prophet may have made this statement against certain hypocrites who had absented themselves from the salah.[21] Nevertheless, even if directed against the hypocrites it is inconceivable that the Prophet, who throughout his mission never dealt harshly with the hypocrites, would say anything of this nature. He always dealt with them gently. Dealing is not confined to only action and interaction; it includes comments and observation in words. If the Prophet had used harsh words, the people around him would certainly have broken away from him. According to all available accounts, the Prophet did not even reproach those who had failed to carry out their duty properly in the battle of Uḥud, although their negligence caused the victory of Muslims to turn into defeat.[22] Being negligent of military duty on the battlefield is more serious than skipping salah in a mosque. If the Prophet did not wish to punish the guilty in the battle of Uḥud, is it rational to assume that he would intend to kill those lagging behind others in prayers?

6–An Unrelated Woman Delousing the Prophet's Head

Al-Bukhārī, Muslim and others have recorded on the authority of Anas ibn Mālik the following tradition: "The Prophet used to frequently visit Umm Ḥarām bint Milḥān, the then wife of ʿUbādah ibn Ṣāmit. One day he visited her. She served him food, and then she started picking lice from his head. The Prophet fell asleep..."[23]

Umm Ḥarām was a Muslim of Madinah. She was the maternal aunt of Anas ibn Mālik, one of the Prophet's assistants.[24] She hailed from the same tribe, al-Najjār, as the Prophet's great grandmother, Salmah bint ʿAmr ibn Zayd ibn Labīd.[25] There does not seem to be any blood or foster relation between the Prophet and Umm Ḥarām. How could, then, one imagine that physical contact occurred between the Prophet and Umm Ḥarām? It is obvious that this tradition represents some sort of attempt to tarnish the Prophet's unblemished and pure character.

Al-Nawawī claims that there exists consensus amongst Muslim scholars that Umm Ḥarām was *maḥram* (an unmarriageable kin) for the Prophet. He also refers to disagreement among scholars over the nature of how she was a *maḥram*. According to Ibn ʿAbd al-Barr, Umm Ḥarām was the maternal aunt of the Prophet through suckling (*riḍāʿah*). He also quotes others anonymously as having said that Umm

Ḥarām was the maternal aunt of the Prophet's father or grandfather through suckling (*riḍāʿah*).[26] Ibn Ḥajar, commentator of al-Bukhārī's *Ṣaḥīḥ*, finds in the tradition permission for an unrelated woman to entertain a male guest, and delouse his head. But this issue he observes has become an intricate one in the eyes of a group of scholars. He also refers to the view of Ibn Abd al-Barr in these words: "Umm Ḥarām or her sister Umm Sulaym, I guess, suckled the Prophet hence one of them was the Prophet's foster mother and the other foster aunt. That is why the Prophet used to sleep beside Umm Ḥarām and received from her the services that are allowed between a male *maḥram* and his female *maḥram* relatives."[27] Yaḥyā ibn Ibrāhīm ibn Muzayn (d.259 AH), a commentator of Imām Mālik's *al-Muwaṭṭa'*, has tried to advance another argument to prove the foster relationship between the Prophet and Umm Ḥarām. He states that the Prophet's great grandmother Salmā and Umm Ḥarām were both from the same tribe, al-Najjār.[28] Ibn Wahb (d.197 AH) is reported to have made two observations on this matter. First, Umm Ḥarām was a foster aunt of the Prophet. Second, Umm Ḥarām was the foster aunt of the Prophet's father or his grandfather.[29] Ibn al-Jawzī refers to some tradition memorizers' view that Umm Sulaym was the foster sister of the Prophet's mother.[30]

It is obvious that most of the scholars, in their bid to maintain the validity of the tradition, have advanced the notion of a foster relation between the Prophet and Umm Ḥarām. According to established history, no woman from Madinah has ever been mentioned by historians as the foster mother of the Prophet. Umm Ḥarām was from Madinah. Al-Dimyāṭī (d.705 AH) emphatically denies any blood or foster relationship between the Prophet and Umm Ḥarām. He argues that the women who suckled the Prophet are known and Umm Ḥarām's name is not among them. He further disproves the theory of a foster relationship between the Prophet's grandfather and Umm Ḥarām. He insists that there was no possibility of any link between Umm Ḥarām and Umm Salmā, the Prophet's great grandmother, who was from Madinah, because the two came from two different families. He gives the genealogy of both.[31] Thus the two are linked to each other but not later than previous four generations. If there was any foster relation between them, he maintains, it could not be considered as the basis of a foster relation between the Prophet and Umm Ḥarām.[32]

As for Ibn al-Jawzī's suggestion that Umm Sulaym, the sister of Umm Ḥarām, was a foster sister of the Prophet's mother, Āminah bint Wahb, this is a far-fetched idea. The idea of a foster sisterhood between Umm Sulaym and Āminah indicates that both were of almost the same age. When the Prophet was born, his mother was thirty years old[33] hence Umm Sulaym was also of the same age. Thus, at the time of the Prophet's entry into Madinah Umm Sulaym was already eighty to eighty-three. Historical calculation may not corroborate it. When the Prophet entered Madinah, Umm Sulaym devoted to the Prophet's service her son Anas ibn Mālik who was then only 8–10 years old.[34] This means that at the time of Anas's birth she was seventy-one to seventy-three. It should be born in mind that Anas was the first and only child through her first husband, Mālik ibn Naḍḍār.[35] Biologically, women in their seventies are unable to conceive due to the menopause, which generally sets in at the age of fifty. Aside from this, Umm Sulaym, after she embraced Islam, married Abū Ṭalḥah and bore him two children, Abū ʿUmayr and ʿAbd Allāh.[36] Is it believable then that at the time of her marriage with Abū Ṭalḥah she was eighty-four years old? History has it that Abū Ṭalḥah had been very much impressed by her features before he proposed to her.[37] Abū Ṭalḥah's proposal to her speaks volumes for her age for he was hardly twenty-five to thirty years old.[38] At that time Umm Sulaym should not have been more than twenty-five to thirty. In this case, she was twenty-three to twenty-eight years junior to the Prophet. It is, then, not possible for Umm Sulaym to have been the foster sister of Āminah.

In light of this, the theory of a foster relation between the Prophet and Umm Ḥarām is untenable, and it seems obvious that the scholars developed this idea on the basis of mere speculation. This is why some scholars like Abū Bakr ibn al-ʿArabī and al-Dimyāṭī have proposed the theory of the Prophet's exclusive privilege.[39] This proposal also strengthens the belief that no foster relationship existed between the Prophet and Umm Ḥarām. The proposal of the Prophet's exclusive right to have physical contact with Umm Ḥarām also seems to be mere speculation. Undoubtedly, the Prophet had several exclusive privileges granted to him by Allah such as marriage with any number of women. But there are unequivocal statements on his exclusive privileges either in the Qur'an or in the Hadith.[40] There is no reference in either of the two sources to his privilege of being deloused by an unrelated woman. In order to declare anything specific concerning the Prophet strong evidence must be provided, mere speculation will not do.

It is unthinkable that the Prophet would have had physical contact with an unrelated woman in the form of delousing, when he himself refused to shake hands with women while conducting their pledge of allegiance.[41] In fact, no one would have raised any questions if the Prophet had done so, that is taken women's hands into his own for this sacred act, yet he avoided it. If this tradition is considered authentic then certain people may misuse it and the Prophet did not do or say anything which could mislead the people. The only way to end the controversies surrounding this tradition, and to maintain the integrity of the Prophet is to declare the tradition to be false.

7–Encouraging a Man to Commit More and More Sins

Muslim and others (though not al-Bukhārī) have recorded on the authority of Abū Ayyūb and Abū Hurayrah the following tradition: "The Prophet said: 'By the One in whose Hands is my soul, if you do not commit sins, Allah will destroy you and bring another people who will commit sins and ask Allah for His forgiveness, Allah will, then, forgive them'."[42]

What are we being told here, that Man should be daring in committing sins, and, if he does not commit sins, he will have no chance to repent and ask Allah for His forgiveness? In other words if a nation remains pious committing a minimum amount of errors only, it may lose the chance of survival. Can anyone imagine that the Prophet would encourage his followers to commit sins so as to be able to seek Allah's forgiveness? It is strange that al-Nawawī, a commentator of Muslim's work, has said nothing on this matter, meaning that he does not seem to have found any problem with the tradition.

The Qur'an reiterates that nations are destroyed because of their sins (6:6; 8:52, 54 etc). Allah has given glad tidings of a blissful life both in this world and the hereafter for only those who do good deeds (2:25; 10:9; 16:97 etc). The Qur'an invites mankind to develop exceptionally admirable qualities (25:62–74), which enable them to easily keep away from sinful thoughts and acts. Believers have been warned against falling victim to the tricks of Satan who always leads man into sin.

Whilst it is true that believers have been advised to always seek Allah's forgiveness for the errors they may have committed in their daily life, this can in no way be construed to mean that mankind has been invited and encouraged to commit more and more sins. A life dominated by sins is a bane, not a boon, and psychologically, if man keeps committing sins deliberately and keeps repenting, he cannot be expected to live a sincerely pious life. Sins when accumulated may turn into chaos (*fasād*) and such a situation is highly condemned in the Qur'an (30:41–42).

The tradition uses the word *dhunūb* for sins. Practically known sins are categorized into two types, major and minor. Major sins (apart from *shirk*) include, illicit sex, unjust killing, theft, robbery, confiscation of someone's rights, misbehavior with parents, dishonesty in dealings etc. It seems that the tradition encourages one to commit not only the minor but also the major sins although it is well known that major sins are cognizable and punishable.

The Prophet established a new society based on new Islamic principles in the Arabian Peninsula, an ideal society in terms of piety and high moral values. Had the Prophet really allowed his people to feel free in committing sins, the Arabs would never have been required to sever their relationship with their past, and the Arabian Peninsula would never have experienced a peaceful era. The Prophet came to discourage people from doing anything wrong. The entire premise of Islam is based on the "promotion of the good and the eradication of evil" (*al-amr bi al-maʿrūf wa al-nahyi ʿan al-munkar*). How could this theory ever be adjusted to the requirements of a tradition which is in total disharmony with both it and basic Islamic principles?

8–ʿUmar ibn al-Khaṭṭāb's Friday Sermon and Āyat al-Rajm

Al-Bukhārī, Muslim and others have recorded on the authority of ʿAbd Allāh ibn ʿAbbās the last Friday sermon of the second Caliph, ʿUmar ibn al-Khaṭṭāb and its background. Only al-Bukhārī has quoted it in detail and below is his version of the story:

> [According to ʿAbd al-Raḥmān ibn ʿAwf, someone reported to ʿUmar the Caliph who was in Makkah for pilgrimage that a particular person observed:] "If ʿUmar should die, I would certainly pledge my allegiance

to so-and-so [Ṭalḥah ibn ʿUbayd Allāh], by God, the election of Abū Bakr was but an expected lapse, which soon came to an end." Upon this ʿUmar became angry and said: "I will surely stand before the people tonight to caution those who want to usurp their leadership." ʿAbd al-Raḥmān ibn ʿAwf, [then, advised him not to do so because the pilgrimage season saw a gathering of all sorts of people including the mean and the ignorant] "who will dominate in the gathering you intend to address, and also because they will take your words but without understanding, and interpret them out of context. So, wait until you return to Madinah, which is the place of hijrah and Sunnah, you will be there with the scholars and the nobles so that when you talk to them, they will grasp your message and interpret correctly." [ʿUmar agreed to this idea, postponed his plan of addressing the people there, and decided to do so in the first gathering in Madinah. On the first Friday upon his return to Madinah, ʿUmar delivered the following sermon]:

"I am going to say something, which I am obliged to say because I do not know whether my death is very close. So he who grasps my words and preserves them in his heart should spread them as far as possible. He who finds himself unable to grasp them should not attribute any lie to me. Verily, Allah raised Muhammad with the truth, and revealed to him the Book. One of the revelations was *Āyat al-Rajm* [concerning stoning to death], which we recited, grasped and memorized. The Prophet enforced the ruling of *rajm* and we did the same after him. With the passage of time, I am afraid, someone might say: 'By God, we do not find *Āyat al-Rajm* in the Book of Allah.' And thus they go astray due to abandonment of an obligation Allah had revealed. Remember! stoning to death is the ruling in the Book of Allah for married men and women who commit adultery and [the act] is established either through the prescribed evidence or through pregnancy or through confession. We also used to read in the Book of Allah – 'Do not attribute your blood relationship to any other than your fathers; this is blasphemy on your part,' or – 'It is blasphemy to attribute your ancestory to any other than your fathers.' Remember! The Prophet said: 'Do not extol me as Jesus the son of Mary was extolled, say only that I am Allah's servant and His Messenger.' It has reached me that someone has said: 'If ʿUmar should die, I would pledge allegiance to so-and-so'. Let no one be beguiled into saying that the election of Abū Bakr was but a sudden lapse, which soon came to an end. Undoubtedly, it was like that but Allah removed its evil impact. There is none among you who could be considered on a par with Abū Bakr. He, who pledges allegiance to someone without consultation with the people, risks himself as well as the person he elects, to be killed. After the Prophet's death we were informed that the Supporters (*al-Anṣār*) remained behind and assembled altogether in the hut of Banū Sāʿidah; and ʿAlī, al-Zubayr and their confidants also remained away from us. The emigrants (*al-Muhājirūn*), then, gathered around Abū Bakr. I said to Abū Bakr: 'let us go to our brethren from the Supporters.' We went to them. When we were close to them, we met two pious persons of theirs who informed us about the consensus [of the Supporters] over the selection of the leader. They asked us about our destination. When we told them that we wanted to see our brethren from the Supporters, the two advised: 'Do not go to them. Carry out whatever we have already decided.' I said: 'By God, we shall certainly approach them.' When we reached the hut of Banū Sāʿidah, we spotted a person covered sitting among them. I asked: 'Who is this?' They answered: 'This is Saʿd ibn ʿUbādah.' I, then, asked: 'What is wrong with him?' They said: 'He is not well.' No sooner had we sat down than their speaker stood and after due praise of Allah said: 'We are the Supporters of Allah and the majority of the Muslim army. And, O Emigrants! You are only a small group; some people from your people came forward attempting to uproot us and prevent us from [our rightful accession to the Caliphate].' When he stopped, I intended to speak – I had already prepared a speech that I liked with a view to delivering it before Abū Bakr, and I used to avoid provoking him. Abū Bakr advised me to wait a while, and I disliked to make him angry. So Abū Bakr himself gave a speech and he was gentler and more sober-minded than I was. By God, he never missed a sentence that I liked in my own prepared speech, but he said the like of it or better than it spontaneously. [He spoke more beautifully than what I had prepared in my speech]. He spoke: 'Whatever good you have said about yourselves, you deserve that, but as for the [issue of Caliphate], it is recognized only for this particular group of the Quraysh. They are the noblest among Arabs with regard to lineage and residence. I have approved for you one of these two men. So give either of them the oath of allegiance'. He, then, took my hand as well as that of Abū ʿUbaydah ibn al-Jarrāḥ who was sitting among us. I hated nothing of what he had said except that proposal. By God, I preferred to be executed without just reason to my leadership of the people among whom there was Abū Bakr. Someone from the Supporters, then, said: 'I am the pillar ... [and propose] that there should be a leader from among us and a leader from among you [the Quraysh].' Thereupon there erupted furor and noise. I isolated myself from the chaos and asked Abū Bakr to stretch his hand. He stretched it; I pledged my allegiance to him, so was done by the Emigrants, and the Supporters followed suit. We, then, pounced upon Saʿd ibn ʿUbādah. Someone said: 'You killed Saʿd ibn ʿUbādah.' I retorted: 'Allah killed Saʿd ibn ʿUbādah.' [In his Friday sermon ʿUmar concluded:] ... By God, we did not find anything more appropriate than the election of Abū Bakr. We were afraid that if we left the place without election of the leader and they elected someone from among themselves, we would have to willingly or unwillingly agree to it or in case of opposition there would be chaos. So, he who pledges allegiance to someone without consultation of other Muslims will risk himself as well as the one to whom he pledged allegiance being killed."[43]

This report consists of several components: 1) the background of ʿUmar's Friday sermon, 2) the introductory part of the sermon, 3) the event of Abū Bakr's election as the first Caliph, 4) the event after the election, and 5) ʿUmar's warning to the people. In order to understand the true nature of this report, we need to analyze each of these five components.

The Background

A certain person makes the observation that he would favor so-and-so after the death of ʿUmar. It is also reported that he added his own understanding of how Abū Bakr was unexpectedly elected to the office of Caliphate. This observation enraged ʿUmar and he decided to speak to the people about the facts related to Abū Bakr's election. The person who made the observation does not ostensibly seem to have said anything wrong. The right to elect a leader is vested in every individual's hands. If someone expressed his desire for a particular person, Ṭalḥah ibn ʿUbayd Allāh as identified by some authorities, it was not illegal or undesirable for him to do so, but in fact his democratic right. Furthermore, there were certain other people like ʿAlī and al-Zubayr who had initially disagreed to the election of Abū Bakr. Their dissent was never considered as harmful for the Ummah. So, if ʿAlī and al-Zubayr were not blameworthy, why was this anonymous person blamed for causing chaos? ʿUmar's anger over his remark is hence somewhat perplexing. Undoubtedly ʿUmar was a somewhat hot-tempered person but after he became a Muslim this disposition surfaced only on religiously serious matters. Had he been a man of uncontrolled temper, he would never have been the successful ruler that he was. It is hard to imagine that ʿUmar became infuriated merely on the grounds of this statement. If he really became disturbed over the observation, it should have been over something other than what has been mentioned in the report.

The Introductory Remarks

ʿUmar begins his Friday sermon with an introduction in which he draws the attention of the audience to two so-called "abrogated"[44] verses of the Qur'an and a hadith. The verses concerned, are *āyat al-Rajm* ["Old man and old woman, if they commit adultery, stone them both surely to death"], and *āyat al-Raghb* ("Do not attribute your blood relationship to any other than your fathers; it is blasphemy on your part, if you do so."). The hadith quoted by ʿUmar in his speech is: "Do not extol me as Jesus the son of Mary was extolled." One wonders what possible link there can be between the main theme of the sermon and these references? It is almost impossible to identify any connection between the two. Arabs were very eloquent in their speech and their hatred of speaking something irrelevant to the occasion is historically well known. ʿUmar was a man of rhetoric and eloquence. It is unlikely that he would make a remark entirely irrelevant to the occasion. Al-Muhallab attempts to make the link. He states that ʿUmar quoted the abrogated verses and the hadith with a view to stressing the point that no one was empowered to arrive at a decision on a matter unstipulated in the Qur'an and the Sunnah.[45] This seems to be a very vague suggestion. Even if accepted, the *Āyat al-Rajm* and *Āyat al-Raghb* have nothing to do with the observation concerning the election of Abū Bakr.

Had there existed any abrogated verses concerning the first Caliph's election only then would ʿUmar's reference to them have had meaning.

The *Āyat al-Rajm*, as referred to by ʿUmar, is not mentioned in the report. If ʿUmar read the other abrogated verse in full, he must have read this one too. According to other sources the *āyat al-Rajm* as quoted by ʿUmar was: "Old man and old woman, if they commit adultery, stone them both to death" (*al-Shaykh wa al-Shaykhah idhā zanayā fa irjumūhumā al-battah*).[46] The first question we need to ask is that is this a Qur'anic verse? Does it corroborate the exemplary eloquence of the Qur'an? Amin Ahsan Islahi, an expert in Qur'anic rhetoric and eloquence, observes:

> If you ponder over this tradition, it seems from every angle the fabrication of a hypocrite. Its purpose is to cast doubt upon the authenticity of the Qur'an, and to create suspicion in unsuspecting hearts that some verses have been excluded from the Qur'an. Consider, first of all, its language. Can anyone with good taste accept it as a Qur'anic *āyah*? It is impossible for any with sound academic taste to even attribute it to the Prophet let alone consider it a Qur'anic verse. Where will you insert this patchwork of jute into the velvet [beauty] of the Qur'an? There is no link whatsoever between the divine language as well as the most eloquent speech of the Qur'an, and the statement [*āyat al-Rajm*].[47]

ʿUmar is shown to have used this verse to prove the validity of the punishment of stoning to death for a married adulterer. Do the words "old man and old woman" necessarily mean married man and woman? The Qur'an never uses a word to convey a message that may not be inherent therein. To do so is against the concept of the Qur'an's eloquence. Islahi views the report concerning *āyat al-Rajm* as a frivolous one, and finds its attribution to ʿUmar as an injustice to him.[48]

Moreover, ʿUmar's statement – "with the passage of a long time, I am afraid, someone might say: by God, we do not find *āyat al-Rajm* in the Qur'an, and go astray because of abandoning an obligation Allah revealed in the Qur'an. Stoning to death is a ruling in the Book of Allah for the married man and woman who commit adultery" – seems to be strange. Is stoning to death a Qur'anic obligation? A Qur'anic obligation is only available therein. What is unavailable in the Qur'an cannot form an obligation. ʿUmar must have been aware of the non-availability of this verse, *āyat al-Rajm*, in the Qur'an, yet he refers to it as a Qur'anic obligation. This is odd.

The Event of Abū Bakr's Election

ʿUmar retold the story of Abū Bakr's election as the first Caliph. On the whole, this story corroborates history. But the minute details of the event seem to be doubtful. For instance, the *Anṣār* (Supporters) have been described as greedy for power not wanting to share this with the *Muhājirūn* (Emigrants) on the grounds that they (the Anṣār) were the real supporters of Islam, whereas the *Muhājirūn* were inferior to them. This picture of the *Anṣār* contradicts the Qur'anic description. The Qur'an says that,

> But those who before them, had homes (in Medina) and had adopted the Faith, [*Anṣār*] – show their affection to such as came to them for refuge, [*Muhājirūn*] and entertain no desire in their hearts for things given to the (latter) [*Muhājirūn*], but give them preference over themselves, even though poverty was their (own lot). And those saved from the covetousness of their own souls, – they are the ones that achieve prosperity. (59:9)

Historically, the *Anṣār* sacrificed almost everything they had for the comfort of the *Muhājirūn*; they gave their hereditary property share to the *Muhājirūn* and they welcomed warmly whoever came to Madinah.[49] Is it, then, believable that the same people would turn overnight and become the enemies of the *Muhājirūn*? It seems doubtful that ʿUmar would describe the *Anṣār* in the way he is reported to have described them in his sermon.

The Event after the Election of Abū Bakr

Immediately after Abū Bakr was elected by both parties (the *Muhājirūn* and the Anṣār), people particularly the *Muhājirūn*, including ʿUmar, attacked Saʿd ibn ʿUbādah, the candidate for leadership on behalf of the Anṣār. This attack almost killed the victim. Here we come to the question as to why he was beaten when the problem had already been resolved amicably. There was nothing wrong on the part of Saʿd ibn ʿUbādah if he was fielded by his people as a potential candidate for leadership. According to ʿUmar, Saʿd was ill, yet he was attacked. If he did anything wrong, he should have been left untouched until he had fully recovered from his illness. Had ʿUmar and others who attacked Saʿd consulted the newly appointed Caliph? If not, why? In the presence of a legal authority, none is authorized to take the law into their own hands. If yes, it is unbelievable that Abū Bakr who was very gentle and kindhearted would have ordered an attack on one of his own Muslim brethren. Would it not have occurred to the attackers that this could cause further rift in the Muslim society? Such a rash step would only be taken by simpletons. In fact, the *Muhājirūn* and the *Anṣār* were all highly astute Muslims and to ascribe such a disgusting act of physical torture to them is to deny their quality of benevolence, as described in the Qur'an itself: "Muhammad is the Messenger of Allah; and those who are with him are strong and firm against the unbelievers, but compassionate among themselves" (48:29).

ʿUmar's Warning to the People

Caliph ʿUmar warned in the end that none should singly tackle the election of the Caliph. But in his sermon he describes how Abū Bakr had proposed two names, ʿUmar and Abū ʿUbaydah for the leadership. It was Abū Bakr's own suggestion. Did he consult others in this matter? Even ʿUmar did the same when he proposed the name of Abū Bakr and pledged his allegiance to him. Had he consulted the community in advance? It seems he did it on his own. When he did so, others followed suit. The person with whose statement ʿUmar had become angry had merely expressed his opinion on the next Caliph. If historical accounts are true, he had proposed the name of Ṭalḥah ibn ʿUbayd Allāh who was one of the most trusted followers of the Prophet from the Quraysh. The person who suggested his name might have thought that Ṭalḥah would prove to be another successful leader of the Ummah. In doing so, he had done nothing wrong as ʿUmar had done exactly the same.

In light of this analysis we may be surmise that what has been attributed to ʿUmar in the form of the Friday sermon is a fabrication, done so in a bid to smear firstly the image of ʿUmar himself, secondly, to blame the *Anṣār* for causing rift in the ranks of the community, and finally to create doubt in the minds of others that the Qur'an was vulnerable to changes. Therefore, this report with its far-reaching negative impact cannot be considered genuine, even though there is no problem in its chain of reporters.

9–Intellectual and Religious Deficiency of Women

Al-Bukhārī, Muslim and others have recorded on the authority of Abū Saʿīd al-Khudrī and Abū Hurayrah the following hadith:

> The Prophet addressed women: "O women! Do charity work. I have been shown that most of the residents of Hell are women." The women asked why. The Prophet said: "You do too much cursing, and are often unfaithful to your family. I have not seen any intellectually and religiously deficient creature as harmful for men as you are." The women asked: "What is our intellectual and religious deficiency, O Prophet of Allah?" The Prophet asked: "Is not the witness of a woman considered half that of man?" The women answered in the affirmative. The Prophet then said: "This is one of [the woman's] intellectual deficiencies." The Prophet proceeded asking: "Do you not abstain from prayer [salah] and fasting during menstruation?" When the women confirmed this, the Prophet said: "This is among [the woman's] religious deficiencies."[50]

This tradition unequivocally declares women to be deficient, both intellectually as well as religiously, as compared to men. In order to ascertain that this statement, supposedly made by the Prophet is accurate, we need to thoroughly analyze the report.

Normally, the answer to a question should be relevant to and in consonance with the issue raised. Here the women ask the Prophet why they will form the majority of the inmates of Hell. The Prophet in response refers to three things, 1) excessive cursing, 2) excessive infidelity, and 3) intellectual and religious deficiencies. The first two reasons are relevant to the issue. The third reason however does not seem to be. The Prophet further clarifies intellectual deficiency, among other things, to mean the inability of a woman to stand as a fully-fledged witness in a case, and concerning religious deficiency as the woman's inability to observe her religious duty of performing obligatory prayer and fasting during menstruation. This is odd, for it is Allah who has determined the woman's witness to be half that of a man's, and it is He who created the menstrual cycle to serve a particular purpose. How could, then, these natural and legal compulsions be regarded as reasons for women to be thrown into Hell? As their perceived intellectual and physical handicaps are not their own handiwork, why should they be held responsible for something which is beyond their control?

The Prophet, according to the report, puts women to blame for playing tricks with men and dominating their minds and hearts, thus misleading them. Again this makes no sense. Is it possible for the less intelligent and the less capable to dominate the more intelligent and the most capable? If women are intellectually deficient, how can they play tricks or outwit men who possess superior intelligence? In fact if anything the reverse applies, for psychologically, the less intelligent are dominated by the more intelligent. If women really do dominate men and mislead them, then the former should be as strong intellectually as the latter.

The Prophet advances, as is claimed, two examples, one to explain intellectual deficiency and the other to prove religious deficiency. The example for intellectual deficiency is a woman's eligibility to be a half witness only. Here it seems intellectual deficiency denotes lack of knowledge. Al-Nawawī mentions three components required of the intellect (*ʿaql*), 1) knowledge, 2) information about the basic and necessary matters related to life, and 3) the power of discernment.[51] This means that deficiency of mind is actually that of knowledge as well as that of discernment. In this case it is, then, not necessarily only the woman's prerogative to suffer from this, for men may also be victims. Thus, why should women alone be referred to as intellectually deficient? Many men are also found lacking in knowledge and having less sagacity. There are also women in their millions who are more sagacious, more knowledgeable, and far more intelligent than men. Umm Salamah, one of the Prophet's wives, once advised the Prophet on a specific issue. After the treaty of *Ḥudaybiyyah*, Muslims in general were very upset due to the humiliating nature of the treaty provisions. When the Prophet asked them to sacrifice an animal to mark the end of the sojourn for ʿ*umrah*, they did not do so, and demonstrated a somewhat silent protest against the apparently unjust treaty. Consequently, the Prophet felt uncomfortable with this approach of his followers, contemplating how to control the situation. Umm Salamah was with him during this journey. She advised him to sacrifice his animal first, assuring him that his action would make the others believe that the Prophet's decision was unalterable, and they would then certainly follow suit. The Prophet did exactly as advised by his wife and the reaction of the followers was the same as that anticipated by Umm Salamah.[52] Was Umm Salamah a woman suffering from intellectual deficiency? ʿĀ'ishah, another wife of the Prophet, is known in history as an extremely intelligent woman, the most intelligent of her time, who was consulted during her life-time on matters of a serious nature by men of the highest intellect including ʿUmar ibn al-Khaṭṭāb. In what category will she be placed, that of *Nāqiṣāt* ʿ*aql* (intellectual deficiency) or that of *Kāmilāt* ʿ*aql* (intellectual perfection)?

The reference to women's half eligibility as witnesses is based on Qur'anic verse 2:282. Does this *āyah* really talk about women's intellectual deficiency? Muhammad Asad observes:

> The stipulation that two women may be substituted for one male witness does not imply any reflection on women's moral or intellectual capabilities: it is obviously due to the fact that, as a rule, women are less familiar with business procedures than men and, therefore, more liable to commit mistakes in this respect.[53]

The *āyah* itself spells out the reason for its stipulation. The two women as witnesses are supposed to help each other because of their unfamiliarity with matters related to monetary transaction. It could be concluded that if the reason of forgetfulness due to unfamiliarity with the matter does not exist, there may not be any need to call two women to stand as witnesses, substituting a male witness. It should be borne in mind that applicability of a ruling requires availability of the relevant situation. If a highly qualified woman particularly in the field of business management is available to act as witness, it seems unfair to still give her half credibility. But in a society where women are generally uneducated and confined to domestic matters, the provision of two women's witnessing may be justified.

The reason given for religious deficiency is women's inability to perform obligatory prayer and to fast during menstruation. As observed earlier menstruation is a natural phenomenon in women and during this time they are not allowed to carry out their religious duties. What is then wrong on the part of women? If they refrain from prayer and fasting, it is not because they want to but because they have to. That being so, how could this then be considered a reason for their supposed religious deficiency? Women do not pray because prayer during menstruation is not binding on them according to Islamic law. This is why they are not even required to make up the missed prayers. Likewise, they do not fast because it is forbidden for them during this time, although in the case of fasting they are required to make them up later. By doing compensatory fasting, a woman manages to redeem the loss, so non-fasting entails no loss at all on the part of women.

Furthermore, the term *Nāqiṣāt ʿaql wa dīn* (intellectually and religiously deficient) is a derogatory and insulting phrase tantamount to calling someone an idiot, and Islam does not allow use of humiliating words:

> O you who have attained to faith! No men shall deride [other] men: it may well be that those [whom they deride] are better than themselves; and no women [shall deride other] women: it may well be that those [whom they deride] are better than them selves. And neither shall you defame one another, nor insult one another by [opprobrious] epithets: ... (49:11)

It is inconceivable that the Prophet would hurt the feelings of women by calling them *Nāqiṣāt ʿaql wa dīn*. His words and acts were the living interpretation of the Qur'an. If the Qur'an prohibits the believers from hurting or offending anyone by the use of such words, would not the Prophet have practiced this to the highest level? Moreover, the Prophet is reported to have expressly shared his feeling toward women in these words: "The love for women has been deposited in my heart."[54] One who was so kindhearted towards them would never have employed such an epithet against them. Al-Bukhārī has recorded ʿAbd Allāh ibn ʿAbbās's observation on women in these words: "Verily, women constitute the majority of the best in the Ummah."[55] It seems Ibn ʿAbbās developed this view about women on the basis of some utterances of the Prophet, and if this is so, the concept of women's intellectual and religious deficiency is seriously questionable.

10–ʿĀ'ishah's Trickery on the Prophet

Al-Bukhārī, Muslim and others have recorded two traditions describing how ʿĀ'ishah played a trick upon the Prophet to hurt his feelings. Both traditions are cited as reported by al-Bukhārī and Muslim:

1–ʿUbayd ibn ʿUmayr reported that he heard ʿĀ'ishah saying that:

> The Prophet used to stay for a period in the house of Zaynab bint Jaḥsh and drink honey in her house. [She said] "Ḥafṣah and I decided that when the Prophet entered upon either of us, we would say, 'I smell *maghāfīr* [a particular flower which gives an unpleasant odor] on you. Have you eaten *maghāfīr?*' When he entered upon one of us, she said that to him. He replied, 'No but I drank honey in the house of Zaynab bint Jaḥsh and I will never drink it again'." Then came the revelation – "O Prophet! Why do you make unlawful what Allah has made lawful for you, seeking to please your wives?..." (66:1–4).[56]

2–ʿĀ'ishah reports:

> The Prophet loved sweets and honey very much. As a routine the Prophet would visit his wives daily after ʿ*Aṣr* prayer one after another. One day when the Prophet visited Ḥafṣah, he stayed with her longer than normal. I checked concerning the reason; I was told that some relative had sent a leather container of honey to Ḥafṣah, and the Prophet drank some honey from the gift. I, then, said: "By God, I will certainly play a trick on him [the Prophet]." I mentioned it to Sawdah and advised her to say to the Prophet, when he drew close to her, whether he took *maghāfīr*; when the Prophet denied [this], [to] ask him about the reason of the smell; since the Prophet was very sensitive to any kind of foul smell, he would, then, say that Ḥafṣah [had] served him honey drink...

ʿĀ'ishah continues,

> "You have to, then, say: 'It seems the bee of that honey derived honey element from *al-ʿurfuṭ* [a smelly plant].' I will do the same to the Prophet." I also advised Ṣafīyyah [the Prophet's other wife] to do the same. When the Prophet visited Sawdah, she was on the verge of disclosing the plan to the Prophet but when the Prophet drew close to her, she said as advised. When the Prophet visited me, I said the same as planned. When the Prophet visited Ṣafīyyah, she did the same. In reaction to the same statement from us the Prophet, on his visit to Ḥafṣah, refused to take honey there. Upon this Sawdah said that they [the Prophet's wives] deprived the Prophet of his favorite drink. I, therefore, warned her to keep silent.[57]

Both these reports contain some clear contradictions. First, which of the two wives did the Prophet stay longer with to drink honey? The first stipulates Zaynab bint Jaḥsh, whereas the second Ḥafṣah. Second, which of the wives did ʿĀ'ishah collude with against the Prophet? The first mentions Ḥafṣah, whereas the second refers to two wives, Sawdah and Ṣafiyyah. As the chains of narrators for both reports are authentic how are we to explain the discrepancies? Any evaluation will be considered an attack on al-Bukhārī and Muslim who are believed to have recorded only authentic traditions in their works. But nevertheless silence on the part of scholars is an offense against the Prophet and his wives. It is obvious that both reports cannot be correct, but identifying the correct one and on what grounds seems to be a very difficult task. Al-Nawawī has tried to resolve the problem. He first acknowledges that conflict exists between the reports and then comments that the first tradition is the correct one in comparison to the second based on two reasons: (1) some scholars like al-Nasā'ī consider the chain of narrators of the first tradition to be stronger than that of the second, and (2) the first report mentions two wives (ʿĀ'ishah and Ḥafṣah), which is in agreement with the Qur'an (66:1–4) which refers to only two women anonymously.[58]

Al-Nawawī is not categorical in his statement about the second report in that he does not clearly mention his stand on the position of the second tradition. Given his discussion, why did he then not declare the second report of both Muslim and al-Bukhārī to be unreliable? He did not do so because this would have brought the authenticity of the two scholars' authentication of Hadith into question. It is regrettable that al-ʿAynī and Ibn Ḥajr, the most respected of commentators on al-Bukhārī's *Ṣaḥīḥ*, did not touch on this apparent conflict at all. Why? Was it not to simply maintain the reliability of the methodology of Hadith examination developed by al-Bukhārī and Muslim, an approach in fact which only serves to put their own reliability at stake? What would have been wrong in simply referring to the issue as al-Nawawī had done in his comment on Muslim's reports? Would honest analysis not have been the best approach?

There is another clear problem in the two reports. Are we really to accept that ʿĀ'ishah the most beloved wife of the Prophet would vow to play a trick on him? The Prophet was loved and respected by all to such a degree that no one, including his wives, would even think of hurting him psychologically or play tricks with him. Ibn Ḥajar and al-Nawawī do not say anything on this matter. Only Badr al-Dīn al-ʿAynī takes note of the problem and observes that ʿĀ'ishah at the time was still young and inexperienced and did not actually intend to hurt the Prophet.[59] This is a plausible explanation to some extent, but the question yet remains as to why the other wives of the Prophet would agree to go along with it. Ḥafṣah was a mature woman who knew very well the negative repercussion of their plan. Why did she therefore not prevent ʿĀ'ishah from carrying it through?

Moreover, the two reports mention not only the plan to trick the Prophet but also ʿĀ'ishah's campaign to make the other wives lie to him concerning the smell of the honey he consumed. It is inconceivable that ʿĀ'ishah would utter a lie or advise others to do so to the Prophet. The practice is condemned in Islam. Again if we excuse ʿĀ'ishah on the grounds that she was young and inexperienced, this does not explain the actions of the other more mature wives. All these valid questions and observations have been entirely ignored by Hadith commentators.

It seems easier to consign the two reports of al-Bukhārī and Muslim to the bin than to even conceive of the Prophet's wives as intending to trick him by speaking lies. The position of the Prophet is far greater than that of Hadith scholars. Moreover, ʿĀ'ishah, Ḥafṣah and the other wives mentioned in the two reports, are considered as the "mothers of believers" and it is incumbent upon all believers to love the Prophet's wives and believe in the integrity of their character. But Muslim scholars in general and Hadith authorities in particular nevertheless insist on the authenticity of the two reports merely because these have been recorded by al-Bukhārī and Muslim. It seems they have more respect for the latter than the Prophet's own wives and care little if the traditions subvert the sanctity of ʿĀ'ishah as long as they preserve that of al-Bukhārī and Muslim. This is utterly unacceptable. It is better to denounce the two reports as fabrications or unreliable than to smear ʿĀ'ishah, as well as the Prophet's other wives, which the reports undoubtedly do.

Amin Ahsan Islahi offers an interpretation which does not adversely affect the Prophet's wives. He states that

> Once the Prophet consumed honey in the house of some of his wives. The honey caused a particular foul smell, which was disliked by some of [them]. Certain kinds of honey give a foul smell. Even if there is no foul smell, some sensitive people particularly women do not like all kinds of smell. People differ in their taste and disposition. Some of the Prophet's wives did not like that particular honey, which gives the smell of *maghāfīr*. When they expressed their aversion to the smell, the Prophet who had a fine taste and was also very sensitive to the feelings of women, vowed never to take honey.[60]

It may be argued here that the Qur'anic statement – "[Say, O Prophet:] 'Would that you two turn unto God in repentance, for the hearts of both of you have swerved [from what is right]! And if you uphold each other against him (*taẓāharā ʿalayhi*), [who is God's message-bearer, know that] God Himself is his Protector, and [that,] therefore, Gabriel, and all the righteous among the believers and all the [other] angels will come to his aid" (66:4) – corroborates the event as depicted in the above reports. Undoubtedly, the two wives of the Prophet did something wrong by backing each other against the wish of the Prophet. But the offense indicated in the Qur'anic statement is that one of the wives of the Prophet disclosed to another wife a secret which the Prophet had shared with her and asked her not to divulge to anyone else. The seriousness of the offense on the part of the two wives was that they had not upheld the Prophet's command concerning the secret. The secret which the Prophet had shared with one of his wives was that he had vowed not to drink honey anymore asking her not to divulge this resolve to anyone.

When finding a problem in any report, Hadith commentators often make the remark that "One or other of the narrators must have become deluded" (*wahima*). It could however, also be said that one or other of the reporters made a mistake. An error in reporting from any narrator in a chain of narrators is something that is very possible. If a reporter by mistake for instance in this case changed the names of the Prophet's wives in his report, some other reporter might have presented the report, advertently or inadvertently, in a modified version. The reporters did not certainly report the event exactly as described by ʿĀ'ishah. Their wordings were not necessarily the wordings of ʿĀ'ishah. While passing the report verbally to others, it would have been quite natural for the narrators to use different words. We can only conclude that this report seems to have been subject to a large degree to some non-precise presentation by reporters.

11–Burning of the Ant Nest

Muslim has recorded a tradition on the authority of Abū Hurayrah that "One of the previous prophets took shelter under a tree, he was bitten by an ant there; he, then, commanded his companions to move from there and burn the anthill in its entirety. Thereupon Allah asked him as to why he had killed all the ants, whilst only one ant had bitten him."[61]

This tradition presents a case of rashness on the part of a prophet. The Qur'an depicts a very excellent image of Allah's prophets. They were all patient, kind, sensible, generous, pious, brave, honest, truthful etc. Of course, the Qur'an does not mention all the prophets that were sent to mankind but it is axiomatic that the prophets who are mentioned in the Qur'an exude the highest qualities, representing the institution of prophethood itself, as well as the character of all those prophets who remain anonymous to us.

It is therefore inconceivable that a prophet would become so infuriated by the bite of an ant that he would have their entire nest burnt.

When an ordinary person is unlikely to react so impetuously how much more ridiculous to presume that a prophet would do so.

Conclusion

To conclude, eleven *aḥādīth* have been read and checked minutely in this chapter, employing the light of human reason. Given the issues raised and the force of logic brought to bear, it would be hard for anyone to digest and accept them, albeit recorded by great Hadith scholars, as authentic. As the maxim goes, "the face is the index of mind," so in this case, the text of a hadith indicates its nature, that is whether it is acceptable. As explained in the beginning of the chapter, human reason is not meant to signify mental power free from all bounds. Having said this however, if the Qur'an declares time and again that human reason is a reliable criterion to judge the truth from the false, then scholars and students from any background should use their reason to discover the truth in Hadith literature.

6

Authentication of Hadith Through Established History

THE STUDY OF HISTORY IS ESSENTIAL and one of its more primary purposes is educative. More than a simple representation of past events, history should ideally be a guide to help humanity correct the mistakes it may have made earlier and to draw inspiration from the very best it may have achieved. The Qur'an presents history in this vein and in the guise of a teacher. Both the Qur'an and the Bible describe the history of many nations and individuals. However, many historical accounts in the Bible seem inaccurate in the light of Qur'anic accounts and a case in point is that of prophet Lot or Lūṭ. The Bible depicts him as a man of low character who becomes sexually involved with his own daughters[1] (though unknowingly), whereas the Qur'an presents him as a man of high character and integrity.[2] In order to authenticate a historical report concerning an event, the established historical account on the matter concerned is to be checked. In case of similarity in both the descriptions reported and the historical event, the report is to be declared as reliable. If there is a clash between the reported event and the well-known historical account, the reported event is to be rejected as unacceptable.

Hadith literature contains many historical accounts including subject matter that in one way or another often deals with history. The reports, at times, corroborate history and at times, contradict it. In a situation where a report contradicts established history, the tradition, regardless of its authenticity in terms of the chain, is to be considered dubious if not declared fabricated.

1–The First to Die after the Prophet, Sawdah or Zaynab?

Al-Bukhārī records the following tradition as to who would be the first to die after the Prophet, on the authority of ʿĀ'ishah:

> Some of the Prophet's wives asked him as to which of them would be the first to die after his death. The Prophet answered: "The one with the longest hand." They, then, measured their hands and found Sawdah to have the longest hand. She was the first to die after the death of the Prophet. When she died, they realized that the meaning of the longest hand was the one most generous in charity, as she loved charity work very much.[3]

This report claims that Sawdah was the first to die after the Prophet's death. However, according to established history, Sawdah died in 54 AH,[4] and it was Zaynab bint Jaḥsh who died before her in 20 AH.[5] This is why the report is defective. Muslim records another tradition on the authority of ʿĀ'ishah, according to which it was Zaynab bint Jaḥsh who was the most generous among the Prophet's wives and it was she who died first after the death of the Prophet.[6] Ibn Ḥajar, after a long discussion on al-Bukhārī's report, concludes that a reporter made a mistake in transmission.[7] Al-Nawawī declares al-Bukhārī's report to be false.[8]

2–Madinah versus Syria as the Place of Abū Sufyān's Death

Al-Bukhārī has recorded on the authority of Zaynab bint Abī Salamah a tradition which states that "When the news of Abū Sufyān's death in Syria reached Umm Ḥabībah, she mourned for three days only."[9]

Muslim and others also record the same report but without identifying Syria as the place of Abū Sufyān's death.[10] Ibn Ḥajar criticizes this statement as an error because, according to established history, Abū Sufyān died in 32 AH in Madinah.[11]

3–Khubayb ibn Isāf or Khubayb ibn ʿAdī, A Combatant in the Battle of Badr

Al-Bukhārī has recorded on the authority of Abū Hurayrah a report, according to which in the battle of *Rajī'* the enemy took several Muslims including Khubayb ibn ʿAdī captive and killed them later on.

Al-Bukhārī's report explains that Khubayb ibn ʿAdī was one of the participants in the battle of Badr and during the battle had killed a Quraysh soldier, al-Ḥārith ibn ʿAmr ibn Nawfal.[12]

Ibn Hishām, Ibn Saʿd, and Ibn Kathīr have compiled a list of Muslim combatants in the battle of Badr and there is only one Khubayb mentioned and he is Ibn Isāf.[13] Ibn Hishām has listed who killed who in the battle of Badr and according to his account Khubayb ibn Isāf, a Muslim from the *Anṣār*, killed al-Ḥārith ibn ʿAmr ibn Nawfal.[14] This means that the information available in the report recorded by al-Bukhārī contains a historical error. Khubayb ibn ʿAdī who participated in the battle of *Rajīʿ*, and was killed by Quraysh later on is not mentioned as having participated in the battle of Badr.

Ibn Ḥajar suggests that the history could be corrected in light of al-Bukhārī's authentic report. His argument is that if Khubayb was not the one who killed al-Ḥārith in the battle of Badr, why did al-Ḥārith's family later kill him in retaliation? At the same time, Ibn Ḥajar refers to a possibility that the killer of Khubayb ibn ʿAdī actually mistook him for Khubayb ibn Isāf. He also suggests another possibility that both Khubayb ibn Isāf and Khubayb ibn ʿAdī may jointly have killed al-Ḥārith.[15] Ibn Ḥajar seems to ignore the fact that mere speculation and presumed possibilities do not change historical facts on the ground.

4–Residence of the Prophet's Daughter, Fāṭimah

Al-Bukhārī records on the authority of Abū Hurayrah a tradition that "the Prophet walked one day silently towards the market of *Banū Qaynuqāʿ* and sat in the courtyard of Fāṭimah's residence."[16]

Al-Dāwūdī (d.828 AH) remarks that certain parts of this report were either omitted or different reports somehow became merged into it. According to him, Fāṭimah's residence was not in the locale of the Jewish tribe, *Banū Qaynuqāʿ*.[17] Ibn Ḥajar agrees that there is an error in the report. He considers the report recorded by Muslim in his *Ṣaḥīḥ* as correct which is why he suggests rectifying al-Bukhārī's report with that of Muslim adding: "...Until he reached the market of *Banū Qaynuqāʿ*, and then he returned until he arrived in the courtyard of Fāṭimah."[18] Muslim's report clearly indicates that the residence of Fāṭimah was not in the Jewish quarter but elsewhere.

5–Punishment for Drinking Alcohol, Eighty Lashes Versus Forty

Al-Bukhārī records a long tradition on the authority of ʿUbayd Allāh ibn ʿAdī ibn al-Khiyār concerning the punishment of al-Walīd ibn ʿUqbah for drinking wine. The last sentence of this states: "Then ʿUthmān ibn ʿAffān called ʿAlī ibn Abī Ṭālib and ordered him to flog al-Walīd. So ʿAlī flogged him with eighty lashes."[19]

Muslim records the same story on the authority of Abū Sāsān Ḥuḍayn ibn al-Mundhir, but his report indicates that al-Walīd was punished with forty lashes for drinking alcohol.[20] Al-Bukhārī himself records another tradition which clearly mentions that ʿUthmān ordered ʿAlī to flog al-Walīd with forty lashes, and ʿAlī did so.[21] So, al-Bukhārī has recorded two sets of hadith on this case. In the second there is a mention of forty lashes instead of eighty as in the first one. Ibn Ḥajar declares the second narration reporting forty lashes as more reliable than the one referring to eighty lashes. He also refers to the report recorded by Muslim declaring it to be more reliable.[22]

6–The Prophet's Age, Sixty-Three Versus Sixty-Five

Muslim records a report on the authority of ʿAbd Allāh ibn ʿAbbās which states that "When the Prophet died he was sixty-five years old."[23]

However, Muslim himself also records a report on the authority of ʿAbd Allāh ibn ʿAbbās and Muʿāwiyah that the Prophet's age at the time of his death was sixty-three.[24]

It is strange that Muslim would consider both traditions to be authentic given the clear difference in number but his decision seems to be based on only the apparent authenticity of the chain of narrators. If he had checked the text against well-known historical facts however, he would certainly have quoted only one of them in his work. Al-Nawawī considers the report mentioning the age of the Prophet as sixty-three to be more authentic.[25] Ibn Saʿd is certain that the Prophet was sixty-three at the time of his death.[26]

7–Duration of the Makkī and Madnī Periods

Muslim records on the authority of ʿAbd Allāh ibn ʿAbbās that the Prophet stayed in Makkah 15 years after his prophethood, and 10 years in Madinah after hijrah.[27] Muslim also records another version of the report but according to this version, as Ibn ʿAbbās mentions, the Prophet stayed in Makkah for 13 years and in Madinah for 10 years.[28] Muslim's report runs counter to established history whereas Bukhārī's does not. Ibn ʿAbd al-Barr has quoted Ibn Isḥāq's view that the Prophet lived 13 years in Makkah after he was appointed God's Messenger and according to other sources, as quoted by Ibn ʿAbd al-Barr, the Prophet lived 10 years in Madinah after hijrah.[29]

8–Time Gap Between the Construction of al-Masjid al-Ḥarām and al-Masjid al-Aqṣā

Al-Bukhārī and Muslim have both recorded on the authority of Abū Dharr the following tradition:

> Abū Dharr says, I asked the Prophet as to which mosque was built on the earth first. The Prophet answered, "*al-Masjid al-Ḥarām.*" I, then, asked, "which one was built after that?" The Prophet said, "*al-Masjid al-Aqṣā'.*" I asked, "What is the time-gap between them?" The Prophet said, "Forty years."[30]

This report contradicts general agreed historical facts. *Al-Masjid al-Ḥarām* was built by Ibrāhīm and Ismāʿīl,[31] and *al-Masjid al-Aqṣā* by Sulaymān[32] and between both the prophets, Ibrāhīm and Sulaymān, there existed a gap of several generations. Ibrāhīm's youngest son, Isḥāq had a son named prophet Yaʿqūb whose son prophet Yūsuf settled in Egypt,[33] where he also invited his other brothers to settle. During Yūsuf's period in Egypt the children of Israel flourished.[34] It seems that after a long spell of prosperity in Egypt, the Israelites gradually degenerated into slavery to the ruling dynasty. It was during these terrible times that Moses was raised to redeem their lost glory.[35] Moses established Hebrew authority over a large area of the Middle East, a few generations after which prophet David came to the throne.[36] It was prophet Sulaymān, his son, who built the mosque in Jerusalem.[37]

Ibn al-Jawzī expresses doubt over the authenticity of this report on the grounds that the time difference between Ibrāhīm constructing the

Ka'bah, and Sulaymān constructing the mosque in Jerusalem, covers more than a thousand years.[38] Al-Qurṭubī, also finds a contradiction between the report and established history, but tries to resolve the problem by referring to an unsubstantiated story of Adam's construction of the Ka'bah and one of his son's construction of the mosque in Jerusalem, thus establishing a time difference of around forty years between the construction of the two mosques.[39] Both al-Ṭabarānī and al-Khaṭṭābī also adopt the same line of argument as al-Qurṭubī. Ibn Ḥajar, in a bid to protect the sanctity of the report, suggests two possibilities: 1) the founder of *al-Masjid al-Aqṣā* was either Adam, the angels or Ya'qūb, and 2) Ibrāhīm was not the founder of the Ka'bah but erected the building on an already existing foundation. He then states his preference for the theory that Ya'qūb was the original architect of the mosque in Jerusalem and Ibrāhīm that of the Ka'bah, trying to validate the forty-year time difference. Nevertheless Ibn Ḥajar remains uncomfortable with this speculation declaring Ibn al-Jawzī's view of the thousand year time difference between the construction of the two mosques to be preferable.[40]

Had the mosque in Makkah already been built, mention would certainly have been made of Adam having been the first architect of the Ka'bah. What the Qur'an actually states about the Ka'bah is that Allah assigned a particular place in Makkah to Ibrāhīm for construction of this place of worship.[41] As for the construction of the mosque in Jerusalem, al-Nasā'ī has recorded on the authority of 'Abd Allāh ibn 'Amrū ibn al-'Āṣ the following tradition: "The Prophet said: 'When Sulaymān the son of David built *Bayt al-Maqdis*, he requested Allah to grant him three things...'"[42] The Qur'anic verse and this authentic hadith therefore establish beyond any doubt that the Ka'bah was built by Ibrāhīm and *al-Masjid al-Aqṣā* by Sulaymān leaving no room for the myth that Adam was the founder of the Ka'bah and his son that of *Bayt al-Maqdis*. We can only conclude that this report is not authentic.

9–Abū Sufyān's Offer of His Daughter in Marriage to the Prophet

Muslim records the following tradition on the authority of 'Abd Allāh ibn 'Abbās:

> Muslims were not paying attention to Abū Sufyān, nor socializing with him. So he said to the Prophet: "O Prophet of Allah! Grant me three things." When the Prophet agreed, he said: "My daughter, Umm Ḥabībah, is the most beautiful woman in Arabia. I will give her to you in marriage." The Prophet, then, accepted...[43]

This report clearly indicates that when Abū Sufyān embraced Islam his daughter, Umm Ḥabībah, (note in Arabic the word *umm* does not necessarily refer to the woman as the mother of so and so) was not yet married to the Prophet, and it was Abū Sufyān who arranged the marriage between the two. However, Abū Sufyān accepted Islam on the eve of the conquest of Makkah, which took place on 20th Ramadan 8 AH[44] whilst his daughter had married the Prophet when she was still in Abyssinia as a Muslim emigrant along with other Makkan Muslims.[45] The sources report that she returned to Madinah along with others from Abyssinia in the year of the *Ḥudaybiyyah* treaty, that is the 6th year after hijrah.[46] *Sīrah* writers have mentioned details of Abū Sufyān's visit to Madinah to persuade the Prophet to postpone his plan of marching towards Makkah. The account of Abū Sufyān's arrival in Madinah includes information on how his daughter, Umm Ḥabībah, as a wife of the Prophet, treated her father. When Abū Sufyān entered the apartment of his daughter and tried to sit on the Prophet's bed, she stopped him from doing so because it belonged to the Prophet whereas he (Abū Sufyān) was a *mushrik* (non-believer).[47] This clearly shows that when Abū Sufyān travelled to Madinah before the conquest of Makkah, he was still a non-believer, and his daughter Umm Ḥabībah was already married to the Prophet.

Al-Nawawī finds a problem in the report because, as he maintains, Abū Sufyān accepted Islam in 8 AH, whereas the Prophet married Umm Ḥabībah in 6 AH.[48] Ibn Ḥazm considers the report fabricated (*mawḍūʿ*) due to two reasons: 1) it contradicts established historical fact for the Prophet married Umm Ḥabībah in Abyssinia long before Abū Sufyān's conversion to Islam, and 2) one of the narrators, ʿIkrimah ibn ʿAmmār, is unreliable.[49] Ibn al-Ṣalāḥ criticizes Ibn Ḥazm's approach stating that ʿIkrimah is a reliable narrator in the eyes of great scholars like Wakīʿ and Ibn Maʿīn. He offers another interpretation of Abū Sufyān's proposal to the Prophet stating that the proposal might have been for the renewal of the marriage between the Prophet and Umm Ḥabībah.[50] Al-Nawawī rejects this suggestion stating that the Prophet is not reported to have renewed his marriage with Umm Ḥabībah, and Abū Sufyān did not mention that he wanted to remarry his daughter to the Prophet. Yet, he conjectures that Abū Sufyān may have intended the renewal of marriage in his statement – "I will give you Umm Ḥabībah in marriage."[51] This is an unjustified attempt to retain the sanctity of the report and Ibn Ḥazm's criticism seems to be strong and tenable.

10–The Prophet's Marriage to Maymūnah

Al-Bukhārī, Muslim and others record on the authority of ʿAbd Allāh ibn ʿAbbās that the Prophet married Maymūnah when he was still in the state of *iḥrām* (pilgrimage attire).[52]

According to Maymūnah herself however, the Prophet married her after having completed his hajj and when out of *iḥrām*.[53] There is an obvious conflict between the two reports. Ibn ʿAbbās states that the Prophet's marriage to Maymūnah took place while the Prophet was still in *iḥrām* whereas Maymūnah states that the marriage took place after the Prophet was out of *iḥrām*. Logically, Maymūnah's statement should be taken as more valid than that of Ibn ʿAbbās and considered more authentic than that offered by others, given that it was she after all who actually got married. According to Saʿīd ibn al-Musayyib, Ibn ʿAbbās made a mistake in his report.[54] Al-Nawawī states that according to many *Saḥābah*, the Prophet's marriage to Maymūnah took place after the Prophet had come out of *iḥrām*.[55] Abū Bakr ibn al-ʿArabī does not accept Ibn ʿAbbās's report as reliable on two grounds: 1) nobody aside from Ibn ʿAbbās reports this statement, and 2) others who have reported differently have been more knowledgeable on the matter than Ibn ʿAbbās.[56]

Moreover, there also exist authentic traditions according to which the Prophet prohibited marriage whilst in the state of *iḥrām*. Muslim has recorded several reports through different chains of narrators which contain the Prophet's statement: "Verily, one who is in the state of *iḥrām* is not allowed to marry or to be married."[57] It is hard to imagine that the Prophet himself would then break the rule. In Ibn ʿAbd al-Barr's opinion Ibn ʿAbbās's report represents an error, even though the chain of the report is authentic, and he prefers the other report narrated by many people.[58] Regardless of the differences of opinion which exist among scholars concerning the matter, ultimately it is reasonable to accept the wife's own account of her marriage to the Prophet as being the most authentic. In conclusion the information given on the authority of Ibn ʿAbbās may be considered a mistake and the report hence deemed unreliable.

7

Moderation in Relation to Authentication of Hadith

ISLAM WAS REVEALED AS A BALANCED way of life, in total consonance with human nature, which tends to prefer that which is moderate and reject or dislike that which is immoderate. Its rules and regulations therefore reflect the principle of balance in all things and anything attributed to Islam which appears to be either exaggeration or extreme, is not an original part of the faith.

The Qur'anic Stand on Moderation

The Qur'an calls the adherents of Allah's messages as an *ummatan wasaṭan* (or justly balanced nation): "Thus have We made of you a nation justly balanced (*ummatan wasaṭan*)" (2:143). In practice this definition means that the Muslim perspective and position on all matters is one of moderation, with true believers avoiding extremism and extravagance in all affairs. Followers are required to abandon excessive materialism and the excessive spiritual deprivation of the followers of earlier prophets. Neither materialism, nor extreme spiritualism, denotes a normal pattern of life, which should accommodate within its boundaries a balanced pursuit of both the material and the spiritual.

Man is a multi-dimensional being and justice demands that all aspects of his life are given due, proportionate care and attention. Features such as family life, social order, economic undertaking, political activity, cultural activity, educational pursuit, intellectual growth, moral sanction, and religious practice, constitute the real makeup and drives of man. Imbalance in any aspect of these will cause a resulting extremity in one or other elements of his life. For instance, if a person takes excessive interest in religious rituals and rites, devoting far more time and energy to these than required, this will certainly have an effect on his family life as well as other social and economic responsibilities. The Qur'an invites man to take the middle path in every situation, stating for instance: "Those who, when they spend, are not extravagant and not niggardly, but hold a just balance between those extremes" (25:67). Although this verse seems to offer advice specific to economic life, it is however far wider in scope. The chief message conveyed is the principle of moderation, applicable everywhere regardless of time and space. Verses 25:63–74 describe a normal believer as one who does not suffer from a superiority complex (63); who does not become entangled in non-issues with anyone, particularly the ignorant (63); who devotes himself sincerely to his Lord (64); who always feels concerned about the end result of his acts in this life (65–66); who remains frugal in his earning and spending (67); who abstains from unjust killing (68); who maintains his chastity (68); who repents for wrong doing (69–71); who desists from false testimony (72); who eschews frivolous acts honorably (72); who tries to have insight into the message of God (73); and who takes care of his family fulfilling his role in the most appropriate manner.

This description speaks volumes of Islam's view of humankind for it requires man to know himself, and to apply a balanced approach to all his affairs, preventing any form of extremism in character or Islamic life. In addition, Allah commands the believers to uphold justice and demonstrate generosity: "Allah commands justice, the doing of good, and liberality to kith and kin" (16:90). The message conveyed is that all acts of mankind should be based on a balance between justice and generosity, an important principle of moderation.

The Prophetic Approach to Moderation

The Prophet kept away from any form of extremism and also advised his followers to be just and balanced in their life, avoiding all sorts of instability. We have for instance the case of ʿUthmān ibn Maẓʿūn, and certain others like him, who were very much inclined to an extreme form of spirituality, wanting to run away from worldly affairs, including marriage. They appealed to the Prophet to allow them to castrate themselves, a request which the Prophet vehemently rejected making it clear that Islam allowed no room for any kind of injury or infliction.

We also have the case of certain individuals who having asked the Prophet's wives about his daily routine, decided to do more with one of them vowing to spend his time always in prayer, another deciding to fast daily, and yet another imposing celibacy upon himself. When the Prophet learnt of their approach, he expressed his displeasure over what they had decided, stating that piety lay not in extremity but in rather a balanced way of life comprising both material and spiritual enterprises.

ʿAbd Allāh ibn ʿAmrū ibn al-ʿĀṣ was very much inclined towards high spirituality with one of his practices being to recite the entire revealed portions of the Qur'an everyday. The Prophet disapproved of this and exhorted him to recite the Qur'an in a stretch of two weeks. He also used to fast everyday, with the Prophet once again advising him not to go to such extremes. While sending Abū Mūsā al-Ashʿarī and Muʿādh ibn Jabal as his representatives to Yemen, the Prophet advised them, among other things, to make things easy for the people and not to make them difficult.

Abū al-Dardā' had lost interest in worldly affairs, including his matrimonial life. He devoted most of his time to prayers. He fasted quite often. He ignored almost totally the conjugal rights of his wife. He did not give rest to his body. He avoided sleep even at night. When Salmān al-Fārsī came to know about this approach of his friend, he advised him to equally pay heed to all of his needs, devotional as well as material. Abū Dardā' was skeptical of his friend's advice. So he took Salmān to the Prophet and sought his guidance on Salmān's advice. The Prophet conformed to the advice of Salmān saying that "your body has rights over you; your eyes have rights over you; your soul has rights over you; your wife has rights over you, hence you must fulfill all these rights due on you." It is clear that the Prophet was not meant to convey anything indicative of extremism but rather only moderation, and all his teachings, actions and sayings represent this. It is for this reason that anything extreme attributed to the Prophet should be rejected as false or fabricated.

Furthermore, the Prophet was sent as a mercy (*raḥmah*) to mankind (21:107). This is indicated in the nature of his character, messages, and teaching, the latter precisely in accordance with human nature. As mentioned earlier, man is generally averse to extremism and had the lessons given by the Prophet been of an extreme nature, man would surely have rejected them outright. The Arabs were the first people addressed by the Prophet and one of the main reasons they accepted his message was because of the beautiful aspect of moderation contained therein.

Moderation: Precise Definition and in Relation to Pertinent Traditions

It is now obvious that moderation appears to be one of the bases of the Islamic message with neither the Qur'an nor the Prophet Muhammad advocating any kind of excessiveness. Moderation therefore is the way of Islam and may be defined as a justly balanced approach to affairs and life, whether conceptual or practical, excluding all forms of excessiveness and extremism therein. Examples of certain traditions are given below to explore the principle of moderation and to gauge how these traditions stand up before it.

1–Ṣalāh al-Tasbīḥ

It is reported that the Prophet taught his uncle ʿAbbās ibn ʿAbd al-Muṭṭalib a special kind of salah which within its cycles contained elements extra to the normal prayer. This is known as the *Ṣalāh al-Tasbīḥ*. Its procedure is as follows: (1) after completing the reading of *al-Fātiḥah* and another surah (as required in normal prayer), in the state of standing the following phrases need to be recited – *Subḥān Allah wa al-Ḥamdu li Allah wa Lā Ilāha illā Allah wa Allahu Akbar* (Glory be to Allah; All praises are due to Allah; There is no god but Allah; and Allah is the Greatest of all) – fifteen times, (2) in the state of *rukūʿ* (bending) one has to recite the same ten times, (3) after rising from *rukūʿ* one has to recite the same ten times, (4) in the state of *sujūd* (prostration) one has to recite the same ten times, (5) the same is to be repeated in every cycle of the prayer which contains four cycles. The significance of this peculiar prayer, as mentioned in the tradition, is that the performer will be granted general pardon for ten categories of his sinful acts, the first sin, the last sin, the old sin, the new sin, the minor sin, the major sin, the deliberately committed sin, the inadvertently occurred sin, the hidden sin, and the open sin.[1]

Ibn al-Jawzī has declared this tradition unreliable due to the occurrence of some unreliable reporters in its chain of narrators. He has quoted this tradition through three chains of narrators:

(1) Hibat Allāh ibn Muḥammad ibn al-Ḥuṣayn, Abū ʿAlī al-Ḥasan ibn ʿAlī ibn al-Mudhahhab, Abū al-Ḥasan al-Dārquṭnī, ʿUthmān ibn Aḥmad ibn ʿAbd Allāh, Abū al-Aḥwaṣ Muḥammad ibn al-Haytham al-Qāḍī, Aḥmad ibn Abī Shuʿayb al-Ḥarrānī, Mūsā ibn Aʿyun, Ṣadaqah ibn Yazīd al-Khurāsānī, ʿUrwah ibn Ruwaym, Ibn al-Daylamī, al-ʿAbbās ibn ʿAbd al-Muṭṭalib, The Prophet;

(2) Al-Ḥuṣayn, Abū ʿAlī ibn al-Mudhahhab, al-Dārquṭnī, Abū Bakr al-Nīsāpurī and ʿAbd Allāh ibn Sulaymān ibn al-Ashʿath, ʿAbd al-Raḥmān ibn Bishr ibn al-Ḥakam, Mūsā ibn ʿAbd al-ʿAzīz, al-Ḥakam ibn Abān, ʿIkrimah, Ibn ʿAbbās, The Prophet;

(3) Ibn al-Ḥuṣayn, Ibn al-Mudhahhab, al-Dārquṭnī, Abū ʿAlī al-Kātib ʿAlī ibn Muḥammad ibn Aḥmad ibn al-Juhm, Aḥmad ibn Yaḥyā ibn Mālik al-Sūsī, Yazīd ibn al-Ḥubāb, Mūsā ibn ʿUbaydah al-Rindī, Saʿīd ibn Abī Saʿīd *mawlā* Abū Bakr ibn al-Ḥazm, Abū Rāfiʿ *mawlā* of the Prophet, The Prophet.

Ṣadaqah ibn Yazīd al-Khurāsānī in the first chain and Mūsā ibn ʿUbaydah in the third chain are unreliable narrators, with Mūsā ibn ʿAbd al-ʿAzīz in the second chain being an unknown person. This is why Ibn al-Jawzī categorizes the report on the special prayer as unreliable even though there exist several other traditions on the same matter. He rejects all of them as unacceptable on the grounds that one or other of the reporters in these chains is weak, unknown or unreliable.[2]

However, even if all or only one of the chains of narrators were authentic, the subject matter of the report is such that it would not allow the tradition to be classified as reliable, for what it reports concerning this special kind of prayer exudes extremity. The Prophet taught a very balanced method of praying the obligatory and supererogatory prayers (salah), in terms of the time and energy involved. This tradition on the other hand relates a method which appears odd in that it demands much time and energy on the part of the performer. In conclusion therefore the tradition can be rejected on the basis of its disproportionate nature, and not merely on the existence of weak and unknown reporters in its chains of narrators.

2–Other Supererogatory Prayers

In Muslim society across the world, particularly in mystic circles, some supererogatory prayers are given special attention and people perform them in the hope of being highly blessed both in this world and in the hereafter. These distinct prayers are the Saturday prayer, Sunday prayer, Monday prayer, Friday prayer, 10th Muharram prayer, 1st Rajab prayer, 15th Shaʿban Night prayer, prayer on the eve of ʿĪd al-Fiṭr, Hajj Day prayer etc. The very basis of such practice lies in the availability of traditions which refer to special supererogatory prayers. An example of one such tradition follows:

> He who prays four cycles of prayer on Sunday night, reciting in each cycle fifteen times *Sūrah al-Ikhlāṣ* [112] after *al-Fātiḥah*, Allah, on the Day of Judgment, will grant him a reward reserved for reading the entire Qur'an ten times and acting upon all the injunctions of the Qur'an; he will be raised from his grave with his face radiant like the full moon; he will be given for each cycle of this prayer one thousand bungalows made of ruby stone; each bungalow will contain one thousand rooms; each room will be furnished with one thousand beds; on each bed will be seated a maiden before whom there will be one thousand male and one thousand female servants."[3]

This and other traditions describing the method of performing special supererogatory prayers and their reward(s) have been rejected as unacceptable simply on the grounds of their defective chains of narrators. However, it is surprising that they were not rejected on the bizarre nature of their content alone, which speaks volumes of their fabrication.

3–Excessive Reward and Punishment

Like the Qur'an, *aḥādīth* also teach man about the rewards for doing good deeds and the punishment for doing evil. The Qur'an provides such information in a general manner stating, for instance, in a number of places, that the denial of the truth will lead to grievous suffering and humiliation, and obedience to Allah and the Prophet will be rewarded graciously on the Day of Judgment. At times, it does mention details of both the reward and the punishment, but nowhere does this seem to be disproportionate. The case of Hadith literature is a little different. One can find therein minute details concerning reward and punishment which appear to be exaggeration. There are for instance traditions, which relate of great reward for negligible good acts, and severe punishment for an insignificant evil act. Such traditions abound in the sources and a few illustrative examples are given below:

(1) He who recites *Subḥān Allah wa bi ḥamdihi*, Allah will plant for him in Paradise thousands of date palm trees, whose roots will be made of gold.[4]

(2) He who reads a particular *duʿā'* while going to bed, 700,000 angels will be raised for each letter of the recitation, who will glorify him and ask Allah for his forgiveness.[5]

(3) He who reads a poetic verse after the night prayer, his prayer of that night will not be accepted.[6]

(4) He who reads words of praise for Allah while going to bed will become as innocent as he was on the day of his birth.[7]

(5) If one remembers Allah only once in the market place, Allah will remember him a hundred times.[8]

(6) If one says in the beginning of night: "May Allah bless Noah and peace be upon him," he will not be stung by a scorpion that night.[9]

(7) If one reads *Al-Ḥamdu li Allah Rabb al-ʿĀlamīn* [All praise is due to Allah, the Lord of all the worlds], an angel will call him [the one reciting these words] from the place from where his words cannot be heard: Allah has indeed come forward to you, so ask Him.[10]

(8) O Ibn ʿUmar! Read from the dawn until the morning prayer one hundred times these words: *Subḥān Allah wa bi Ḥamdihi; Subḥān Allah al-ʿAẓīm; Astaghfir Allah*, the world will be at your feet with all its treasures; and Allah will create out every word you recite an angel who will glorify its reward until doomsday."[11]

(9) One who devotes himself to Allah for forty days, from his tongue will gush out springs of wisdom.[12]

(10) One hour pondering is better than sixty years of devotion.[13]

Hadith scholars have declared these traditions to be fabricated. However, one need not examine their chains to determine this, for the examination of text alone is indicative enough of this. According to Ibn al-Qayyim reports consisting of exaggeration in reward and punishment are evidently unreliable.[14]

4–Denunciation of the Rich

A number of traditions reported in the sources denounce rich people and association with them. For example:

(1) Allah curses the poor [man] who honors the rich for the sake of wealth. He who does so, Allah will take away one third of his religion.[15]

(2) The Prophet advised his wife ʿĀ'ishah that "The secrets of your joining me in the life hereafter are that (1) you do not have any relations with rich people and (2) you do not put on a dress without adding a patch on it."[16]

These traditions are fabrications and without question unacceptable. Ibn al-Jawzī condemns them as lies.[17] The Qur'an time and again invites its followers to be generous in making financial contributions to the cause of Islam, in helping the poor meet their needs, in developing military power, and advancing the Islamic state in all aspects of growth and development. If people do not devote their time and energy to earn wealth, to invest it and to save it, how will a positive response to the call of Allah come about?

5–Condemnation of Certain Sections in the Muslim Community

Hadith literature contains many traditions attributed to the Prophet, which condemn certain sections of the Muslim community disproportionately. For example:

(1) The optimist [*Murji'ite*], the supporter of human freedom [*Qadarite*], the rejecter [*Shiʿite*], and the rebellious [*Kharijite*], one fourth of their faith in the unity of God will be withdrawn, and Allah will throw these disbelievers into Hell to abide therein forever.[18]

Ibn al-Jawzī has declared this tradition to be fabricated.[19]

6–Disapprobation of Certain Individuals

There exist a number of traditions which are taken for granted as acceptable by the Muslim community, which condemn and curse certain well known figures in history. For example:

(1) The Prophet cursed Yazīd ibn Muʿāwiyah because he would kill Ḥusayn, the grandson of the Prophet before the eyes of people who would not help the victim, and said: "Yazīd and the people who would not help Ḥusayn will be subjected to grievous suffering."[20]
(2) The brother of Umm Salamah, the Prophet's wife, had a son named al-Walīd. The Prophet disapproved of this name, saying: "You have named the child with a name of your pharaohs; there will certainly be a person who will be named al-Walīd who will be far more mischievous to this Ummah than the Pharaoh was to his people."[21]
(3) The Prophet said: "There will soon be in my Ummah a person named Wahb; Allah will grant him wisdom; and also there will be another man by the name of Ghaylān who will be far more harmful for my Ummah than Satan."[22]

Ibn al-Qayyim very categorically denounced these traditions as fabricated.[23] He did so on the basis of the unacceptable nature of their text. However, he also classified them as unreliable due to the existence of unreliable reporters in their chains of narrators.[24]

7–Unreasonable Admiration of Some Companions

Traditions doting unnecessary praise on some Companions of the Prophet abound in the literature. For example:

(1) The Prophet said: "Abū Bakr is the best of my Ummah and the most pious person in my Ummah; ʿUmar is the most beloved and the most just in my Ummah; ʿUthmān is the most modest and the most generous in my Ummah; ʿAlī is the most intelligent and the smartest in my Ummah; ʿAbd Allāh ibn Masʿūd is the most trustworthy and the most honest in my Ummah; Abū Dharr is the most pious and the most truthful in my Ummah; Abū al-Dardā' is the most devoted to Allah in

my Ummah; and Muʿāwiyah is the most clement and the kindest in my Ummah."[25]

(2) The Prophet said: "Verily, Allah made me His friend just as He did Abraham; in Paradise my residence and that of Abraham will be in front of each other, whereas al-ʿAbbās will be placed in between the two friends of Allah."[26]

These traditions reflect exaggeration and are hence unreliable.

8–The Amazingly Peculiar Significance of Qur'anic Surahs

There are traditions which describe the significance of Qur'anic surahs in a proportionate manner, and there are traditions which depict the advantages of Qur'anic surahs in an inordinate way. For example:

(1) The Prophet said: "If one hears *Sūrah Yā Sīn*, the reward of spending ten *dīnār* in the path of Allah is credited into his account; if he reads it, the reward [equivalent] of twenty hajj is adjusted for him; if he writes it and drinks its potion, there enter into his heart one thousand satisfactions, one thousand lights, one thousand blessings, one thousand mercies, and one thousand sustenances, and from his heart are removed all kinds of ill-will and diseases."[27]

(2) The Prophet said: "One who reads *Sūrah al-Dukhān* at night, seventy thousand angels pray to Allah for his forgiveness until the following morning."[28]

(3) The Prophet said: "If one reads *Sūrah al-Ikhlās* after ablution one hundred times followed by his reading of *Sūrah al-Fātiḥah*, Allah writes for each letter ten good deeds, effaces ten evil deeds, raises him to ten levels [higher], builds in Paradise one hundred castles, makes his deeds of that day equivalent to the deeds of a prophet; [makes his] reading of the surah [equivalent to] reading the whole Qur'an thirty-three times. This surah serves as freedom from polytheism, causes the angels to be present with him, chases Satan away, echoes around the throne of God as to the name of its reader until God looks at him, [and] if Allah looks towards him, he will never be punished."[29]

Ibn al-Jawzī finds these traditions to be enormously excessive hence unreliable merely on the grounds of their defective chains of narrators.

However, they should be denounced as unreliable merely on the nature of their exorbitant statements and not simply from verification of their chain.

9–Incredible Position of One who Reads the Qur'an

Almost the entire Muslim world attaches great significance to the reading and memorization of the Qur'an. These hugely praiseworthy actions are based on authentic traditions found in the most authentic works of Hadith. However, alongside this position Muslims also hold many misconceptions concerning the position of the memorizers and readers of Qur'an, some of which are so remarkable in their incredibility that one cannot help but entertain misgivings as to their authenticity. Two such traditions are given below:

> (1) The Prophet said: "If one reads one third of the Qur'an, he is granted one third of prophethood; if one reads two thirds of the Qur'an, one is given two thirds of prophethood; if one reads the whole Qur'an, he is virtually in the perfect position of prophethood; he will be told on the Day of Judgment to read the Qur'an and become elevated a level higher for each verse recited; when the process of elevation will be over, he will be granted two things: (1) immortality, and (2) everlasting blessings."[30]
> (2) The Prophet said: "If one who was taught the Qur'an by Allah complained of poverty, Allah would write poverty between his eyes to remain there until Doomsday."[31]

These traditions are undoubtedly fabrications. In addition, their chains of narrators are all deficient.

10–Unnecessary Praise of Cities and Towns

Traditions which heap great praise on certain cities and towns abound in the memory of Muslims as well as in their literature. For example:

> (1) The Prophet said: "ʿAsqalān is one of those brides from where Allah will raise on the Day of Judgment seventy thousand martyrs."[32]
> (2) The Prophet said: "Four gates of Paradise are opened into the world, Alexandria, ʿAsqalān, Quzwayn, and Jeddah; the position of

Jeddah is superior to these cities just as the House of God in Makkah is superior to all the other mosques in the world."[33]

Ibn al-Jawzī counts these and other similar traditions as unreliable on the grounds of deficiency in their chains of narrators. However, once again, the words and statements are enough to consider them as lies attributed to the Prophet.

11–Classification of Week Days

There are traditions in which certain days of the week have been praised whilst other days have been condemned. These are undoubtedly fabrications. For example, the Prophet said:

> Saturday is the day of beguilement because the Quraysh wanted to beguile that day; Sunday is the day of construction and plantation because Paradise was built and planted that day; Monday is the day of travel and business because one son of Adam killed another on that day; Wednesday is the day of evil omen causing errors and letting the young grow old because Allah sent the tornado to destroy the people of ʿĀd on that day, Pharaoh was born that day, Pharaoh proclaimed godhood that day, and he was destroyed on that day; Thursday is the day of visiting the ruler and getting needs fulfilled because Abraham entered the court of the Egyptian ruler and got his wife back along with having his needs fulfilled [on that day]; and Friday is the day of proposal and marriage because the prophets proposed and solemnized their marriages on that day for blessings.[34]

8

Al-Bukhārī's Chapter on Predetermination: An Evaluation and Interpretation

One of the most widely respected Hadith scholars in Muslim history, and perhaps the most famous, is al-Bukhārī. His *al-Jāmiʿ al-Ṣaḥīḥ* also commonly known as *Ṣaḥīḥ al-Bukhārī,* is widely considered by many to be the most authentic book after the Qur'an.[1] So esteemed is the text in fact, that its contents are generally held to be unquestionable. *Al-Jāmiʿ al-Ṣaḥīḥ* has exerted great influence on the Muslim mind, and the work is widely read and referred to throughout the Muslim world as a source of Islamic law.

Al-Jāmiʿ al-Ṣaḥīḥ contains a chapter on predestination entitled *Kitāb al-Qadar* (book of predestination) consisting of twenty-seven traditions relating to the concept of a fore-written destiny for man; the evident message for believers is that human life, in all its detail, including man's final destination, has been predetermined, even before a person's coming into the world. The great significance that these traditions have for Muslim understanding of human responsibility cannot be underestimated, and seen in this context the chapter and traditions contained therein need careful examination.

Debate over a fore-written destiny has existed in the Muslim world since the first Islamic century. The main arguments advanced in favor of the theory are based on certain Qur'anic *āyāt* as well as certain traditions, particularly those recorded by al-Bukhārī in *Kitāb al-Qadar*. As emphasized in previous chapters, and according to the general approach of *muḥaddithūn*, the authenticity of traditions is heavily dependant on authenticity of reporters. Al-Bukhārī is believed to have been scrupulous in ascertaining the reliability of the *sanad* of his selected traditions leaving no gap. According to this criteria, the traditions mentioned in *Kitāb al-Qadar* are conceivably sound. However, from the standpoint of textual content (*matn*) there may be some cause for questioning. Many scholars have tried to interpret these traditions in one way or another and these interpretations are available in well-known commentaries on *Ṣaḥīḥ al-Bukhārī*. This chapter is a humble attempt to critically review these interpretations and advance a new interpretation of most of the twenty-seven traditions contained in the chapter *Kitāb al-Qadar*. All the traditions that will be cited are authentic in terms of their chain of narrators (*sanad*).This reinterpretation is based on a so far untouched methodology that is not applied by Hadith commentators. The objective of the exercise is to reassert the validity of *aḥādīth* in Muslim life on the one hand, and to identify probable errors in the text of reports, on the other.

The General Approach in Hadith Interpretation

Almost all the well-recognized works of Hadith have been interpreted by Hadith scholars with some works such as al-Bukhārī's having multiple commentaries by different Hadith authorities. A deep study of Hadith commentaries will reveal that there exists no well-defined and articulated methodology for interpreting Hadith. Generally, five methodological components are available in Hadith commentaries. First, the commentator examines the chain of narrators (*sanad*) in a bid to prove the reliability or unreliability of reports. Second, the message contained in the tradition is highlighted or further elaborated upon in light of well-known scholars' views. Third, the commentator spends time to identify reports from other sources with a view to developing a complete picture of the tradition in view. Fourth, the commentator, at times, describes the background of a particular hadith. Fifth, the scholar at times advances his own view either favoring or rejecting the views of others.

Every so often the commentator seems to lose the objectivity required for examination, and which is consequent upon the methodology mentioned. Well-known commentators of al-Bukhārī's work include al-Ṭībī, al-Kirmānī, Ibn Ḥajar, al-ʿAynī (d.855 AH), al-Qasṭalānī (d.923 AH), al-Sindī (d.1138 AH), and Hamzah Muhammad Qasim. They have all used almost the same methodology as mentioned above in their commentaries.

Reflection on the Meaning of the Term *Al-Qadar*

Al-Farāhīdī (d.175 AH) cites the literal meaning of *al-qadar* as being the appropriate judgment (*al-qaḍā' al-muwaffaq*).[2] Al-Rāghib al-Aṣfahānī identifies the literal meaning as power (*al-qudrah*). When it is attributed to man, he further elaborates, it signifies his ability to do something; when it is ascribed to Allah, it denotes His infinite power shared by none.[3] Al-Fayrūzābādī (d.817 AH) describes its original import as being final judgment (*al-qaḍā'*), command (*al-ḥukm*), the real form of a thing (*mablagh al-shay'e*), and capacity (*al-ṭāqah*). The meaning of the statement *qadar Allāh al-rizq*, he explains, is "Allah determined the sustenance."[4] Allah's distribution of sustenance is due to His limitless power.

Al-Kirmānī defines *al-qadar* as the command of Allah.[5] Ibn Ḥajar quotes scholars anonymously as having said that *al-qaḍā'* is the general outlines of the divine judgment existing from eternity, and that *al-qadar* is the minute details of that judgment.[6] Al-Qasṭalānī puts it otherwise stating that *al-qadar* is the basis and *al-qaḍā'* is its precise detail.[7] It seems Muslim scholars' understanding of *al-qaḍā'* vis-a-vis *al-qadar* is based on mere speculation. Hamzah Muhammad Qasim considers *al-qadar* as Allah's knowledge of things before their occurrence.[8] He strengthens his view by advancing anonymous scholars' statements that "*al-qadar* signifies that Allah knew the measures of things and their times before their creation; and that He caused what was in His knowledge to come into existence."[9] Ibn Taymiyyah (d.727 AH) identifies *al-qadar* as having a twofold meaning a) Allah's eternal knowledge about creation's future deeds, about all aspects of man's obedience, his rebellion, his sustenance, his lifespan, and his position whether rewarded or condemned. b) Allah's comprehensive willpower over everything, including man's acts.[10] It seems that Ibn Taymiyyah expounded the idea of the two dimensions of *al-qadar*, keeping in view the approach of two groups of Muslim scholars, the *qadarite* and the *jabarite* in terms of their theological debate over man's freedom to act. Although his view represents a particular group of theologians, he adopts a moderate approach between the two extremes. However, not everything moderate is necessarily right. The first component of Ibn Taymiyyah's explanation supports very much the Jabarite view and the second one validates the Qadarite stand. His view is not actually a moderate one. As a matter of fact, what the scholars have stated concerning *al-qadar* refers to the fatalistic theory of predetermination hence *kitāb al-qadar* may be rendered into English as the chapter on predetermination. The question of whether the term *al-qadar* implies predetermination or not, may easily be resolved by looking at its Qur'anic usage. The Qur'an uses the word *qadar* with all its variant forms (noun, verb, adjective, singular, plural etc.) one hundred and thirty two times, with the meaning of the word *qadar* varying with variation of context. An honest reading of all the relevant *āyāt* in the Qur'an reveals that the word *qadar* has been applied with around fourteen shades of meaning:

(1) power (e.g. 2:264; 16:75–76; 21:87; 57:29; 90:5; 97:1–3),
(2) estimation (e.g. 6:91; 22:74; 39:67; 74:18–20),
(3) balance (e.g. 34:11),
(4) capacity (e.g. 13:17),
(5) empowerment (e.g. 77:23),
(6) restriction (e.g. 13:26; 17:30; 29:62; 30:37; 34:36; 34:39; 39:52; 42:12; 65:7; 89:16),
(7) due proportion (e.g. 25:2; 65:3; 80:19),
(8) scheduled time (e.g. 20:40; 77:22),
(9) decree (e.g. 54:12),
(10) encompassing (e.g. 48:21),
(11) overpowering (e.g. 5:34),
(12) measure (e.g. 15:21; 23:18; 42:27; 43:11; 54:49; 73:20),
(13) final judgment (e.g.15:60; 27:57), and
(14) determination (e.g. 54:12).

Some of these shades of meaning belong to both the human and divine aspects (power, empowerment), while some are exclusively associated with man (estimation, balance, capacity, accessibility), and others attributed to God alone (determination, final judgment, measure, restriction, due proportion, scheduled time).

The Qur'an does not mention the determination of God or His final judgment in the sense of a predetermination of all the minute details of human life. Logically, the concept of predetermination hardly fits into the Qur'anic framework. The Qur'an places only two created beings (humans and jinn) as being morally responsible for their acts (6:112; 6:128; 6:130; 7:179; 51:56; 55:39) and as such man's moral thoughts and acts may not be deemed as predetermined. The physical and intellectual features of man however may be considered fully predetermined just as in the case of animals, animate and inanimate beings, celestial creatures, earthly and heavenly phenomena etc.

In order to substantiate the idea of predetermination of human life in all its detail scholars advance the Qur'anic statement: "It is Allah who created you and all that you do" (37:96). Ibn Ḥajar (d.857 AH) claims, in the light of a tradition recorded by Muslim, that this *āyah* was revealed in response to the Quraysh's argument concerning human freedom to act. He derives from this *āyah* that everything in human life is predetermined with all its details.[11] This *āyah* (37:96) does not speak about the creation of human acts but is actually that part of prophet Ibrāhīm's statements made to his people who worshiped idols made of stones and wood. He wanted to make his people realize their error in worshipping idols. His main argument was that Allah was the Creator not only of themselves but also of the materials they used for carving idols hence the creation's worship of creation was a folly. Reading an *āyah* in isolation of its context is wrong and leads to misunderstanding and misinterpretation.

Evaluation and Interpretation of Traditions in *Kitāb al-Qadar*

What follows is an evaluation and reinterpretation of al-Bukhārī's chapter on predestination with reference to the *aḥādīth* contained therein. Note, the *aḥādīth* are numbered according to their number in *Kitāb al-Qadar* and not consecutively.

Hadith No. 1 Prefixing of Man's Destiny in the Mother's Womb

ʿAbd Allāh ibn Masʿūd quotes the Prophet as having said:

> [as regards your creation], verily, everyone of you is gathered in the womb of his mother for forty days, then in the form of *ʿalaqah* [leech] for the same period, and thereafter in the form of *muḍghah* [chewed lump] for the same period. Then Allah sends an angel to write four words: He writes his deeds, time of his death, means of his livelihood, and whether he will be wretched or blessed [in religion]. Then the soul is breathed into his body. So a man may do deeds characteristic of the people of the [Hell] Fire, so much so that there is only the distance of a cubit between him and Hell, and then what has been written [by the angel] surpasses, and so he starts doing deeds characteristic of the people of Paradise and enters Paradise. Similarly, a person may do deeds characteristic of the people of Paradise, so much so that there is only the distance of a cubit between him and it, and then what has been written (by the angel) surpasses, and he starts doing deeds of the people of the (Hell) Fire and enters the (Hell) Fire."[12]

Critical Analysis and Interpretation

The chain through which this tradition has been narrated is: Hishām ibn ʿAbd al-Malik (d.227 AH) from Shuʿbah ibn al-Ḥajjāj (d.160 AH) from Sulaymān ibn Mihrān al-Aʿmash (d.147 AH) from Zayd ibn Wahb (d.96 AH) from ʿAbd Allāh ibn Masʿūd from the Prophet. All four reporters (Hishām, Shuʿbah, Sulaymān and Zayd) following the Companion ʿAbd Allāh ibn Masʿūd are known as *thiqah thabt* (highly reliable), *thiqah ḥāfiẓ mutqin* (perfectly authentic), *thiqah ḥāfiẓ* (highly authentic), and *thiqah jalīl* (respectably authentic) respectively.[13] This particular chain perfectly well meets the three main criteria of continuity (*ittiṣāl*), integrity (*al-ʿadl*), and retentive memory (*al-ḍabṭ*). This leaves the text of the report. Does it fulfill the other two criteria, *ʿadm al-shudhūdh* (non-anomaly) and *ghayr al-ʿillah* (non-deficiency)? Note that out of these five criteria developed by the great Hadith scholars for authentication of traditions the first three are applied to the chain and the last two mainly to the text. There is no denying the fact that the last two criteria are also, at times, applicable to the chain.

The opening statement of the report outlines the duration of the first three stages of the human fetus in the mother's womb. The first stage, which has been mentioned anonymously in the report, is apparently *nuṭfah* as specified by the Qur'an (23:13). It lasts for forty days. The subsequent two stages, *ʿalaqah* and *muḍghah* hold on for the same period each. The total period for the first three stages of the embryo is thus one hundred and twenty days i.e. seventeen weeks. Information on embryological development is now well established and no longer a subject for speculation. Modern scientific discoveries in the field of Genetic Engineering have long provided all the minute details of the embryonic and fetal stages. According to Genetic Engineering, the embryonic period enters the fetal period after two weeks. The above three stages as mentioned in the report constitute the embryonic period. If modern scientific terms are used to describe the three embryonic stages, they are zygote (*nuṭfah*), blastocyst (*ʿalaqah*), and differentiation (*muḍghah*). A brief description of the three stages may further clarify the matter. When a sperm is deposited in the vagina, it travels through the cervix and into the fallopian tubes. A single sperm penetrates the mother's egg cell, and the resulting cell is called zygote (*nuṭfah*). The zygote spends the next few days traveling down the fallopian tube and divides to form a ball of cells, which continue dividing further. As a result, there forms an inner group of cells with an outer shell. This stage is called blastocyst (*ʿalaqah*). The blastocyst reaches the uterus (*raḥim*) at roughly the fifth day, and implants into the uterine wall on about day six. It adheres tightly to the endometrium (lining of the uterus), where it receives nourishment through the mother's bloodstream. The cells of the embryo now multiply and begin to take on specific functions. This process is called differentiation (*muḍghah*), which produces the varied cell types that make up a human being. This stage is a very critical stage in human formation.[14] Scientific discovery puts the duration of the embryonic period at roughly two weeks, whereas the above report calculates it at seventeen weeks. This is strange. How can a compromise be affected between the two claims?

One may easily raise doubt over the equivalence of the scientific terms for the embryonic stages (zygote, blastocyst, and differentiation) to the terms used in the hadith (*nuṭfah*, *ʿalaqah* and *muḍghah*). It may be suggested that the terms used in the report represent the fetal period and not the embryonic period. The clear solution to this problem is available in the Qur'an. The relevant verses read:

> Indeed, We created man from quintessence of clay; then We placed him as *nuṭfah* in a firmly fixed place of rest [fallopian tube]; then We made *nuṭfah* into ʿ*alaqah*; then of that ʿ*alaqah* We made *muḍghah*; then We made out of *muḍghah* bones (ʿ*iẓām*) and clothed the bones with flesh (*laḥm*); then We developed out of it a new creation (*khalq ākhar*): Hallowed, therefore, is Allah, the best to create. (23:13–14)

From this Qur'anic statement, one may identify altogether six stages, three embryonic (*nuṭfah*, ʿ*alaqah*, and *muḍghah*) and three fetal (ʿ*iẓām*, *laḥm* and *khalq ākhar*). Semantically, *nuṭfah* refers to the seminal fluid, which when deposited in the fallopian tubes causes conception. ʿ*Alaqah* literally signifies leech. This naming of the second embryonic stage is remarkable. At this stage the embryo really adheres tightly to the uterine wall just like a leech sticks to a relevant surface. Scientifically, the embryonic stage of this nature is called blastocyst, which, as mentioned earlier, adheres to the uterine wall, hanging from there. *Muḍghah* denotes a chewed form of a thing. Biologically, it is this stage of the embryo that produces varied cell types, which make up a human being. The Qur'anic statement (23:13–14) is in total conformity with modern biology. The literal meaning of the embryonic terms, as stated in the Qur'an, also supports scientific accuracy on the matter. To consider *nuṭfah*, ʿ*alaqah* and *muḍghah* as the stages of the fetal period, and not of the embryonic period is to discredit the Qur'anic statement.

Professor Keith Moor, one of the pioneers of IVF conception, admits the miraculous nature of the Qur'anic statement. According to him, the stages of ʿ*alaqah* and *muḍghah* are so minute that they are completely invisible to human eyes and can only be observed through a microscope. He declares that these stages form the embryonic period. He is of the view that the Prophet or anyone else could not have formulated this Qur'anic statement (23:13–14) because of the non-availability of microscopes or any other such tools during the Prophet's time. The microscope was developed in the 16th century, roughly a thousand years after the Qur'an's revelation. He acknowledges that the Qur'anic description of the embryonic stages is exactly the same as that of modern scientific discovery. Keeping in mind the Qur'an's statement and the findings of science one may feel uncomfortable by the statements made in the report and cited in al-Bukhārī.[15]

It is most probable that one or other of the reporters (not ʿAbd Allāh ibn Masʿūd, a Companion) erred (*wahima*) in reporting the duration. Yaʿqūb ibn Sufyān (d.277 AH) was one of the most reliable authorities in Hadith (*thiqah ḥāfiẓ*).[16] He comments on the position of Zayd ibn Wahb, the reporter who narrates the report from ʿAbd Allāh ibn Masʿūd, in these words: "There is many a deficiency in his reports."[17] Al-Dhahbī protests this observation of Yaʿqūb and says: "He is not right."[18] Ibn Ḥajar echoed the same sentiment.[19] But neither al-Dhahbī nor Ibn Ḥajar advanced any argument to rebut Yaʿqūb's observation of Zayd ibn Wahb. The objective here is not to discredit the authentic position of Zayd ibn Wahb, but to show the possibility of the mishandling of his reports by others. This message may be derived from the observation made by Yaʿqūb ibn Sufyān. It seems that the mention of the embryonic period as spreading over seventeen weeks is a later insertion in the hadith. This, hence, refers to a defect (*ʿillah*) in the report in which case the report is deemed defective (*maʿlūl*).

Muslim recorded a tradition on the same subject on the authority of Ḥudhayfah ibn Asīd al-Ghifārī (d.42 AH) that:

> I heard the Prophet to have said: "Forty two days after the position of *nuṭfah* [zygote], Allah entrusts to it an angel who fashions it and makes its ears, eyes, skin, flesh and bones. He [the angel] then, asks Allah whether [it is] male or female. He writes what Allah determines. He, then, asks about its lifespan. He writes what Allah decrees. He, then, asks about its sustenance. He writes what Allah decides. The angel, then, goes out with the document in his hand. He does not add to what he was commanded nor does he exclude anything from there."[20]

This tradition is no less significant than the one recorded by al-Bukhārī. This is an authentic report. In terms of the chain of narrators it has an edge over al-Bukhārī's report in that Muslim's chain contains two Companions, ʿĀmir ibn Wāthilah and Ḥudhayfah ibn Asīd with the former reporting from the latter. All the other reporters after ʿĀmir ibn Wāthilah are reliable sources. This equally authentic report contradicts al-Bukhārī's. As we have seen al-Bukhārī's report puts the point of human destiny as being after seventeen weeks, whereas Muslim's report puts this after only six weeks. Muslim's tradition is in consonance with scientific fact. In such cases of conflict between two equally reliable traditions, only one of them is to be accepted. Rationally speaking, Muslim's report emerges stronger than al-Bukhārī's. The former does not have any internal defect (*ʿillah*) and is in agreement with modern findings in the field of Genetic Engineering. Consequently, al-Bukhārī's report appears to be strange and peculiar (*shādhdh*) because it is in conflict with the comparatively more reliable report of Muslim.

The second statement in al-Bukhārī's tradition concerns the determination of four things for man, however, only three are specifically mentioned, with the fourth missing from the report. The stated three things are his sustenance, his lifespan, and his position as one of being rewarded or condemned. Ibn Ḥajar agrees that the mention of "deed" is missing from the list of four items.[21] He identifies the fourth item from two other reports of al-Bukhārī, one from the chapter on the Beginning of Creation (*Bad'u al-Khalq*) and the other from that on the Unity of God (*al-Tawḥīd*). But there is once again an error in the report under "Beginning of Creation." One item (lifespan) is missing there. It mentions only three: deed, sustenance and being rewarded or condemned.[22] The report under "Unity of God" certainly mentions all the four items.[23] Undoubtedly, the fourth item is known from other reports but what about the position of the report in view? Does it not, then, become defective (*muʿallal*) and strange (*shādhdh*)? Badr al-Dīn al-ʿAynī suggests that the item "deed" was not mentioned in the report as quoted from al-Bukhārī's *kitāb al-qadar* due to it being well-known.[24] One may respond with the question, are the two items (sustenance and lifespan) out of the three items already mentioned in the report concerned not well known? Certainly, they are as well known as the unmentioned "deed." Al-ʿAynī's argument does not go down well. It seems Ibn Ḥajar and al-ʿAynī are both aware of this particular defect of al-Bukhārī's report but do not want to declare it strange (*shādhdh*) hence the feeble justification. Al-Bukhārī has recorded the same report in four places, *kitāb bad'u al-khalq*, *kitāb aḥādīth al-anbiyā'*, *kitab al-qadar*, and *kitāb al-tawḥīd*. Out of these four reports only two (in *kitāb aḥādīth al-anbiyā'* and *kitāb al-tawḥīd*) mention all the four items, while the other two (*kitāb bad'u al-khalq* and *kitāb al-qadar*) state only three items. This situation is certainly one of strangeness (*shudhūdh*).

The third statement in al-Bukhārī's report explains that a person does evil deeds (of the people of Hell) throughout his life but shortly before his death destiny (*al-kitāb*) overtakes him and he begins doing good deeds (of the people of Paradise) hence he deserves entry into Paradise; and vice versa that a person does good deeds throughout his life but shortly before his end destiny overtakes him and he commits evil deeds and hence is thrown into hellfire. There seems to be a very apparent contradiction between this component of the report and the second one as mentioned above. According to the second statement there is only one destiny (*al-kitāb*) prepared by the angel, which comprises four items, deed, sustenance, lifespan and the end result. This determination of four things is enough to conclude that man is bound to act in accordance with what had been written while he was still in his embryonic or fetal stage of life. The third statement refers very clearly to one more destiny (*al-kitāb*) made by man himself. It is on the basis of this freedom that he chooses to act according to his preference. The fore-written destiny overtakes him at a later stage of his life and the person concerned starts doing deeds accordingly. No commentator of al-Bukhārī seems to have realized this incongruity in the report. The first part of the tradition specifies a fore-written detailed destiny, whilst the last part mentions a man-made destiny, which is ultimately dominated by natural destiny. A very natural question arises, how can it be possible for man to act on his own for a considerable period of time in his life, and not in accordance with his fore-written destiny? Does the fore-written destiny take effect only at the last stage of man's life?

This idea that a natural destiny can overtake man, and can snatch Paradise from him, sends out a frightening message, that man stands coerced at the hands of the unseen. It hardly fits into the Qur'anic framework concerning man's position. Man is in charge of the earth (*khalīfah*), placed in a situation of test, and will be rewarded or punished in accordance with his good or bad deeds: (1) "Behold, your Lord said to the angels: 'I will create the inheritor of the earth.'" (2:30), (2)

"It is He who has made you the inheritors of the earth: He has raised you in ranks, some above others, so that He may try you by means of what He has bestowed upon you." (6:165), (3) "If Allah had so willed, He could surely have made you all one single community but [His plan is] to test you in what He has given you." (5:48), (4) "Behold, We have willed that all beauty on earth be a means by which We put men to test – as to which of them are best in conduct." (18:7), (5) "He who has created death as well as life, so that He might put you to a test [and thus show] which of you is best in conduct..." (67:2). Positions of *khilāfah* and *ibtilā'* require, to the extent of necessity, freedom of thought, choice and action. The end result, man's ultimate destination, is to be based on his performance in this life. If the end result is already forewritten, then the ideas of *khilāfah* and *ibtilā'* become a mockery.

It is said that al-Bukhārī's report does not represent the predetermination of man's destiny in all its detail, but reflects Allah's omniscience (Allah is all-Knowing, and knows how things will be).[25] Undoubtedly, Allah is omniscient; nothing is hidden from Him; the present, the past and the future are all in His eternal knowledge. The Qur'an has categorically mentioned this: "And that Allah encompasses all things with His knowledge" (65:12). However, al-Bukhārī's report does not make any reference to the knowledge of God but rather uses the word *kitābah* (writing). Did the Arabs of the Qur'an's time use, even though metonymically, the word 'writing' in the sense of knowing? Certainly not. If the report had stated that Allah had foreknowledge of the future of man yet to be born, there would be no problem. But the report describes four components of man's life in such a way that it looks like predetermination of human destiny, with man enjoying no freedom at all.

Ibn Ḥajar has also researched the nature of al-Bukhārī's report. According to his analysis, the tradition has not only been merely reported on the authority of ʿAbd Allāh ibn Masʿūd but there are other Companions involved i.e. ʿAbd Allāh ibn ʿUmar, Abū Hurayrah, Anas ibn Mālik, Ḥudhayfah ibn Asīd etc. He manages to identify around forty different chains (*isnād*) through which this report has been transmitted. He also expresses his confidence in being able to uncover many more sources of this tradition, were he to delve deeper into the search.[26] He remains short of declaring the tradition as *mutawātir* (recurrent), but what he says leads ultimately to this conclusion. *Ḥadīth Mutawātir* has two main classifications: literal (*lafẓī*) and conceptual (*maʿnawī*).[27] The report does not fall under the category of literal recurrence (*tawātur lafẓī*). The reporting in all the available reports is not literally the same and a few examples may be enough to substantiate this conclusion. Al-Bukhārī himself has recorded seven traditions on the same subject i.e. predetermination of human destiny.[28] Out of these seven reports four have been narrated on the authority of ʿAbd Allāh ibn Masʿūd, and the remaining three on the authority of Anas ibn Mālik. The reports of ʿAbd Allāh contain two versions. Two of them mention determination of four items but only three are counted therein. The narration of Anas has another variation. It mentions the determination of gender (male or female) in place of "deed." Muslim has recorded around eight chains for the same tradition, two on the authority of ʿAbd Allāh ibn Masʿūd, five on that of Ḥudhayfah ibn Asīd, and one on that of Anas ibn Mālik.[29] In the report by Ibn Masʿūd human destiny is determined after one hundred and twenty days pass over various embryonic stages, whereas according to the report through Ḥudhayfah ibn Asīd, it takes place only after forty, or forty-two, or forty-five days. The predetermined items in the reports on the authority of Ḥudhayfah vary from one another. In one version (Hadith No. 6667) the number of the determined items are six: end result, gender, deed, effect, lifespan and sustenance. In another version (Hadith No. 6668) the determined items are only three: gender, lifespan, and sustenance. It is interesting to note that both these reports end with the statement: "There does not take place any addition or reduction in what was decided." Certainly, the two reports contradict each other. In another version of Ḥudhayfah's report (Hadith No. 6670), the items determined are six: gender, physical nature (normal or abnormal), sustenance, lifespan, conduct, and end result (whether condemnation or reward). Here in this report, one item (physical nature) is different. Does this situation refer to the unity in meaning or to the disunity in meaning? It is difficult to prove the continuity (*tawātur*) of al-Bukhārī's report due to the variations which exist in the other versions of the report. Logically, each report remains in the category of solitary (*āḥād*) reports.

While interpreting al-Bukhārī's report, neither al-Ṭībī, nor Ibn Ḥajar, nor al-ʿAynī, nor al-Qasṭalānī discuss the implication of its message on one's faith. In all likelihood they probably avoided saying anything on the matter because they asserted their view in their respective introductory notes to their commentary of al-Bukhārī's *kitāb al-qadar*. They have emphatically declared that neither the Jabarites nor Qadarites are right in their belief; and that only the stand of Ahl al-Sunnah is correct. Jabarites see man's life as absolutely predetermined. They claim that man enjoys no freedom at all; what he does is preordained. Qadarites attribute to man freedom of thought, choice and action and do not agree with the idea of a fore-written destiny. Ahl al-Sunnah find themselves treading the middle path, avoiding both extremes. They insist that there does exist a fore-written destiny but this does not adversely affect man's freedom to choose and act. It is not proper to be engaged here in the discussion as to which group holds the most valid attitude.

It is undeniable that al-Bukhārī's report goes against both ahl al-Sunnah and Qadarite opinion, but gives support to those with a fatalistic approach towards life. Some might suggest the total rejection of the report on the one hand (based on it being replete with internal defects), and designating it as strange (*shādhdh*) on the other because of other more authentic versions. This is not reasonable. It seems appropriate to identify the errors contained in the report and rectify them in accordance with other available versions. A careful scrutiny may help scholars to recast the report, which may resemble something like the following possible version:

> Forty two days after the stage of *nuṭfah*, Allah entrusts it to an angel who fashions it, and makes its ears, eyes, skin, bones and flesh. He, afterwards, in accordance with the command of Allah determines its gender (*dhakar* or *unthā*), its lifespan (*ajal*), its deed (*ʿamal*), its physical feature (*sawīyyun* or *ghayr sawīyy*), its sustenance (*rizq*), and its disposition (*shaqiyy* or *saʿīd*). By God, a person performs good deeds throughout his life, but at a time close to the end of his life destiny (*al-kitāb*) overtakes him and he begins to do evil deeds until he dies hence he enters Hell. Likewise, a person does bad deeds throughout his life but shortly before the end of his life destiny (*al-kitāb*) overtakes him and he begins to do all that ultimately leads him to Paradise.

This carefully remolded form of the tradition in *kitāb al-qadar* stands in need of a highly rational as well as universally acceptable interpretation.

Nuṭfah (zygote) refers to the beginning of conception. Roughly six weeks after conception the fetus undergoes rapid growth, and the baby's main external features begin to take form. Eyes, ears, skin, bones and flesh etc. start growing at this stage. According to modern scientific discovery in Genetic Engineering, the first six weeks of the fetus are very crucial; formation of human organs take place during this period. It is, then, during this crucial period that Allah determines man's destiny. The gender of the baby is determined. Whether it is male or female is decreed in the womb of the mother. The physical features of the baby are also established in the fetal stages. If it is born handicapped, this is because it was formed like this during pregnancy.

Now we need to understand how and in what form the *ajal* (lifespan), *rizq* (sustenance), *ᶜamal* (deed), and *shaqiyy* or *saᶜīd* (disposition) are conditioned. Human lifespan is governed by certain divinely decreed rules. According to these, man, at times, lives a long age and, at times, a very short life. Man has hardly any control over this dimension of his destiny. Yet, man has been granted certain privileges to prolong his life. Aḥmad ibn Ḥanbal records a tradition of the Prophet on the authority of Rāfiᶜ ibn Makīth: "A good deed expands life and charity work saves one from tragic death."[30] Al-Tirmidhī has recorded a tradition of the Prophet on the authority of Sulaymān that "Nothing but a good deed extends [one's] lifespan."[31] *Rizq* (sustenance) may not necessarily mean a fixed amount of livelihood. It may be taken as the area of interest, ability and propensity towards certain particular economic activities. This is why people have different abilities in the economic field. Some people are highly intelligent by birth, and some are mediocre. Thus people earn their livelihood on the basis of their respective aptitude. One may not deny the role of man in his economic life. The amount of wealth may increase and, at times may decrease. This is easy to understand. A person obtains a job with a specified salary. When his employer finds him hard working, very honest, regular, punctual, and more productive, he rewards him by affecting his promotion and increasing his salary. Conversely, if he finds the employee irregular, lazy and non-productive, he may either fire him or demote him decreasing his salary. In the same way Allah may also increase or decrease the amount of man's sustenance keeping his performance in view. Once the Prophet prayed for his personal assistant (voluntary attendant), Anas ibn Mālik: "O Allah! Increase him in wealth and children, and bless him for what you have already bestowed upon him."[32] The *ʿamal* (deed) denotes mental, physical and moral abilities to think, to decide, to choose, and to act. This is why people differ from one another in their intellectual and physical abilities. The Prophet taught his people to pray to Allah in these words: "O Allah! I seek refuge in You from evil hearing, evil sight, evil speech, evil thought, and evil desire."[33] This advice of the Prophet in itself indicates that man has certain freedom in his choice of action, and in order to act rightly he seeks the help of Allah. Almost all the Hadith works contain a chapter entitled *kitāb al-Daʿawāt* (Chapter on Invocation to God), which consists of a number of *aḥādīth* encouraging believers to seek Allah's help to abstain from evil deeds and to do good deeds. This substantiates the idea that man has freedom of thought and action to the extent that he can easily demonstrate his position as a human being, that is one who thinks and acts according to his own will. This is his special feature.

The concept of determination of *shaqiyy* or *saʿīd* may not necessarily be in the sense of condemnation or reward. According to al-Fayrūzābādī, *shaqā'* literally means harshness/hard-heartedness (*shiddah*) and difficulty (*ʿusr*).[34] *Shaqiyy* is a person who is very hard and harsh in his natural disposition and can easily lose his temper. He is short as well hot tempered. The term *shaqiyy al-qalb* signifies a person who is hard-hearted. The word *saʿīd* originally means happy. A person who is of a happy temperament is *saʿīd*. Such a person meets and behaves with others smilingly and merrily. These two words may be deemed as the expression of man's natural temperament. *Shaqiyy* is hot tempered and *saʿīd* is cool-minded. These two terms also refer to human behavior. Abū Dāwūd has recorded a tradition on the authority of Abū Hurayrah: "Verily, Allah has taken away from you the pre-Islamic criteria of superiority based on ancestral pride. There are now only two people, a believer who is God-conscious and a transgressor who is hard-hearted."[35] It is evident from this tradition that people stand divided into groups on the basis of their conduct. Those who fear Allah and submit to him are believers; and those who reject the message of Allah and do not stand in awe of Allah are transgressors. In the hadith the word *shaqiyy* has been used as opposite to *taqiyy* (God-conscious). *Shaqiyy*, therefore, will mean a person who out of his harshness rejects submission to Allah. These two categories of people are to be seen everywhere in every society. The notion that the two terms (*shaqiyy* and *saʿīd*) refer to the predetermined position of man either as condemned or as rewarded runs counter to the Qur'anic declaration. In *Surah Hūd* (11) *āyāt* 25–100 we have a description of the story of the people of Noah, *ʿĀd*, *Thamūd*, the people of Lot, the people of *Madyan*, and the Pharoah and his people. The conclusion of these stories has been given in verses 11:101–109. Three statements in this concluding remark are noteworthy. *Āyah* 11:101 reads: "It was not We who wronged them but they wronged their own souls..." and *āyah* 11: 105–106 reads: "Among those are condemned (*shaqiyy*) and rewarded (*saʿīd*). Now those who will have brought wretchedness upon themselves (*al-ladhīna shaqū*) will be in the fire...", "...and of those [that are gathered together], some will be wretched *(shaqiyy)* and some, happy *(saʿīd)*. Now as for those who [by their deeds] will have brought wretchedness upon themselves, (*al-ladhīna shaqū*) [they shall live] in the fire...." These three *āyāt* (11: 101, 105 & 106) hold the wrongdoers responsible for their ill fate. Their position as condemned and rewarded is determined only on the Day of Judgment. When Adam was sent down to the earth to begin his life, he was assured of guidance from Allah in these words: "There shall certainly come unto you guidance from Me: he who follows My guidance will not go astray (*yaḍillu*), and neither will he be unhappy (*yashqā*)" (20:123). Here unhappiness (*shaqā'*) is consequent upon rejection of guidance hence happiness (*saʿādah*) is consequent upon acceptance of guidance.

The last part of the tradition speaks of the domination of destiny (*al-kitāb*) over man, due to which he will deserve either Paradise or Hell. Apparently, the tradition teaches that a person once known as pious will be forced by destiny to perform evil deeds so as to justify his entry into Hell; and that a person known for his bad deeds will be coerced into acting righteously so as to let him enter Paradise. If the meaning of this statement is that man is denied freedom, then this will surely contrast with the divine attribute of justice. The corollary of

Allah's justice is that man should be rewarded or punished on the basis of his performance. Most probably, destiny (*al-kitāb*) signifies the general rules of guidance and misguidance, reward and punishment. The guidance or misguidance are both dependent, to the extent of necessity, upon man. It is the will of man, which takes initiative to accept or reject God's message. The Qur'an says: "By it He causes many to stray and many He leads into the right path; but He causes not to stray but the iniquitous" (2:26). The dominance of destiny over man means that human life is governed by the eternal divine rule of righteousness and evildoing. A person who performs good deeds may not necessarily be sincere in his approach. His good deeds might be all mere show hence the general impression about him will be that he is a pious man. His insincerity will not remain hidden from the eyes of the people around him for long. He will become exposed one way or another for his insincerity and hypocrisy. Ultimately, his insincerity will cause him to enter Hell. Human destiny reads that the insincere person will be punished. A person who performs bad deeds may not necessarily be an insincere person. He might be sincere and God-fearing in his heart but circumstances may have forced him to commit evil. This is why he appears as a man destined for Hell. Since he is sincere and wishes to do only good, he will be helped by Allah to give up his bad deeds and do only what is good. Thus, due to his sincerity and concern to do good destiny will guide him on how to fulfill his wish, and, then, good deeds will take him to Paradise.

Hadith No. 2 (Human Destiny)

> The Prophet said: "Allah appoints an angel for the womb of the mother. He says: 'O my Lord! This is *nuṭfah*. O my Lord! This is *ʿalaqah*. O my Lord! This is *muḍghah*.' When Allah willed to accomplish its creation, the angel says: 'O my Lord! Male or female; fortunate or unfortunate [*shaqiyy* or *saʿīd*]; what about the sustenance, what about the lifespan?' Thus, these things are written in the womb of the mother itself."[36]

The report's chain runs as follows: Sulaymān ibn Ḥarb (d.224 AH) from Ḥammād ibn Zayd (d.197 AH) from ʿUbayd Allāh ibn Abī Bakr ibn Anas (d.uncertain) from Anas ibn Mālik (d.93 AH) from the Prophet. The three reporters after Anas ibn Mālik (Sulaymān, Ḥammād, and ʿUbayd Allāh) are known as *thiqah imām ḥāfiẓ* (perfectly authentic authority), *thiqah thabt faqīh* (genuinely authentic jurist), and *thiqah* (authentic) respectively.

Al-Bukhārī has recorded this tradition also in *kitāb al-ḥayḍ* and *kitāb aḥādīth al-anbiyā'*. The authority there is the same i.e. Anas ibn Mālik. The wordings of these two reports are almost the same as in the above-mentioned report. One may not find any variation in meaning between the three versions of the report. Muslim has also recorded the same report in *kitāb al-qadar*.

This tradition does not mention the duration of the period covering the embryonic stage. It seems quite rational to remain silent about the precise timing of the fetal growth and determination of human life with its four basic dimensions: gender, disposition, sustenance, and life-span. It is strange to note that this tradition does not refer to deed. It is hard to believe that the Prophet did not mention anything about it. One's deeds form a very crucial part in human life. One could suggest that the Prophet himself might have described details of human destiny in various ways. On occasions he might have mentioned only four items, at other times only three, on some occasion he counted six items, to someone he talked about some items and to someone else he added an item. This suggestion may not be substantiated. The Prophet must have received this information (that is concerning the determination of human destiny in its fetal stage) from Allah. It is therefore not to be supposed that he would have altered it whilst sharing it with his Companions.

Where there are missing elements in the reported tradition, the error may be attributed only to the narrators coming after the Companions of the Prophet. One may also theorize that, in the case of the above-mentioned tradition, Anas himself condensed the Prophet's statement.

The possible interpretation of the determination of human destiny has already been made under the first tradition on the authority of ʿAbd Allāh ibn Masʿūd. There is no need to repeat the same ideas here again.

Hadith No. 3 (Preordainment)
The Prophet said: "The pen has become dry on what you are destined to receive."[37]

This tradition has been recorded on the authority of Abū Hurayrah (d.59 AH). Since it is not included in *kitāb al-qadar* as a full-fledged report, al-Bukhārī has not given it its full chain. Its complete chain and the text are available in *kitāb al-nikāḥ*. In order to have a justified understanding of this tradition, it is important to read the full report in *kitāb al-nikāḥ*.

> It is related that Abu Hurayrah said: "I said, 'Messenger of Allah, I am a young man and I fear fornication for myself. I cannot afford to marry.' He was silent. Then I repeated the like of that and he remained silent. Then I repeated the like of that yet again and he was silent. Then I said the like of that and the Prophet, may Allah bless him and grant him peace, said, 'Abu Hurayrah, the pen is dry, having written what you will encounter, whether you are castrated or not.'"[38]

Its chain comprises six narrators: Aṣbagh ibn al-Farj (d. 225 AH) from ʿAbd Allāh ibn Wahb from Yūnus (d.159 AH) from Ibn Shahāb al-Zahrī (d.125 AH) from Abū Salamah (d.2 AH) from Abū Hurayrah. They are all highly authentic reporters.

This report gives rise to many questions. Why did Abū Hurayrah not find means to marry? Did he not do anything to earn his livelihood? Was he a person below the poverty line or an indigent? If yes, why? How did he, then, manage to meet his daily needs? Did he depend on others for his sustenance? If wealthy people were supporting him economically, why did they fail to see his inability to afford marriage? The answer to these and many other related questions may render the report doubtful.

Abū Hurayrah was a member of the Madinan Islamic society where everyone was always ready to help the other. He was inclined towards learning, memorizing and disseminating the Prophet's teachings devoting most of his time to these activities. This devotion to intellectual pursuits left him with no opportunity to earn a decent livelihood requiring him to depend heavily on charity. The people knew of his interest and contribution and must have respected him as well as supported him materially for his needs. If society took care of his daily needs, is it to be supposed they would be ignorant of his need for a wife? Al-Bukhārī himself has recorded a report which relates that the Prophet solemnized the marriage of a poor man to a woman merely on the condition that the groom teach the bride the Qur'an; the Prophet making it clear to the groom before marriage that his teaching of the Qur'an to the bride would be deemed as his dowry for her.[39] Abū Hurayrah deserved the same treatment. When he shared his problem with the Prophet, he well knew that he would find a way out of his predicament.

Abū Hurayrah sought the Prophet's permission to castrate himself to eliminate the sexual needs of his body, speaking volumes for the seriousness of the challenge he was facing. The report indicates that the Prophet did not take his Companion's complaint and request seriously as apparent from the response. It is however inconceivable that the Prophet would treat the matter lightly brushing it aside as simply predetermined destiny. The Prophet's advice to Abū Hurayrah to be patient until his destiny brought into effect what had already been written for him contrasts with the Prophet's approach in general. Abū Hurayrah was afraid of committing wrong if an immediate solution was not in place. The Prophet was duty bound to resolve the problems of his people. His apparent observation that "it does not matter whether you castrate or not" (suggesting that he did not see anything wrong in castration) goes against his own judgment: "There is no room for any kind of injury or physical affliction." Muslim jurists are all unanimous that castration is totally prohibited in Islam. The basis for this view is the Prophet's own verdict given in response to the problem of his Companions, including ʿUthmān ibn Maẓʿūn who had also sought the Prophet's permission to castrate himself.[40] What was wrong for ʿUthmān ibn Maẓʿūn to do must also have been wrong for Abū Hurayrah. Logic demands that the Prophet would not have left the decision to Abū Hurayrah and would in no uncertain terms have discouraged the young man from crippling himself. Furthermore, there does not seem to have been any real obstacles in arranging a marriage for Abū Hurayrah, with the dowry either possibly paid from the official exchequer or by some generous member of society.

Al-ʿAynī raises an issue concerning the phrase "dry pen." Referring to the view of al-Karmānī that this signifies the immutability of the written command of Allah, he rebuts this idea and quotes an *āyah* which states that "Allah effaces whatever He wills and retains whatever He wills" (13:39). According to this Qur'anic statement al-ʿAynī argues Allah changes what He wants to change. Thus, he seeks to emphasize that predetermined destiny is not absolute; it may be modified if Allah so wills.

Ibn Ḥajar seems to be in favor of the immutability of a fore-written destiny and to strengthen his argument cites a dialogue between the governor of Khurāsān, during al-Mamūn's time, ʿAbd Allāh ibn Ṭāhir and a scholar of the time, al-Ḥusayn ibn al-Faḍl. The former saw a contradiction between the tradition – "The pen has dried on what has been written down" – and the Qur'anic statement: "Every day He is in new splendor" (55:29). He asked the latter to explain this and received the reply that the *āyah* refers to what Allah displays and not to what he creates afresh. Upon this, the governor was very much impressed and out of appreciation kissed the scholar's forehead.[41] However, although the governor was satisfied with what al-Ḥusayn had stated this is not necessarily the case for all.

There are other *āyāt* that spell out unequivocally the continuous directing of affairs by Allah, i.e. "He still regulates all affairs" (13:2), and "He directs the affairs from the heavens to the earth" (32:5). Abdullah Yusuf Ali interprets the second Qur'anic statement (32:5) in these words: "In the immense past was Allah's act of creation: it still continues, for He guides, rules, and controls all affairs."[42] While interpreting *āyah* 55:29, Abdullah Yusuf Ali observes: "Allah's is still the directing hand in all affairs. He does not sit apart, careless of mankind or of any of His creatures. But His working shows new splendor every day, every hour, every moment."[43]

The drying up of the pen, as stated by the Prophet in the report, means that Allah has determined the basic and general laws for everything and that those predetermined rules are absolute. However, as for the details of life, they are made, written, modified, and rewritten every moment in accordance with the situation and time involved.

Hadith No. 4 (The Predestined Role of Man)

> A man said, "O Allah's Apostle! Can the people of Paradise be differentiated from the people of the Fire?" The Prophet replied, "yes." The man said, "Why do people [try to] do [good] deeds?" The Prophet said, "Everyone will do the deeds he has been created to do or he will do those deeds which will be made easy for him to do."[44]

The chain of this report is as follows: Ādam ibn Abī Ayās (d.221 AH) from Shuʿbah from Yazīd ibn Abī Yazīd al-Rishk (d.130 AH) from Muṭarrif ibn ʿAbd Allāh (d.220 AH) from ʿImrān ibn Ḥuṣayn (d.52 AH). All the narrators of this tradition are highly reliable.

Ibn Ḥajar states that the man's question referred to the angels or some other creation which Allah has informed us of, concerning the symptoms of both the people of Paradise and those of Hell.[45] This is mere speculation with no substantial evidence to prove its accuracy. It would seem that Ibn Ḥajar reached this far-fetched assumption under the impact of a theological debate taking place during his era between various groups of theologians. Ibn Ḥajar hailed from a theological group other than the Qadarite (exponents of human liberty and the doctrine of free will) or Jabarite (inclined to the doctrine of predestination) and this would explain why he advances an interpretation which surely contests the belief of others whilst substantiating the view of his own particular group. An objective examination of the question leaves little room for doubt that the questioner wanted to know whether people could be recognized as to their final fate on the basis of their acts, and not the meaning the author of *Fatḥ al-Bārī* derives. The answer given by the Prophet was in the affirmative, by which he meant that the people of Paradise would look different from those of Hell on the basis of their deeds. The second question asked might not have been what al-Bukhārī has recorded i.e. "Why do people [try to] do [good] deeds?" The question recorded by Muslim seems to be more pertinent and intelligible: "What should, then, be the act?" Al-Bukhārī's question leads to one direction and Muslim's to another. According to the question recorded by the latter, the questioner wanted to know as to what kind of special deeds might make someone distinctly destined for Paradise.

It is odd that Ibn Ḥajar does not find any difference between the question quoted by al-Bukhārī and that by Muslim reading the same message in both. The Prophet's answer to the second question has also become the subject of controversy between the version of the report recorded by al-Bukhārī and that by Muslim. In al-Bukhārī's version the narrator is uncertain as to which word was used by the Prophet. In Muslim's version the narrator does not express any doubt. Muslim's version is preferable to al-Bukhārī's because Muslim's wordings get referred to in al-Bukārī's report. When the Prophet stated that everyone is facilitated towards his/her deeds, he actually elucidated the following Qur'anic statements:

> (1) And He inspired it as to its wrong and its right. (91:8)
> (2) Thus, as for him who gives [to others] and is conscious of God, and believes in the truth of the ultimate good for him shall We make easy the path towards [ultimate] ease. But as for him who is niggardly, and thinks that he is self-sufficient, and calls the ultimate good a lie – for him shall We make easy the path towards hardship (92:5–10)

In these *āyāt* Allah vividly states that man has been equipped with the capability to do either good or evil and that man's preference is honored; should he want to act rightly, he is helped further to continue in this; and if he chooses to act sinfully, he finds the path smooth for him. Whether he chooses to act rightly or wrongly, the choice is man's and to claim that man is forced to act in accordance with what is predetermined for him is to challenge the Qur'anic statements quoted above.

In his commentary on this tradition Ibn Ḥajar quotes a dialogue between Abū al-Aswad al-Dawliyy and ʿImrān ibn Ḥuṣayn as recorded by Muslim. The latter asked the former his opinion on people's deeds, their efforts in this regard, whether deeds are predetermined and predestined or whether they represent people's choice of acceptance or rejection of their prophets' message. Al-Dawliyy replied that deeds had already been predetermined, to which Ibn Ḥuṣayn commented that this would be an injustice to man. Al-Dawliyy trembled with horror at this remark stating that everything was the creation of Allah and in His control and that Allah would not be questioned for what He did but rather they would be questioned. At this Ibn Ḥuṣayn expressed good wishes for the former and said that he did not mean what he had asked but was testing his understanding. Thereafter Ibn Ḥuṣayn narrated a tradition:

> Two tribesmen of Muzaynah met the Prophet and shared their concern with him: "Are people's efforts which they make every moment in their life mere manifestation of the predetermined destiny or will their destiny be shaped in future in accordance with their acceptance or rejection of the message of prophets?" The Prophet responded to this query saying that man's fate has already been predetermined and the Qur'an conforms to it.[46]

This report, as recorded by Muslim, gives the impression that the mission of all prophets was meaningless and that their role in guiding mankind of little use for whether humanity acted rightly or wrongly their destiny had already been written. This message conflicts with the Qur'an which in a number of *āyāt* makes it crystal clear that prophets were raised one after another to show man the right path and that the fate of man depends on his reaction to the message they conveyed. A few *āyāt* are enough to substantiate the significance of the role that prophets play in affecting human destiny:

> [We sent all these] apostles as heralds of glad tidings and as warners, so that men might have no excuse before God after [the coming of] these apostles: and God is indeed Almighty, Wise. (4:165)

> O mankind! Verily, there has come unto you the Messenger with the truth from your Lord. So believe in him, it is better for you. But if you disbelieve, then certainly to Allah belongs all that is in the heavens and the earth. (4:170)

> Who receives guidance receives it for his own benefit; who goes astray does so to his own loss. (17:15)

These *āyāt* clearly show that Messengers were sent to mankind to guide them and to teach them right from wrong, and that it is man's own choice which either takes him to the path of benefit or that of loss.

In the dialogue cited between Abū al-Aswad al-Dawliyy and ʿImrān ibn Ḥuṣayn, Abū al-Aswad is reported to have said: "Allah will not be asked but the people will be asked." This is true. But it begs the question, how will people be questioned for actions committed in precise accordance with a predetermined destiny? Logically, people can only be questioned if they have enjoyed the freedom to choose and act. In the absence of freedom, questioning a man and considering him responsible for his actions is little more than injustice. The report claims that two individuals from the Muzaynah tribe asked the Prophet about the status of human actions, whether these were predestined or whether man had freedom to choose the path shown by God's Messengers. The question is purely philosophical and this as well as the way it is posed demonstrates the intelligence of the questioners for it cannot have come from simple Arabs who at the time of revelation were not theologians. It would therefore appear that the questioners were used as mouthpieces by those with a vested interest to have their question expressed and to give it credibility.

In Muslim's report the Prophet is said to have cited Qur'anic *āyah* 91:8, "And He inspired it as to its wrong and its right," as confirmation of the existence of a predetermined human destiny. However, it is inconceivable that the Prophet quoted this *āyah* to prove what it does not do. Verse 91:8 expresses the capability of man to act freely to do both good and bad. This innate ability of man is God-given.

It is worth noting that Muslim's report is not available in any other sources of tradition including the other five books of Hadith literature. A solitary tradition, which is entirely in contrast with the Qur'an is unreliable.

Hadith No. 6 (Natural Innocence)

The Prophet is reported to have said: "No baby is born but with natural innocence (*fiṭrah*); it is his parents who make him a Jew or Christian. It is like your live-stock giving birth to its young. Do you find any of them with its ears chopped? It is you who cut their ears."[47]

The chain of narrators of this tradition is as follows: Isḥāq ibn Ibrāhīm (d.238 AH) from ʿAbd al-Razzāq ibn al-Hammām (d.211 AH) from Maʿmar ibn Rāshid (d.154 AH) from Hammām ibn Munabbih (d.132 AH) from Abū Hurayrah. All the narrators are reliable.

Al-Bukhārī has recorded the same tradition in *kitāb al-janā'iz* on the authority of Abū Hurayrah but through a different chain. In this report there is a slight variation and it reads as follows: "The Prophet said: 'Every baby is born with its natural innocence; it is only his parents that make him a Jew or Christian or Magian. It is just as the animal gives birth to its baby. Do you, then, find its ear slit?'"[48]

One may wonder why this tradition has been included in *kitāb al-qadar*. The tradition puts the issue of predetermination to rest for it does not refer to human destiny as governing people's fate but rather blames parents for turning their children into Jews or Christians or Magians, parental contribution therefore playing a considerable part in one's ultimate belief structure. Likewise, a child born into a Muslim family and raised as a Muslim becomes a Muslim because of his parents' contribution, with Islam being consequent upon his parents' efforts. Where does a destiny predetermined in the mother's womb fit into all this? We can only conclude therefore that this statement of the Prophet apparently conflicts with traditions emphasizing the role of a predetermined destiny.

Hadith No. 8 (Prohibition on Snatching Others' Rights)

"The Prophet said: 'No woman should seek her sister's divorce so as to find the bowel empty and arrange her own marriage, as she will get what has been determined for her.'[49]

The chain runs as follows: ʿAbd Allāh ibn Yūsuf (d.218 AH) from Mālik ibn Anas from Aū al-Zinād ʿAbd Allāh ibn Zakwān (d.130 AH) from ʿAbd al-Raḥmān ibn Hurmuz al-Aʿraj (d.117 AH) from Abū Hurayrah from the Prophet. All the narrators are highly authentic. This tradition has also been recorded by al-Bukhārī in four additional places on the authority of Abū Hurayrah but with a slightly different chain.[50]

The tradition teaches Muslim women to place their trust in Allah and seek His help in marriage; one is not allowed to snatch away what others have but should make concerted effort in the right direction. Modern society is facing many crises, one of which is a shortage of suitable husbands for women. This leads to the very obvious problem of jealousy arising between unmarried and married women, further exacerbated by a climate of free mixing allowing unmarried women access to married males. Where free mixing leads to a tenuous relationship of sorts divorce becomes the ultimate outcome with the waiting woman seizing the opportunity to enter the life of someone who had belonged to someone else. This tradition is equally applicable to a man who may ask his brother to divorce his wife so as to marry her.

Hadith No. 9 (Allah is the Sole Owner of Everything)

> Once a messenger of one of the daughters of the Prophet came to the Prophet and informed him that her son was breathing his last breath. The Prophet, then, sent a message to her to keep patient and hope for Allah's mercy, as everything happens at its scheduled time and also because what Allah gives is His and what He takes back is His.

The chain of narrators of this report is: Mālik ibn Ismāʿīl (d.217 AH) from Isrā'īl ibn Yūnus (d.160 AH) from ʿĀṣim ibn Sulaymān (d.140 AH) from Abū ʿUthmān ʿAbd al-Raḥmān al-Nahdī (d.95 AH) from Usāmah ibn Zayd (d.54 AH). All The narrators are highly authentic.

The same report has been recorded by al-Bukhārī in five additional places.[51] The whole incident as cited in all the reports may be described as follows: One of the daughters of the Prophet sent a message to him that her son was breathing his last, and requested the Prophet to visit her. The Prophet sent words of solace to her saying: "Verily what Allah takes away is His and what He has given is His. Everything to Him has its appointed schedule. Be patient and hope for Allah's mercy." She, then, sends another message to the Prophet urging that he visit her. Upon receiving this the Prophet goes to her place along with Saʿd ibn ʿUbādah, Muʿādh ibn Jabal, Ubayy ibn Kaʿb, Zayd ibn Thābit and many others. The dying child is put into the Prophet's lap. The breathing sound of the baby is very dry and the Prophet's eyes fill with tears. Saʿd states: "What is this O Prophet of Allah!" The Prophet answers: "This is compassion which Allah has put into the hearts of His servants. Allah showers His merciful servants with mercy."

This tradition conveys several messages; first that death is certain, second, that man's life belongs to Allah hence it is His prerogative to let it remain as long as He wills, third, that death occurs at its time scheduled by Allah, fourth, that the relatives of the dying person should keep patient and hope for something good from Allah, fifth, that visiting the dying person is a nice tradition, sixth, that man has been made by Allah very soft-hearted, and seventh, that Allah is with those who show compassion to others.

Hadith No. 11 (The Prophet's Prophesies)
Ḥudhayfah ibn al-Yamān states that

> The Prophet delivered a speech to us in which he left nothing out concerning what would happen until doomsday. One who understood it remembered it; one who ignored it lost it. If I see something I will recognize it, even though I might have forgotten it, just as a person recognizes another person who appears after a long disappearance.[52]

The chain of narrators is: Mūsā ibn Masʿūd (d.220 AH) from Sufyān al-Thawrī from Sulaymān al-Aʿmash from Abū Wā'il Shaqīq ibn Salamah (d.100 AH) from Ḥudhayfah ibn al-Yamān (d.36 AH).

This chain appears to be very defective due to the inclusion of Mūsā ibn Masʿūd. Many Hadith scholars have given negative observations about him. Bundār declares him weak (*ḍaʿīf*) in Hadith. He wrote his traditions but later on abandoned them. Abū Ḥātim mentions that he is famous for reporting from al-Thawrī but used to distort (change as a result of misplacing of the diacritical marks, *taṣḥīf*) reports. According to al-Tirmidhī, he was considered weak in reporting. Ibn Ḥibbān has included his name in the list of authentic reporters but accepts that he erred in reporting. ʿAmr ibn ʿAlī al-Fallās comments that anyone with insight into Hadith never reported from him. Ibn Khuzaymah does not deem him reliable. Abū Aḥmad al-Ḥākim viewed him as weak. Abū ʿAbd Allāh al-Ḥākim states that he made a lot of errors and his memory was defective. Al-Sājī observed that he used to distort reports.[53] Aḥmad ibn Ḥanbal was of the view that the source of Mūsā was not the famous Sufyān al-Thawrī but someone else.[54] These observations from some of the greatest scholars in the field of Hadith throw suspicion on the position of Mūsā and thus render him unreliable. Therefore, the report, even though it has been recorded by al-Bukhārī, may not be considered authentic.

In addition the wording of the report also renders it doubtful. The report states that the Prophet described in this speech everything that was going to happen on earth until doomsday. If this were the case, his speech would have to be a very lengthy one, taking weeks if not months to complete. This is no doubt exaggeration and of rather an extraordinary kind. In the known history of the Prophet there is no reference to such a speech. Furthermore, the Prophet never did anything frivolously and if he had really mentioned all the events that were to take place in the future, what would have been the wisdom behind this? Would this detailed information have served any purpose to his mission? It is more likely that during his speech the Prophet mentioned various significant events that were to take place in the future.

Al-Bukhārī has recorded another report on the authority of ʿUmar ibn al-Khaṭṭāb in *kitāb bad'u al-khalq* that: "The Prophet stood among us and informed us about many things right from the beginning of creation until the entry of people into Paradise or Hell. There were those who remembered it and also those who forgot it."[55] This report is not as exaggerated as the first one and there is no problem in accepting that the Prophet shared certain important information concerning the future with his Companions. As the report mentions, many people forgot the Prophet's prophesies, and many remembered them. Now the question arises: did those who remembered the future predictions made by the Prophet communicate them to others? If yes, where are those reports? Hadith sources are replete with such predictions of the Prophet. Non-availability of such predictions gives rise to doubt as to the authenticity of the report mentioned above. It is strange that al-Bukhārī could not investigate the integrity of a reporter (Mūsā ibn Masʿūd) in the chain he used.

Hadith No. 12 (Predetermined End Result)

ʿAlī reports that

> We were sitting with the Prophet. While nudging the ground with his stick, he raised his head and said: "For every one of you has been predetermined a place either in Hell or in Paradise." Upon this someone retorted: "O Prophet of Allah! Shall we not, then, resign [ourselves] to

fate?" The Prophet said: "No, you have to act because each one of you is facilitated towards his destiny." The Prophet, then, read the *āyah*: "Thus, as for him who gives [to others] and is conscious of God, and believes in the truth of the ultimate good for him shall We make easy the path towards [ultimate] ease. As for him who gives in charity and fears Allah, and believes in the best, We will make smooth for him the path of ease (92:5–7)."[56]

The chain of this report is: ʿAbdān ʿAbd Allāh ibn ʿUthmān (d.221 AH) from Abū Ḥamzah Muḥammad ibn Maymūn (d.168 AH) from Sulaymān al-Aʿmash from Saʿd ibn ʿUbaydah (d. uncertain; after 100 AH) from Abū ʿAbd al-Raḥmān ʿAbd Allāh ibn Ḥabīb (d.70 AH) from ʿAlī ibn Abī Ṭālib. All these reporters are highly authentic.

The same report with slight variations is available in eight more places.[57] All these versions have been quoted mainly through three authorities: Saʿd ibn ʿUbaydah from Abū ʿAbd al-Raḥmān from ʿAlī. The main variation among these versions of the report is in the first statement of the Prophet. Out of nine versions only three refer to the fact that "For every one of you has been predetermined a place either in Hell or in Paradise." The remaining six versions contain the statement: "For each of you a place in Paradise and a place in Hell have been reserved." The former version of the report from *kitāb al-qadar* refers to the predetermination of one's ultimate destination, either in Paradise or in Hell, meaning that the end result of every human being has already been decided in eternity. The problems associated with this sort of interpretation have already been discussed at length, namely that predetermination is injustice to man and his position as *khalīfah* on the earth. There is no reason for taking this statement attributed to the Prophet as being correct. What has been reported in the other six versions, that "for each of you a place in Paradise and a place in Hell have been reserved" seems to be quite reasonable. Humanity has been told time and time again in the Qur'an that man's bad deeds will take him to Hell and his good deeds to Paradise. For example: (1) Yea! Those who earn evil and by their sinfulness are engulfed – they are destined for the fire: therein to abide; (2:81). (2) "He that works evil will not be requited but by the like thereof: and he that works a righteous deed – whether man or woman – and is a Believer – such will enter the Garden (of Bliss): Therein will they have abundance without measure" (40:40).

In light of the Qur'anic clarification, the statement that for everyone has been reserved a place either in Paradise or in Hell seems to be correct. It is up to mankind to act in accordance with deserving one or the other. As the statement attributed to the Prophet in the report cited in *kitāb al-qadar* is in absolute contrast with the Qur'an we therefore cannot accept it as correctly reported.

The question as to whether one should resign oneself to fate indicates a misunderstanding on the part of the questioner. He might have thought that as places in Paradise and Hell had already been allotted and one's place was assured one way or another it would not matter how he acted. The Prophet's answer reveals the misunderstanding of the questioner. The Prophet emphatically states "No, you must act because each of you is led smoothly to the end result." This statement does not mean that man is bound to act in accordance with his predetermined fate. Since the Prophet quotes Qur'anic verses 92:5–7 to confirm his view, there does not remain any room for confusion. These verses explain that the path of man is made smooth according to the choice of man. One who believes in the unity of God, does good deeds, fears Allah and takes care of the less fortunate people around him, his path leading to Paradise will be made smooth. Likewise, one who rejects the message of Allah, does not act righteously, and does not help others around him, his path leading to Hell will be made smooth.

In three versions of the report (hadith nos. 1362, 4948, and 4949), the following statement has been attributed to the Prophet: "One who is from among the rewarded (*ahl al-saʿādah*) will be facilitated to act righteously; and one who is from among the condemned (*ahl al-shaqā'*) will be facilitated to act sinfully." There is no indication in this statement that the two positions, of reward and condemnation, have been predetermined in eternity. Those who take the initiative towards a righteous life are the *ahl al-saʿādah* and those who choose to lead an iniquitous life should be considered as *ahl al-shaqā'*. There is complete conformity between this understanding and verses 92:5–7 as quoted by the Prophet.

In two versions of the report (hadith nos. 1362 and 4948) there is a statement attributed to the Prophet that "and there is no human being but he/she has been predestined as either condemned or rewarded [*wa illā qad kutibat shaqiyyah aw saʿīdah*]." This statement is taken as evidence for the existence of a predetermined human destiny. Although it would appear so, it may also be interpreted otherwise. Keeping in mind Qur'anic statements concerning the Day of Judgment, generally mentioned in the past tense, it may be stated that man by his actions is certain to be either among the rewarded or among the condemned. This is definite especially given use of the past tense for there is no denying the fact that application of the past tense is used at times for confirmation and to indicate the certainty of a matter.

Hadith No. 13 (Companions of Hell)

During the expedition of Khaybar the Prophet said about a combatant who claimed to be a Muslim that he was a dweller of Hell. In the war the man fought bravely and was seriously injured. The people approached the Prophet and informed him of the man's bravery and serious injury. The Prophet once again confirmed his position as a dweller of Hell. Some Muslims felt uncomfortable by this. In the meantime when the pain of the injury became unbearable, the man killed himself by thrusting an arrow into his neck. Some people rushed to the Prophet and said: "O Prophet of Allah! Allah has confirmed your statement. He committed suicide." Upon this the Prophet asked Bilāl to announce: "None but the believer will enter Paradise; and Allah, indeed, makes the iniquitous support Islam."[58]

The chain of this report is: Ḥibbān ibn Mūsā (d.233 AH) from ʿAbd Allāh ibn al-Mubārak from Maʿmar ibn Rāshid from Muḥammad ibn Muslim ibn al-Shihāb al-Zuhrī from Saʿīd ibn al-Musayyib (d.100 AH) from Abū Hurayrah. All these narrators are highly authentic.

The same report has been recorded by al-Bukhārī in *kitāb al-maghāzī*. That report is also on the authority of Abū Hurayrah. But there is a slight change in other names of the narrators.[59]

It seems that the brave combatant in the Muslim army was considered a true believer for when the Prophet cited the position of the man as a dweller of Hell, his followers were surprised for they had found him to be apparently serious in his dedication. Until, that is, he committed suicide when he showed himself to be otherwise, for a true believer cannot do anything prohibited in Islam and maintains his faith throughout life until death. The man's taking of his own life speaks volumes for his level of commitment and insincerity to his faith, for had he been a true believer he would never killed himself simply on account of acute pain or injury. Generally, the message derived from this tradition is that the combatant was a Muslim who became sinful before the end of his life and thus entered Hell because he had been destined to be doomed. This however may not be the correct derivation. The announcement the Prophet made through Bilāl clarifies matters. Bilāl announced: "None but the believer will enter Paradise; Allah, indeed, makes the iniquitous support Islam." As the man was sinful, non-serious in his belief and an untrue Muslim his mere association with Muslim society and army could not save him from Hell. He fought bravely not because he was sincere towards Islam but because he was an Arab. Arabs of the pre-Islamic era were by nature extremely courageous. They loved war and they loved to die in the battle field. This particular person supported Islam to show his valor and warlike chivalry. It is the law of Allah that He allows Islam to be supported by both Muslims as well as, at times, by non-Muslims.

The tradition declares that only the faithful will enter Paradise. The quality of faithfulness implies constancy, dedication, and commitment. For believers it means a form of constant allegiance that lasts to the end of one's life. Although, granted, a sincere believer will be helped by Allah to die with faith, the main role is that of man. A believer must do his utmost to remain sincerely faithful throughout his life and the Qur'an invites believers to do so: "O you who believe! Be conscious of Allah with full consciousness and do not let death overtake you but in the state of Islam" (3:102).

Hadith No. 14 (Dwellers of Hell)

There existed a certain brave and courageous man who appeared to be one of the finest representatives of the Muslims during a military expedition led by the Prophet. The Prophet however looked upon him and said, 'Whoever wants to see a dweller of Hell should look at this man'. Someone from among the Muslims followed the man and found him to be amongst the toughest of all in the fighting against the non-believers until he became seriously injured; at this point he committed suicide by pricking an arrow through his shoulder. The man who witnessed this rushed to the Prophet and declared: 'I bear witness that you are the Prophet of Allah'. The Prophet asked as to what had happened. So he recounted the whole story from the Prophet's observation of his final destination to his suicide. The Prophet then, said: "A man acts sinfully but he is actually a dweller of Paradise; and a man acts righteously but he is a dweller of Hell; the deeds that count are ones done towards the end of [one's] life."[60]

The chain of this report is: Saʿīd ibn Abī Maryam (d.224 AH) from Abū Ghassān Muḥammad ibn Muṭarrif (d.160 AH) from Abū Ḥāzim Salamah ibn Dīnār (d.144 AH) from Sahl ibn Saʿd (d.99 AH). All these narrators are highly reliable.

This tradition is similar to hadith no. 13 in that it describes the Prophet's prophecy that the man's destination would be Hell and how this was proven true when he eventually committed suicide. However it contains one additional piece of information, the Prophet's statement that whether one acts righteously or not, this ultimately has no bearing on one's final destination, for it is what one does at the end of one's life that determines whether one will enter either Paradise or Hell. Hence man's final destination is consequent upon the nature of his last actions in life.

People have unnecessarily read into this statement corroboration for the predetermination of human destiny theory whereas all it simply says is that the outward does not necessarily reflect the inner. A man may be famous for his piety and good actions, but he might not be sincere in his beliefs and acts; sooner or later he will be exposed committing those sins which lead him to Hell. It should be noted that someone who habitually sins but feels remorse for his evil deeds and who may at times try to change his life by turning over a new leaf is not in the same category. His concern and effort to change and repent will one day materialize and he will be helped by Allah to repent and live a good life hence assuring his entry into Paradise. In other words, the basic element which determines one's fate is sincerity or hypocrisy.

Hadith No. 15 (Position of a Solemn Vow)

ʿAbd Allāh ibn ʿUmar reports that the Prophet prohibited making a solemn vow (*al-nadhar*) and said: "It does not cause anything to happen; it rather serves as a way to extract wealth from the miser."[61]

The chain of this report is: Abū Nuʿaym al-Faḍl ibn Dukayn (d.219 AH) from Sufyān ibn ʿUyaynah (d.198 AH) from Manṣūr ibn al-Muʿtamir (d.132 AH) from ʿAbd Allāh ibn Murrah al-Hamdānī (d.100 AH) from ʿAbd Allāh ibn ʿUmar (d.73 AH). All the reporters are highly authentic.

Al-Bukhārī has recorded the same tradition in *kitāb al-aymān wa al-nudhūr*. Its chain is the same with the exception of al-Bukhārī's direct source. Here the source is Khallād ibn Yaḥyā (d.213 AH).[62]

It is not clear why al-Bukhārī has included this tradition in *kitāb al-qadar* for it would have been sufficient to include it in the chapter on oaths and vows. It is likely that he wanted to convey the message that nothing can cause anything to happen except by way of *al-qadar* (predetermined human destiny).

In terms of the hadith itself it would seem that the Prophet was instructing people to keep away from making vows due to the frivolous nature of this act. Essentially, there is no room in Islam for anything meaningless and when one makes a vow one is apparently in effect offering a bribe to Allah stating if 'You do this for me, I will do that for You'. For example one may plead "O Allah! Please, give me a promotion in my job and I will feed one hundred poor people." This is not allowed for it allows one to imagine that Allah might fulfill one's wish in exchange for something. In order to implore Allah, Muslims have been taught to pray earnestly to Him. Whereas invocation is desirable and indeed rather highly appreciated, vows are not, and definitely reprehensible. Another reason behind the prohibition of vows is their pagan origin. Arabs in the pre-Islamic era used to give a kind of spiritual bribe to their deities.

We need to distinguish however, between this type of vow and that mentioned in verse 76:7 of the Qur'an: "They fulfill their vows and they fear the day whose evil will be wide-spreading." This verse not only allows but it also admires those who fulfill their vows. The reference here is not to the bribe-like vows mentioned in the hadith but to the vows that a Muslim automatically makes as a faithful servant of Allah. Obedience to Allah and His Prophet, taking care of the unfortunate, honoring one's words in daily transactions, these are the most desirable and hence appreciable vows.

Hadith No. 16 (The Role of Vows)

> The Prophet said [that Allah said], "Vowing does not bring to the son of Adam anything I have not already written in his fate, but vowing is imposed on him by way of fore ordainment. Through vowing I make a miser spend of his wealth."[63]

The chain of this report is: Bishr ibn Muḥammad (d.224 AH) from ʿAbd Allāh ibn al-Mubārak from Maʿmar ibn Rāshid from Hammām ibn Munabbih from Abū Hurayrah. All the narrators are reliable.

The message in this tradition is the same as that in the previous one (hadith no. 15). The emphasis here is on the position of Allah's determination. Undoubtedly, nothing can happen without the command of Allah. The wording of the report suggests that it is a *ḥadīth qudsī* (the sayings of the Prophet Muhammad as revealed to him by Allah). But there is no reference to this in the report. The use of the first person "I" cannot be in this case referring to the Prophet because he is not the one who determines destiny. Surprisingly, al-Bukhārī did not notice this.

Hadith No. 17 (The Power of Allah)
Abū Mūsā al-Ashʿarī says:

> We were in a military expedition under the leadership of the Prophet. Whenever we climbed and descended the valley, we raised our voice in glorifying Allah. The Prophet came close to us and said: "O people! Relax, be lenient to yourselves. You are not invoking the deaf and the absent, but you are entreating the All-Hearing, the All-Seeing." Then he said: "O ʿAbd Allāh ibn Qays! Should I not teach you an utterance, which is from among the treasures of Paradise. The utterance is: 'There is no might nor power but with Allah'."[64]

The chain of this report is: Muḥammad ibn Muqātil (d.226 AH) from ʿAbd Allāh ibn al-Mubārak from Khālid ibn Mihrān al-Ḥadhdhā' (d.141 AH) from ʿAbd al-Raḥmān ibn Mull Abū ʿUthmān al-Nahdī from Abū Mūsā al-Ashʿarī. All the reporters except Khālid al-Ḥadhdhā' are reliable. Some Hadith scholars have expressed doubt about Khālid's authenticity. Abū Ḥātim says: "His traditions are written but not used for argument. Aḥmad ibn Ḥanbal never paid attention to a tradition which contained the name of Khālid al-Ḥadhdhā' in its chain; he never heard anything from Abū ʿUthmān al-Nahdī."[65]

It has been reported by Khālid al-Ḥadhdhā' from Abū ʿUthmān al-Nahdī. As mentioned, Khālid never heard anything from the latter. In this case, the report is not a direct transmission of Khālid from his disclosed source. But his name does not render the report unreliable. Al-Bukhārī has recorded the same report through different chains in five additional places.[66] All the reporters of these chains are highly reliable.

There are three evident messages in this tradition. First, the faithful believer has always to remember Allah regardless of the situation. Second, the remembrance of Allah should not cause any harm to man hence one's voice in glorifying Allah should be moderate as Allah can hear if man remembers Him in his heart. Third, the statement, "There is no might nor power but with Allah," constitutes a basic component of Islamic faith. The wisdom behind the inclusion of this report in *kitāb al-qadar* is not intelligible for there does not appear to be any ostensible link between this report and the concept of *al-qadar* as subscribed to by al-Bukhārī.

Hadith No. 18 (Protection of Allah)

The Prophet said: "No successor came to power in succession but he was surrounded by two kinds of retinues, one advising and encouraging him to do good, and the other advising and compelling him to do evil; the one who is protected is only he who is protected by Allah."[67]

The chain of this report is: ʿAbdān ʿAbd Allāh ibn ʿUthmān from ʿAbd Allāh ibn al-Mubārak from Yūnus ibn Yazīd from Muḥammad ibn al-Shihāb al-Zuhrī from Abū Salamah ibn ʿAbd al-Raḥmān ibn ʿAwf (d.94 AH) from Abū Saʿīd al-Khudrī (d.74 AH). All the reporters of this chain are reliable.

Al-Bukhārī has also recorded this report in *kitāb al-aḥkām* on the authority of the same Companion but with a slight difference in the chain.[68]

This tradition conveys several messages both to people in general and to authorities in particular. First, man is normally surrounded by two categories of people, the good and the bad. Second, good people help him to do good things and bad friends encourage him to commit evil deeds. Third, this situation is equally applicable to people in power. Fourth, man whether ordinary or powerful is too weak to identify those who bode him well and those who seek to be his enemy. Fifth, man may easily be deceived by his bad companions. Sixth, man is always in need of Allah's help. Seventh, only Allah can help man to keep safe from the conspiracies of his enemies. Political history, corruption, and intrigue stand witness to the veracity of the Prophet's statement. Corridors of power are not immune and kings, monarchs, rulers and dictators have all succumbed to the deception of evil elements circulating amongst them, causing them to deviate from the right path and ultimately lose their lives. True indeed is the Prophet's statement that "the one who is protected is only he who is protected by Allah." Only Allah can save man from falling into his own people's trap.

Hadith No. 19 (Sexual Pleasure is Predetermined)

The Prophet said:

> Verily Allah has written for Adam's son [humans] the pleasure of sexual liaison, which he will definitely receive; the sexual liaison of the eye is sight, [and] that of the tongue conversation, the human self desires and craves it and the sexual organ confirms it and rebuts it.[69]

The chain of this report is: Maḥmūd ibn Ghaylān (d.239 AH) from ʿAbd al-Razzāq ibn al-Hammām from Maʿmar ibn Rāshid from ʿAbd Allāh ibn Ṭāwūs (d.142 AH) from his father Ṭāwūs ibn Kaysān from ʿAbd Allāh ibn ʿAbbās from Abū Hurayrah. All these reporters are highly authentic.

The beginning of the report contains an observation by ʿAbd Allāh ibn ʿAbbās that: "I did not find any other example of very minor sin more suitable than the one cited in the report narrated by Abū Hurayrah from the Prophet." The message being given thus concerns the issue of minor sinful acts committed in relation to an illicit sexual relationship. Exploring the beauty of a woman other than one's wife, becoming involved with her in unnecessary conversation, desiring to become closer to her, all these constitute forerunners to a final sexual act. As long as these minor acts of pleasure do not ultimately lead to an affair, they fall under the category of minor sin, and of course if they do result in sex, then they all constitute major sin. The sexual act itself, whether in its minor or major form, is full of inherent joy and pleasure, elements placed in the human instinct by Allah and it is to fulfill this natural urge for pleasure that man is attracted to the opposite sex. Any kind of contact between men and women, whether physically or visually, brings ecstasy to both. It is this simple fact which has been highlighted in the tradition.

Ibn Ḥajar believes that the act of sexual liaison has been predetermined for man. Hence man cannot escape his destiny and the predestined act of illicit sex will definitely take place in man's life. In support he advances Ibn Baṭṭāl's view that

> Everything that Allah has written for man already existed in His knowledge hence man is bound to be overtaken by written destiny; man, indeed, does not find any way to keep it away from him; when he commits a prohibited act, he stands condemned because destiny is hidden from him and he is at the same time empowered to act righteously. Thus, the view of the Qadarites and Jabarites becomes rebutted.[70]

Ibn Baṭṭāl goes too far in defense of his view and in the refutation of others. Why does he derive from wherever possible only one message, that Allah has predetermined man's life with all its activities and minute details? The tradition itself simply asserts that pleasure through sexual behavior is ingrained in human nature. Man derives great pleasure from looking at, speaking to, and touching a woman. This enjoyment is not man-made. It is God-made.

One may ask however why minor pleasurable acts have been termed by the Prophet as *zinā* (sexual liaison). This is allegorical. Man is aroused and gains sexual pleasure not only by the final act of intercourse but also equally by all the acts occurring before it. ʿAbd Allāh ibn Masʿūd has said that, "the eyes enjoy sex with sight; the lips commit sex with a kiss; the hands delight sexually by touch; the legs feel ecstatic with walking to the place of sexual liasion."[71]

Ibn Ḥajar finds another clue in the report to support the theory of predetermined destiny. Concerning the statement "the human self desires and craves it; and the sexual organ confirms it and rebuts it," he states:

> what flows from here is that the man himself does not create his act. He desires, for instance, to have sex but, at times, the sexual organ does not obey him in this; he finds himself incapable due to an unknown reason. If man was the creator of his act, he would never fail to fulfill his desire. It is proven by this that a human act is consequent upon [a] forewritten destiny, which either enables man to fulfill the act or snatches away his ability to do so.[72]

Although Ibn Ḥajar derives this interpretation, this is not the meaning of the statement. The statement initially mentions that the human self desires and hence does many things in advance to maximize pleasure. These acts prior to sex may or may not lead to copulation. The reference in this statement is to the final act of sexual intercourse through which man receives optimum pleasure. In the case of intercourse the act turns into a major sin; and if the sexual act cannot take place, all the acts preceding it will remain under the category of minor sin, which are generally forgiven due to one reason or another.

Hadith No. 20 (The Cursed Tree)

Commenting on *āyah* 17:60 "...and so We have ordained that the vision which We have shown thee – as also the tree [of Hell,] cursed in this Qur'an – shall be but a trial for men..." ʿAbd Allāh ibn ʿAbbās explained that it referred to "the actual vision that the Prophet saw with his [own] eyes during his nocturnal journey to Jerusalem and not a dream; and the cursed tree [mentioned] in the Qur'an [was] the tree of *Zaqqūm*."[73]

The chain of this report is: ʿAbd Allāh ibn al-Zubayr al-Ḥumaydī (d.219 AH) from Sufyān ibn ʿUyaynah from ʿAmr ibn Dīnār (d.126 AH) from ʿIkramah ibn ʿAbd Allāh (d.106 AH) from ʿAbd Allāh ibn ʿAbbās. All these narrators are highly reliable.

This is not a tradition of the Prophet but a statement attributed to ʿAbd Allāh ibn ʿAbbās who was a great scholar of the Qur'an. The report presents his interpretation of āyah 17:60 which refers to the Prophet's night journey from Makkah to Jerusalem as a dream. Ibn ʿAbbās interprets it as a true vision which Allah showed the Prophet. This miraculous journey seemed unbelievable for people and the Prophet's announcement in effect served as a litmus test for many in Makkah. There were those who believed in the truthfulness of the claim and those who rejected it as mere concoction. According to the *āyah*, the cursed tree mentioned in the Qur'an – 37:62; 44:43; and 56:52 – as the tree of *Zaqqūm* also served as a test for the people.

The wisdom behind the inclusion of this report in *kitāb al-qadar* is doubtful. Ibn al-Tīn seems to have identified why, writing that the "reason for its inclusion here in this chapter is [that] it indicates that Allah takes away from non-believers, due to their rejection of the truth, the ability to see the truth in the message of the Prophet."[74] This explanation contrasts with the concept of test as stated in the *āyah* itself. If the vision took place with a view to testing people as to whether they accepted the Prophet as the true Messenger of God, it would not have been an imposition. A test entails freedom of thought and choice and one should keep in mind that due to their God-given freedom of thought and choice the same Arabs who had rejected the Prophet's message initially submitted to God later on.

Hadith No. 21 (Adam and Moses Debate)
The Prophet said:

> Adam and Moses argued. Moses said to Adam: "O Adam! You are our father. You disappointed us and caused our expulsion from Paradise." Adam said to Moses: "O Moses, Allah had chosen you for direct conversation and written with His hand the message. Do you blame me for something Allah had determined about me forty years before my creation?" The Prophet repeated the statement – "Adam argued with Moses" thrice.[75]

The chain of this report is: ʿAlī ibn ʿAbd Allāh al-Madāʾinī from Sufyān ibn ʿUyaynah from ʿAmr ibn Dīnār from Ṭāwūs ibn Kaysān from Abū Hurayrah. All these reporters are highly authentic. Al-Bukhārī has recorded the same report in four additional places on the authority of Abū Hurayrah however with a different chain of narrators.[76]

This report is objectionable on several counts. Firstly, Moses addresses Adam by name and it is not befitting for a prophet to address his father by his name. This runs counter to the principle of *iḥsān* (excellent treatment) given to all the prophets including Moses (2:83). Second, a son is not supposed to condemn the father for his error. If he is bound to refer to his father's mistake, he has to apply once again the principle of *iḥsān*. Moses's words are very harsh and unbecoming of a pious son towards a pious father. Third, why did Moses condemn Adam for something for which Allah had forgiven him? It is well known that after repentance a person should not be reminded of his past errors. Fourth, why did Moses blame Adam? Was he unaware that it was Satan who lured Adam into breaking the rule? In fact Allah has categorically mentioned that it was Satan who caused Adam to be expelled from Paradise: "O children of Adam! Do not allow Satan to seduce you in the same way as he caused your parents to be driven out of Paradise" (7:27).

Since Moses received revelation, he must have been informed of Satan's role in Adam's expulsion from the Garden. According to Allah, Satan is to be blamed for this, not Adam, and yet, according to the report, Moses blames Adam. This is strange and rather unbelievable.

In response to objections raised against the report al-Māzarī, a commentator of Muslim's work, refers to various interpretations.[77] 1) A son may be allowed on certain occasions to condemn his father. May be so, but this does not explain why Moses found himself obliged to condemn Adam and indeed there is no need to speculate on this either. 2) The law (shariʿah) of both Adam and Moses differed therefore no problem existed with regard to a son blaming his father. This is inapplicable for the parent-children relationship is an eternal one, inherent in human nature from time immemorial, and Allah must have revealed the principles of this relationship to all his prophets. Furthermore, as we saw earlier the concept of *iḥsān* already existed in Moses's law and governed the relationship of the two parties. 3) Moses's blame of Adam is ineffective and causes no harm for Adam no longer resides in the world of responsibility but in the Hereafter. Ibn ʿAbd al-Barr conjectures that Moses's blaming of Adam was an exception to the rule that "none should be blamed for something against which he has already repented."[78] This is an oft-applied justification in a situation where no rational or moral argument exists. It seems that both al-Māzarī and Ibn ʿAbd al-Barr fail to recall that in the hereafter no one will ever blame the other because empty talk and frivolous acts (*laghwa*), are an impossibility in the hereafter (19:62; 52:23; 56:25; 78:35; 88:11).

One might here refer to prophet Abraham, who also argued with his father (19:41–48), in a bid to justify Moses's questioning of Adam. There is an essential difference between the two cases. Moses condemned Adam for a fault he had already been forgiven for, whereas Abraham did not condemn his pagan father for his idol worship but implored him persuasively to abandon his illogical act of idol worship. Condemnation (*dhamm*) and persuasion (*naṣīḥah*) are two different things. Condemning elders is not desirable but persuading elders to eschew wrong is a highly commendable act.

Al-Ṭībī uses the tradition to reject the views of the Jabarite school, on the one hand, and to condemn Muʿtazilite scholars on the other.[79] This in itself casts suspicion on the genuineness of the tradition and it is not unlikely that it was fabricated in a bid to derail others.

Hadith No. 22 (The Exclusive Rights of Allah)

Muʿāwiyah ibn Abī Sufyān wrote to al-Mughīrah ibn Shuʿbah to write back to him concerning what he had heard the Prophet saying just after the prayer. So Ibn Shuʿbah dictated a response to his scribe, Warrād, and sent this to Ibn Shuʿbah stating that "I heard the Prophet saying just after prayer: 'There is no God except Allah alone, there is no partner with Him; O Allah! None can intercept what You grant; none can give back what You withhold; none's endeavor can be of any help to him against You.'"[80]

The chain of this report is: Muḥammad ibn Sinān (d.223 AH) from Fulayḥ ibn Sulaymān (d.168 AH) from ʿAbdah ibn Abī Lubābah (d.uncertain; after 100 AH) from Warrād (d. uncertain; before 100 AH).

All the narrators are reliable cxcept Fulayḥ ibn Sulaymān. Hadith scholars have expressed their reservation on his authenticity. Yaḥyā ibn Maʿīn states for instance that "...he is weak. His reports do not form the basis of argument," Yaḥyā ibn Saʿīd avoided his reports and al-Nasā'ī, al-Ḥākim and ʿAlī ibn al-Madā'inī considered him weak.[81]

This report has been recorded by al-Bukhārī in three other places.[82] The chains of these three versions are highly reliable.

The Prophet's quoted recitation and utterance immediately following the prayer is a serious reminder that Allah's position in relation to man is always to be remembered. Unlike most other faiths, Islam makes Allah's attributes crystal clear. For instance where in other scriptures He is at times challenged by man, Islam teaches Muslims never to challenge Allah; He is All-Powerful, and everything in the heavens and the earth belongs to Him and is in His dominion. This tradition emphasizes that Allah can release as well as withhold His blessings. No human being can prevent Him from what He decides. But Allah's granting or withholding of His blessings is not a blind act for Allah acts consciously. He blesses those who deserve them and condemns those who do not: "We bestow of Our mercy on whom We please, and We do not cause to be lost the reward of those who do good" (12:56). Being grateful to Allah causes man to increase in His favor whereas ingratitude leads to suffering: "And remember, your Lord caused to be declared: 'If you are grateful, I will increase more favor to you; but if you show ingratitude, truly My punishment is terrible indeed'." (14:7)

The last part of the utterance – "*lā yanfaʿo dha al-jadd minka al-jadd*" – is interpreted variously. Some translate *al-jadd* as wealth, and others as worldly comfort, effort, or grand family lineage.[83] All the meanings appear to carry certain weight and in situations where controversy arises over the meaning of a particular word, the best course of action is to select that meaning which closely maintains the coherence of the statement concerned. Examining the utterance as a whole, one may construe *al-jadd* to mean worldly power and effort thus rendering the whole statement as coherent. In other words the actual meaning would then be: "There is no God except Allah alone, there is no partner with Him; O Allah! None can intercept what You grant; none can give back what You withhold; none's endeavor can be of any help to him against You."

Hadith No. 23 (Seeking Refuge with Allah)

The Prophet said: "Seek refuge with Allah from tortuous effort in life, destructive wretchedness, a tragic end, and the rejoicing of the enemy."[84]

The chain of this tradition is: Musaddad ibn Musarhad (d.228 AH) from Sufyān ibn ʿUyaynah from Sumayy (d.130 AH) from Abū Ṣāliḥ Zakwān (d.101 AH) from Abū Hurayrah. All these reporters are highly authentic.

Al-Bukhārī has also recorded the same tradition in *Kitāb al-Daʿwāt* on the same authority but with a slight variation in the chain. Al-Bukhārī's direct source here is ʿAlī ibn ʿAbd Allāh al-Madā'inī, in place of Musaddad. There is a problem in this report. Sufyān ibn ʿUyaynah states that "the original hadith contained only three things; I added one more; I no longer remember which one I added."[85] The tradition, then, suffers from interpolation (*idrāj*). Since it is not clear what the addition is, it is not safe to be relied upon.

Al-ʿAynī claims that this tradition stands as proof that man is not the creator of his acts. His seeking refuge with Allah, he further argues, illustrates man's inability to prevent hardship and sorrow from affecting him for had he been able to control events around him and prevent evil or harm from touching him man would never have sought refuge with Allah. It is for this reason that al-Bukhārī has quoted verses 113:1–2 from the Qur'an: "Say: 'I seek refuge with the Lord of the daybreak from the evil of what He has created...'," under the subheading under which hadith no. 23 has been recorded in al-Bukhārī. These verses plainly show that Allah is the Creator. Is there any Muslim who could possibly claim to be the creator of anything? Some scholars do believe that man has been given freedom to act and hence to the extent of necessity makes his own decisions and acts accordingly. When the Qur'an and the Hadith are interpreted in the light of theological debates it is a sad reflection upon the nature of scholarship. Neither the Qur'an nor the Hadith address philosophers, connected as they are to the situation prevailing at the time of the Prophet. Man is a vicegerent of this earth. Fixated in the time and place into which he is born, he possesses some power and ability to mould his life and develop it for the better, but his ability to do so is fairly limited. He cannot go beyond a certain demarcated line and is required to seek Allah's help in discharging his duties properly as well as to seek refuge with Allah from what lies beyond his capacity. In sum, this tradition teaches man to always invoke Allah the Almighty to protect him from hardship and evil.

Hadith No. 24 (Allah the Controller of Hearts)

ʿAbd Allāh ibn ʿUmar states: "The Prophet used to quite often swear [take an oath] with these words: 'No, by the One who changes the heart (*lā wa muqallib al-qulūb*)'."[86]

The chain of narrators of this tradition is: Muḥammad ibn Muqātil from ʿAbd Allāh ibn al-Mubārak from Mūsā ibn ʿUqbah (d.141 AH) from Sālim ibn ʿAbd Allāh (d.106 AH) from ʿAbd Allāh ibn ʿUmar. All these narrators are highly authentic. Al-Bukhārī has also recorded this tradition in two additional places.[87] The chains are slightly different but the final authorities are the same i.e. Sālim from his father.

The Prophet invariably took an oath only by Allah and, according to the sources, on different occasions used different words and attributes of Allah in his oaths. Ibn Ḥajar has referred to four such phrases used by the Prophet: (1) by the One in whose Hand is my soul/by the One in whose Hand is the soul of Muhammad, (2) by the One who changes the heart, (3) by Allah, and (4) no, by Allah, then.[88]

The Prophet's practice acted as a guide for his followers that an oath should not be taken in any other manner except by Allah or any of His attributes. There is hardly any apparent link between this hadith as recorded by al-Bukhārī and other *aḥādīth* in *kitāb al-qadar*. This hadith rather strengthens the idea that Allah makes decisions every moment on every matter whatsoever. The predestination theory may not be justified in the light of this hadith. Such discrepancies in Hadith reporting give rise to doubt concerning the authenticity of certain hadith.

Hadith No. 26 (Tragic Death Caused by an Epidemic)

ʿĀ'ishah asked the Prophet about the plague. The Prophet said:

> It was a cause of suffering Allah used to send to whom He willed. But Allah has now made it a source of mercy for the believers. Anyone who is in a town afflicted with the plague and does not leave it out of patience and hoping for Allah's reward; he knows that nothing will

befall him except what Allah has destined for him, and he also knows that one who dies of the plague in this situation will be rewarded like the martyr.[89]

The chain of this report is: Isḥāq ibn Ibrāhīm from al-Naḍr ibn Shamayyil (d.204 AH) from Dāwūd ibn Abī al-Furāt (d.167 AH) from ʿAbd Allāh ibn Buraydah (d.105 AH) from Yaḥyā ibn Yaʿmar (d.89 AH) from ʿĀ'ishah. All the reporters of this chain are highly authentic.

Al-Bukhārī has recorded the same report in two more places on the authority of ʿĀ'ishah, but with slightly different chains.[90]

Islam advises its adherents to be patient in all situations. A town afflicted with an epidemic is often cut off from the outside world and under quarantine no one may enter or leave it. People live in fear of the fatal disease. Of course only Allah can save people from this scourge. If inhabitants choose to flee who would remain to take care of the sick and dying? Muslims believe that death is bound to overtake them, thus escaping a diseased town does not guarantee an escape from death. Humanity matters tremendously in the teachings of Islam.

This tradition of the Prophet advises believers to place their trust in Allah and invites them to always remember that the source of life and death is Allah alone. Undoubtedly, the faithful believer always stands to gain and never loses. He gains in life and loses nothing in death, rewarded magnificently and deservedly in the Hereafter. So, one who dies of the plague whilst bearing patiently and hoping for Allah's blessing for his suffering will be rewarded on the Day of Judgment with the reward of a martyr. The word martyr is significant; it implies great self-sacrifice, one who makes an utmost endeavor to serve Islam and when the time comes, is prepared to lay down his life for Allah's message. This causes him to be termed *shahīd*. Believers try their best to help those afflicted with an epidemic. They do not fear death as they believe that death and life are in the hands of Allah. Of course whilst taking care of the sick they may succumb to the disease and this is the great sacrifice they make. Serving humanity sincerely is a great cause. This is why one who dies of disease while serving patients deserves special treatment in the Hereafter.

This hadith does not fit into the theme al-Bukhārī has proposed. It rather goes against that theme. Even great commentators like Ibn

Ḥajar and al-ʿAynī failed to justify the inclusion of this hadith in the Chapter.

Hadith No. 27 (Allah's Will)
Al-Barā' ibn ʿĀzib reports:

> I saw the Prophet carrying the soil along with us on a day during the battle of Khandaq; he sang: "By God, if it were not the will of Allah we would not be guided to the right path, nor would we be able to pray or fast. O Allah! Send down to us peace of mind and make us strong in the unwanted battle imposed by the pagans who have oppressed us."[91]

The chain of this tradition is: Abū al-Nuʿmān Muḥammad ibn al-Faḍl (d.224 AH) from Jarīr ibn Ḥāzim (d.170 AH) from Abū Isḥāq ʿAmr ibn ʿAbd Allāh (d.129 AH) from al-Barā' ibn ʿĀzib (d.72 AH). All these reporters are highly authentic.

Al-Bukhārī has recorded the same report in four additional places on the authority of al-Barā' ibn ʿĀzib, but with slightly different chains.[92]

These poetic lines represent the true spirit of the Qur'an: (1) "Praise be to Allah Who has guided us to this felicity: never could we have found guidance, had it not been for the guidance of Allah" (7:43), (2) "Allah sent down His tranquility to His Messenger and to the believers" (48:26), (3) "They prayed: 'Our Lord! Pour out constancy on us and make our steps firm: help us against those who reject faith'" (2:250), (4) "And fight them on until there is no more persecution, and religion becomes Allah's in its entirety" (8:39).

These beautiful lines of poetry then reflect the concern of the Prophet and his earnest entreaty to Allah. The tradition teaches us how to appeal to Allah. The first part is a *duʿā'* in praise of Allah followed by a reference to need. Invocations to Allah speak not only of one's wishes but also form a practical approach to life. One has to do one's best to remain firmly on the true path and must also be aware that guidance is not earned by man but is exclusively Allah's gift and a great privilege. In the same vein tranquility also descends from on high. Victory and failure are both in the hands of Allah, hence it is Allah alone who is to be entreated. Man must not exult or feel arrogant for his faith, his possessions or his achievements, for all that he has, has been granted by Allah and arrogance and self-righteousness of this sort may cause him to lose everything as well as his true belief and sincerity.

When the Prophet stated: "Never could we have found guidance, had it not been for the guidance of Allah" this is not to be misconstrued. When Allah sent down the Qur'an, He already provided the whole of humanity with what it needed for guidance. Man's role then and now has been to read, understand and apply it, indeed Allah has equipped humanity with the capacity, ability and prowess to do so. Without the Qur'an, man, however intelligent and powerful he might be, can never reach the level of guidance that it defines for even if he were to develop something on his own in the name of guidance, it would be akin to mere groping in the dark. Persecution is the scourge of humanity and liberation from persecution at the hands of the persecutor has always been one of the main objectives of all Allah's prophets: "We sent Our Messengers with clear signs, and sent down with them the Book and the Balance so that humanity might stand with justice" (57:25). The Last Prophet wanted to bring peace and justice to mankind whilst the pagans insisted on persecution of people. In order to achieve his goal the Prophet Muhammad had to resort to military action. Islam has not come to be subdued but it has come to enlighten mankind so as to ensure justice for humanity.

NOTES

CHAPTER 1

1. Ibn al-Athīr, ʿIz al-Dīn, *Al-Kāmil fī al-Tārīkh* (Beirut: Dār Iḥyā' al-Turāth al-ʿArabī, 1989), vol.2, pp.277–278.
2. Fallatah, Umar ibn Hasan Uthman, *Al-Waḍʿ fī al-Ḥadīth* (Damascus: Maktabah al-Ghazāly, 1981), vol.1, p.183.
3. Ahmad Amin, *Fajr al-Islām*, 5th edn.(Cairo: Compilation, Translation, and Publication Committee Press, 1930), p.258; Abu Zahw, Muhammad, *Al-Ḥadīth wa al-Muḥaddithūn*, 1st edn.(Cairo: 1958), p.480.
4. Muslim, ibn al-Ḥajjāj al-Qushayrī, *Ṣaḥīḥ* (Beirut: Dār Iḥyā' al-Turāth al-ʿArabī, 2000), "Muqaddimah," report no. 1–4.
5. Abu Shahbah, Muhammad, *Al-Isrā'iliyyāt wa al-Mawḍūʿāt fī al-Tafsīr* (Cairo: Majmaʿ al-Buḥūth al-Islāmiyyah, 1973), pp.32–34.
6. Subhi al-Salih, *ʿUlūm al-Ḥadīth wa Muṣṭalaḥuhu* (Beirut: Dār al-ʿIlm li al-Malāyīn, 1959), pp.266–267.
7. Ibn al-Jawzī, ʿAbd al-Raḥmān ibn ʿAlī, "*Kitāb al-Mawḍūʿāt*" (Beirut: Dār al-Kutub al-ʿIlmiyyah, 1995), vol.1, pp.328–329.
8. Ibid., p.330.
9. Ibid., p.331.
10. Ibid.
11. Ibid., p.334.
12. Ibid., p.335.
13. Ibid., p.338.
14. Ibid.
15. Ibid., p.323.
16. Ibn al-Athīr, vol.2, p.76.
17. Ibn al-Jawzī, "*Kitāb al-Mawḍūʿāt*," vol.1, p.325.
18. Ibid., p.254.
19. Ibid., p.259.
20. Ibid., pp.268–271.
21. Ibid., p.277.
22. Ibid., p.278.
23. Ibid., p.286.
24. Ibid., vol.2, p.290.
25. Ibid., vol.1, p.17.
26. Ibid., pp.352–353.
27. Ibid., p.15.
28. Ibid.
29. Ibid.
30. Ibid., p.64.

31. Ibid., p.146.
32. Ibid., p.404.
33. Ibid., p.396.
34. Ibid., p.375.
35. Ibid., p.90.
36. Ibid., p.206.
37. Ibid., p.207.
38. Ibid., p.16.
39. Ibid., pp.84–87.
40. Ibid., p.200.
41. Ibid., p.202.
42. Ibid., p.203.
43. Ibid., p.204.
44. Ibid., p.205.
45. Ibid., vol.2, p.22.
46. Ibid., p.23.
47. Ibid., vol.1, p.354.
48. Ibid., vol.2, pp.189–227.
49. Ibid., p.245.
50. Ibid., p.252.
51. Ibid., p.254.
52. Ibid., p.188.
53. Ibid.
54. Ibid., vol.1, p.20.
55. Ibid., p.22.
56. Ibid.
57. Ibid., p.142.
58. Ibid., p.143.
59. Ibid., pp.241–242.
60. Muslim, "*Kitāb Faḍā'il al-Ṣaḥābah*," tradition no.2542.
61. Ibn al-Jawzī, "*Kitāb al-Mawḍūʿāt*," vol.1, pp.350–351.
62. Ibid., p.17.
63. Ibid., p.18.
64. Ibid., vol.2, p.347.
65. Ibid., p.182.
66. Ibid., pp.33–67.
67. Ibid., p.30.
68. Ibid., vol.2, p.166.
69. Ibid., pp.340–345.
70. Ibid., vol.1, pp.357–372.
71. Muslim, "Muqaddimah," p.51.
72. Ibid., p.52.
73. Ibid.
74. Ibid., p.50.
75. Ibid.
76. Ibid., pp.50–51.
77. Ibid., p.51.
78. Ibid.
79. Ibid.
80. Ibid.
81. Ibn al-Jawzī, "*Kitāb al-Mawḍūʿāt*," vol. 1, p.25.
82. Ibid.
83. Ibid.

CHAPTER 2

1. Fallatah, *Al-Waḍʿ fī al-Ḥadīth* (Damascus: Maktabah al-Ghazāly, 1981), vol.1, p.178.
2. Abū Dāwūd, Sulaymān ibn al-Ashʿath, *Sunan* (Beirut: Dār al-Kutub al-ʿIlmiyyah, 1996), vol.3, "*Kiāb al-Adab*," hadith no.5180.
3. Ibid., hadith no.5183.
4. Fallatah, vol.1, p.180.
5. Muslim, *Ṣaḥīḥ* (Beirut: Dār al-Ma ʿrifah, 1997, with the commentary by al-Nawawī), vol.1, "Muqaddimah," p.39, hadith no.21.
6. Ibid., pp.39–40, hadith nos.22–24.
7. Muslim, vol.1, "Muqaddimah," p.44, hadith no.27.
8. Ibid., pp.44–45, hadith nos.28–29.
9. Ibid., pp.45–46, hadith no.30.
10. Ibid., pp.46–47, hadith no.32.
11. Ibid., pp.48–49, under hadith no.32.

12. Al-ʿAsqalānī, Ibn Ḥajar, Aḥmad ibn ʿAlī, *Hadiyy al-Sārī* (Riyadh: Dār al-Salām, n.d.), p.8.
13. Kamil Muhammad, Muhammad Uwaydah, *Aʿlām al-Fuqahā' wa al-Muḥaddithīn: Al-Imām al-Bukhārī* (Beirut: Dār al-Kutub al-ʿIlmiyyah, 1992), p.9.
14. Kamil Muhammad, *Aʿlām al-Fuqahā' wa al-Muḥaddithīn: Muslim ibn al-Ḥajjāj* (Beirut: Dār al-Kutub al-ʿIlmiyyah, 1995), p.14.
15. Tahan, Mahmud, *Taysīr Muṣṭalaḥ al-Ḥadīth* (Kuwait: Maktabah Dār al-Turāth, 1984), pp.34–35.
16. Ibn Kathīr, Abū al-Fidā Ismāʿīl, *Al-Bāʿith al-Ḥathīth*, 4th edn. Ahmad Muhammad Shakir, ed. (Beirut: Dār al-Kutub al-ʿIlmiyyah, 1994), p.19.
17. Ibid., p.42.
18. Ibn Kathīr, p.20.
19. Tahan, p.146.
20. Ibid.
21. Al-Suyūṭī, Jalāl al-Dīn, *Tadrīb al-Rāwī* (Beirut: Dār al-Kutub al-ʿIlmiyyah, 1989), vol.1, p.252.
22. Al-Khair Abadi, Muhammad Abul Laith, *Takhrīj al-Ḥadīth: Nash'atuhu wa Manhajuhu* (Kuala Lumpur: Dār al-Shākir, 1999), pp.268–274.
23. Ibid., p.265.
24. Mālik ibn Anas, *Al-Muwaṭṭa'* (Beirut: Dār Iḥyā' al-Turāth al-ʿArabī, 1985), vol.1, "*Kitāb al-Zakāh*," tradition no.52.
25. Muslim, vol.4, "*Kitāb al-Zakāh*," tradition nos.2275–2279.
26. Al-Khair Abadi, p.265. The example is not correct because what is referred to as addition is not addition but the part of the original statement of the Prophet. Al-Khair Abadi relies for this contention on al-Tirmidhī who claims that the words "from the Muslims" form addition. Vide, al-Timidhī, *Sunan*, "*Kitāb al-Zakāh*," tradition no.675.
27. Muslim, vol. 4, "*Kitāb al-Zakāh,*" tradition no.2377.
28. Al-Khair Abadi, p.266. He has used this tradition as an example of confusion (*iḍṭirāb*) because Ibn ʿAbd al-Barr (d.463 AH) has declared the tradition as *muḍṭ arab*. On what basis he considers all these five traditions as one. Probably these are really five, and not only one.
29. Abū Dāwūd, "*Kitāb al-Ṣalāh*," tradition no.970.
30. Al-Suyūṭī, *Tadrīb al-Rāwī*, vol.1, p.268.
31. Al-Khair Abadi, p.267.
32. Ibn al-Jawzī, "*Kitāb al-Mawḍūʿāt*," vol.1, "Muqaddimah," p.23.
33. Ibid., pp.11–14.
34. Al-Dumayni, Misfir Ghuram Allah, *Maqāyīs Naqd Mutūn al-Sunnah* (Riyadh: self published by the author, 1403 AH), pp.55–56.
35. Ibid., pp.69–70.
36. Ibid., p.90
37. Ibid. p.96.
38. Ibid., p.121.
39. Ibid., p.139.

40. Ibid., p.144.
41. Ibid., p.146.
42. Ibid., p.150.
43. Ibid., p.156.
44. Ibid., pp.167–180.
45. Ibid., p.185.
46. Ibid. p.196.
47. Ibid., p.208.
48. Ibid., p.124.
49. Ibid., p.310.
50. Ibid., p.352.
51. Ibid., p.384.
52. Ibid., p.406.
53. Ibid., pp.439–440.
54. Ibid., p.461.
55. Ibid., p.478.

CHAPTER 3

1. Al-Tirmidhī, Muḥammad ibn ʿĪsā, *Sunan* (Beirut: Dār Iḥyā' al-Turāth al-ʿArabī, 1995), vol.5, "*Kitāb al-Manāqib*," hadith no.3892.
2. Al-Bukhārī, Muḥammad ibn Ismāʿīl, *Ṣaḥīḥ* (Beirut: Dār Iḥyā' al-Turāth al-ʿArabī, 1400 AH), vol.1, "*Kitāb al-ʿIlm*," hadith no.103.
3. Ibid.
4. Muslim, vol.3, "*Kitāb al-Janā'iz*," hadith no.2151.
5. Al-Zarkashī, Badr al-Dīn, *Al-Ijābah*. Said al-Afghani, ed. (Beirut: al-Maktab al-Islāmī, 1980), pp.67–68.
6. Ibid., pp.85–86.
7. Ibid., p.104.
8. Ibid., p.139.
9. Muslim, vol.5, "*Kitāb al-Ṭalāq*," hadith nos.3681–3704.
10. Ibid., hadith no.3694.
11. Al-Qurṭubī, Muḥammad ibn Aḥmad, *Al-Jāmiʿ li Aḥkām al-Qur'ān* (Beirut: Dār al-Kutub al-ʿIlmiyyah, 2000), vol.4, part 7, p.77.
12. Al-Dumayni, Misfir Ghuram Allah, *Maqāyīs Naqd Mutūn al-Sunnah* (Riyadh: Self published by the author, 1403 AH), p.287.
13. Ibid., p.297.
14. Ibn al-Qayyim, Muḥammad ibn Abū Bakr, *Al-Manār al-Munīf fī al-Ṣaḥīḥ wa al-Ḍaʿīf*. Abd al-Fattah Abu Ghuddah, ed. (Ḥalab: Maktab al-Maṭbūʿāt al-Islāmiyyah, 1982), p.80.
15. Al-Bukhārī, vol.2, "*Kitāb al-Anbiyā'*," hadith nos.3357–3358; Muslim, vol.8, "*Kitāb al-Faḍā'il*," hadith no.6097.
16. *Al-Muʿjam al-Wasīṭ*. Ibrahim Mustafa and others, eds. (Istanbul: Al-Maktabah al-Islāmiyyah, n.d.), p.511.
17. Al-Aṣfahānī, al-Rāghib, *Al-Mufradāt fī Gharīb al-Qur'ān* (Beirut: Dār al-Ma ʿrifah, 1998), p.280.
18. Ibn Ḥajar, *Fatḥ al-Bārī* (Riyadh: Dār al-Salām, 2000), vol.6, p.473.
19. Ibn al-ʿArabī, Abū Bakr, *Aḥkām al-Qur'ān* (Beirut: Dār al-Kutub al-ʿIlmiyyah, 1996), vol.3, pp.262–263.
20. Al-Qurṭubī, *Al-Jāmiʿ li Aḥkām al-Qur'ān* (Beirut: Dār al-Kutub al-ʿIlmiyyah, 2000), vol.6, part 11, pp.198–200.
21. Ibn al-Jawzī, *Zād al-Masīr fī ʿIlm al-Tafsīr* (Beirut: Dār al-Kutub al-

ʿIlmiyyah, 2002), vol.3, part 4, pp.266–268.

22. Al-Ālūsī, Al-Sayyid Maḥmūd, *Rūḥ al-Maʿānī* (Beirut: Dār Iḥyā' al-Turāth al-ʿArabī, 1999), vol.9, part 17, pp.85–87.
23. Islahi, Amin Ahsan, *Tadabbur-i-Qur'ān* (Delhi: Taj Company, 1997), vol.5, pp.162–163.
24. Al-Rāzī, Fakhr al-Dīn, *Mafātīḥ al-Ghayb* (Beirut: Dār Iḥyā' al-Turāth al-ʿArabī, 1997), vol.8, p.156.
25. Mawdūdī, Sayyid Abul A'lā, *Tafhīm al-Qur'ān* (Lahore: Idara Tarjuman al-Qur'ān, 1997), vol.3, pp.167–168.
26. Sayyid Qutb, *Fī Ẓilāl al-Qur'ān* (Cairo: Dār al-Shurūq, 1996), vol.4, p.2387.
27. Al-Bukhārī, vol.4, "*Kitāb al-Qadar*," hadith no.6594; Muslim, vol.8, "*Kitāb al-Qadar*," hadith no.6665. The translation given is of the tradition as recorded by Muslim.
28. Proponents of predestination point to two particular verses of the Qur'an: (1) "Dost thou not know that God knows all that occurs in heaven as well as on earth? All this, behold, is in [God's] record: verily, [to know] all this is easy for God" (22:70). (2) No calamity can ever befall the earth, and neither your own selves, unless it be [laid down] in Our decree before We bring it into being: verily, all this is easy for God. [Know this,] so that you may not despair over whatever [good] has escaped you nor exult [unduly] over whatever [good] has come to you: for, God does not love any of those who, out of self-conceit, act in a boastful manner" (57:22–23). However, *āyah* 22:70 simply shows that Allah knows all that exists in the heaven and on earth. His knowledge is preserved in the Book. It in no way conveys a message concerning predestination. As for *āyah* 57:22–23 when understood and interpreted in the light of other *ayāt* which highlight man's freedom to think, choose, and act, it will mean that Allah has outlined laws and principles for the universe, that are immutable and written in the Book. The Book does not contain precise information of each and every event related to man. For example, Mr A suffers burns from a fire on 29th of July 2009 at 3pm at his house number ...etc. Is this event written in the Book with such precise detail? Certainly not. What is written in the Book is that fire burns; whatever comes in contact with fire will get burnt; the fire will not cause anyone, anything, any place to feel cold.
29. Al-Bukhārī, vol.4, "*Kitāb al-Marḍā*," hadith no.5673, and "*Kitāb al-Riqāq*," hadith no.6464; Muslim, "*Kitāb Ṣifāt al-Munāfiqīn*," hadith nos. 7042–7054. The words of the tradition quoted above are from Muslim.

30. Ibn Ḥajar, *Fatḥ al-Bārī*, vol.11, "*Kitāb al-Riqāq*," p.357.
31. Ibid., p.358.
32. Al-Ālūsī, vol.7, part 14, p.502.
33. Ibn ʿAṭṭiyyah, Ibn Ḥajar, *Fatḥ al-Bārī*, vol.11, p.358; Ibn ʿAṭṭiyyah, *Al-Muḥarrar al-Wajīz* (Beirut: Dār al-Kutub al-ʿIlmiyyah, 2001), vol.3, p.391.
34. Al-Bukhārī, vol.2, "*Kitāb al-Jihād wa al-Siyar*," hadith no.2946; Muslim, "*Kitāb al-Īmān*," hadith nos.124–130.
35. Ibn Ḥajar, *Fatḥ al-Bārī*, vol.1, p.105.
36. Al-Nawawī, Muḥy al-Dīn, *Al-Minhāj: Sharḥ Ṣaḥīḥ Muslim* (Beirut: Dār al-Maʿrifah, 1997), vol.1, p.160.
37. Muhammad Asad, *The Message of the Qur'ān* (Gibraltar: Dar al-Andalus, 1980), p.58.
38. Al-Bukhārī, vol. 2, "*Kitāb Aḥādīth al-Anbiyā'*," hadith no.3407; Muslim, vol.8, "*Kitāb al-Faḍā'il*," hadith no.6101.
39. *The Holy Bible* (Authorized King James Version, The Gideons International, 1978), Genesis 32:22–32.
40. Ibn Ḥajar, *Fatḥ al-Bārī*, vol.6, p.538.
41. Ibid.
42. Muslim, vol.8, hadith no.6100.
43. Al-Nawawī, vol.8, p.128.
44. Al-Bukhārī, vol.4, "*Kitab al-Qadar*," hadith no.6614; Muslim, vol.8, "*Kitāb al-Qadar*," hadith nos.6684–6689. The translation given above is based on the report according to Muslim's report no.6684.
45. Ibn Ḥajar, *Fatḥ al-Bārī*, vol.11, p.622.
46. Ibid., p.621.
47. Ibid., p.623.
48. Muslim, vol.9, "*Kitāb Ṣifāt al-Munāfiqīn*," hadith no.6985.
49. Ibid., "*Kitāb al-Tawbah*," hadith no.6942.
50. Ibid., hadith no.6943–6944.
51. Ibid., hadith no.6945.
52. Ibn Mājah, Muḥammad ibn Yazīd al-Qazwīnī, *Sunan* (Beirut: Dār al-Maʿrifah, 1997: along with the commentary of al-Sindī), vol.4, "*Kitāb al-Zuhd*," hadith no.4341.
53. Muslim, vol.4, "*Kitāb al-Zakāt*," hadith no.2348.
54. Al-Nawawī, *Al-Minhāj: Sharḥ Ṣaḥīḥ Muslim*, vol.9, pp.87–88.
55. Muslim, vol.9, "*Kitāb al-Tawbah*," hadith no.6943.
56. Ibid., vol.5, "*Kitāb al-Riḍāʿ*," tradition no.36636; al-Bukhārī, vol.2, "*Kitāb Aḥādīth al-Anbiyā'*," tradition no.3399.
57. Al-Nawawī, vol.5, p.301.
58. Ibid.
59. Al-ʿAynī, Badr al-Dīn, *ʿUmdat al-Qārī: Sharḥ Ṣaḥīḥ al-Bukhārī* (Beirut: Dār al-Kutub al-ʿIlmīyyah, 2001), vol.15, p.291.
60. Ibn Ḥajar, *Fatḥ al-Bārī: Sharḥ Ṣaḥīḥ al-Bukhārī,* vol.6, p.444.
61. Muslim, "*Kitāb al-Salām*," tradition no.2225–2226; al-Bukhārī, vol.4, "*Kitāb al-Ṭibb*," tradition no.5753.

62. Al-ʿAynī, *ʿUmdat al-Qārī: Sharḥ Ṣaḥīḥ al-Bukhārī,* vol.21, p.406.
63. Ibn Ḥajar, *Fatḥ al-Bārī: Sharḥ Ṣaḥīḥ al-Bukhārī,* vol.6, pp.75–78.
64. Al-Zarkashī, Badr al-Dīn, *Al-Ijābah,* Saʿid al-Afghani, ed. (Beirut: Al-Maktab al-Islāmī, 1980), pp.103–104.
65. Ibn Ḥajar, *Fatḥ al-Bārī: Sharḥ Ṣaḥīḥ al-Bukhārī,* vol.6, p.76.

CHAPTER 4

1. The Qur'an, 4:59.
2. Al-Bukhārī, vol.4, "*Kitāb al-Iʿtiṣām bi al-Sunnah,*" Bāb no.20.
3. Muslim, vol.2, "*Kitāb al-Ṣalāh,*" hadith nos.1137–1139.
4. Ibid., hadith nos.1142–1144.
5. Ibid., "*Kitāb al-Ṭaharah,*" hadith no.783.
6. Ibid., hadith no.776; al-Bukhārī, vol.1, "*Kitāb al-Wuḍū',*" hadith no.180.
7. Al-Nawawī, *Al-Minhāj: Sharḥ Ṣaḥīḥ Muslim,* vol.2, pp.261–262.
8. Muslim, vol.3, "*Kitāb al-Janā'iz,*" hadith nos.2146–2150.
9. Ibid., hadith no.2151.
10. Al-Zarkashī, *Al-Ijābah,* p.72.
11. Ibid., pp.76–77.
12. Ibid., p.77.
13. Ibid., pp.81–83.
14. Ibid., p.93.
15. Ibid., p.94.
16. Ibid., p.97.
17. Ibid., p.97.
18. Ibid., p.98.
19. Ibid., p.100.
20. Ibid., pp.109–110.
21. Ibid., pp.110–111.
22. Ibid., p.101.
23. Muslim, vol.6, "*Kitāb al-Aqḍiyah,*" hadith no.4447.
24. Ibid, hadith no.354; al-Bukhārī, vol. 2, "*Kitāb al-Rahn,*" hadith nos.2515–2516.
25. Muslim, vol.8, "*Kitāb al-Qadar,*" hadith no.6712–6715.
26. Muslim, vol.8, "*Kitāb Faḍā'il al-Ṣaḥābah,*" hadith nos.6322–6326; al-Bukhārī, vol.4, "*Kitāb al-Daʿwāt,*" hadith no.6344.
27. For example see, Al-Bukhārī, vol. 4, "*Kitāb al-Daʿwāt,*" hadith nos.6375–6377.
28. Al-Bukhārī, vol.1, "*Kitāb al-Wuḍū',*" hadith no.233; Muslim, vol.6, "*Kitāb al-Qasāmah,*" hadith nos. 4329–4335.
29. Al-Bukhārī, vol.1, "*Kitāb al-Wuḍū',*" hadith no.220; Muslim, vol.2, "*Kitāb al-Ṭahārah,*" hadith nos. 657–659.
30. Al-Bukhārī, vol.1, "*Kitāb al-Wuḍū',*" hadith no.216.
31. Muslim, vol.2, "*Kitāb al-Ṭahārah,*" hadith no.654.
32. Al-Nawawī, *Al-Minhāj: Sharḥ Ṣaḥīḥ Muslim,* vol.6, pp.155–156.
33. The Qur'an, 7:157.
34. Al-Bukhārī, vol.4, "*Kitāb al-Ḥudūd,*" hadith no.6858; Muslim, vol.6, "*Kitāb al-Aymān,*" hadith no.4287.
35. Ibn Ḥajar, *Fatḥ al-Bārī,* vol.12, "*Kitāb al-Ḥudūd,*" p.229.
36. Ibid.

37. Al-Nawawī, *Al-Minhāj: Sharḥ Ṣaḥīḥ Muslim,* vol.6, p.134.
38. Al-Bukhārī, vol.1, "*Kitāb al-Īmān,*" hadith no.30; Muslim, vol.6, "*Kitāb al-Aymān,*" hadith no.4289.
39. Muslim, vol.6, "*Kitāb al-Aymān,*" hadith no.4274.
40. Al-Bukhārī, vol.6, "*Kitāb al-Ḥudūd,*" hadith no.4408.
41. Muslim, vol.5, "*Kitab al-Musāqāt,*" hadith nos.3987–3990.
42. Al-Nawawī, *Al-Minhāj: Sharḥ Ṣaḥīḥ Muslim,* vol.5, "*Kitāb al-Musāqāt,*" p.477.
43. Ibid., p.478.
44. Muslim, vol.5, "*Kitāb al-Musāqāt,*" hadith nos.4014–4018; al-Bukhārī, vol.2, "*Kitāb al-Ijārah,*" hadith no.2281.
45. Ibid., vol.8, "*Kitāb al-Shiʿr,*" tradition nos.5853–5855; Al-Bukhārī, "*Kitāb al-Adab,*" tradition no.6155.
46. Al-Zarkashī, *Al-Ijābah*, p.111.
47. Muslim, vol.8, "*Kitāb Faḍā'il al-Ṣaḥābah,*" tradition nos.6334–6345; al-Bukhārī, "*Kitāb al-Ṣalāh,*" tradition no.453.

CHAPTER 5

1. Al-Zamakhsharī, Maḥmūd ibn ʿUmar, *Al-Kashshāf* (Beirut: Dār al-Kutub al-ʿIlmiyyah, 1995), vol.3, p.287.
2. Muslim, vol.5, "*Kitāb al-Riḍāʿ,*" hadith no.3585–3590.
3. Al-Nawawī, vol.5, pp.273–274.
4. Muslim, vol.5, "*Kitāb al-Riḍāʿ,*" hadith nos.3588–3589.
5. This is the summery developed on the basis of information available under the biographies of Abū Ḥudhayfah, his wife Sahlah bint Suhayl, Sālim. See for the detail, Ibn al-Athīr, *Usd al-Ghābah* (Beirut: Dār al-Ma ʿrifah, 1997), vol.4, pp.416–417 (for Abū Ḥudhayfah), vol.5, pp.316–317 (for Sahlah bint Suhayl), vol.2, pp.260–262 (for Sālim).
6. Muslim, vol.7, "*Kitāb al-Imārah,*" hadith nos.4811–4812.
7. Al-Nawawī, vol.5, p.274.
8. Muslim, vol.5, "*Kitāb al-Riḍāʿ,*" hadith nos.3575–3581. In these traditions three different terms have been used to refer to foster relationship: 1) *al-Maṣṣah*, 2) *al-Raḍʿah*, and 3) *al-Imlājah*. All these three words mean sucking milk directly from the breast.
9. Al-Bukhārī, vol., "*Kitāb aḥādīth al-Anbiyā',*" hadith no.3340 & 3361; Muslim, vol.2, "*Kitāb al-Īmān,*" hadith nos.474–481.
10. Muslim, vol.8, "*Kitāb al-Faḍā'il,*" hadith nos.6109–6110.
11. Al-Bukhārī, vol.1, "*Kitāb al-Ghusl,*" hadith no.278; Muslim, vol.2, "*Kitāb al-Ḥayḍ,*" hadith no.768.
12. Al-Nawawī, vol.8, p.126.
13. Ibn Ḥajar, *Fatḥ al-Bārī*, vol.1, p.501.
14. Muslim, vol.9, "*Kitāb al-Tawbah,*" hadith no.6954.
15. Ibn al-Athīr, *Al-Kāmil fī al-Tārīkh* (Beirut: Dār Iḥyā'

al-Turāth al-ʿArabī, 1994), vol.5, p.394.

16. Muslim, vol.5, "*Kitāb al-Liʿān*," hadith nos.3736–3748.
17. Ibn al-Athīr, op. cit., vol.5, p.394.
18. Muslim, vol.3, "*Kitāb al-Masājid*," hadith nos.1479–1483; al-Bukhārī, vol.1, "*Kitāb al-Adhān*," hadith no.644.
19. Muslim, vol.8, "*Kitāb al-Faḍā'il*," hadith no.6061.
20. Abū Dāwūd, vol.3, "*Kitāb al-Adab*," hadith no.5268.
21. Muslim, vol.3, "*Kitāb al-Masājid*," hadith no.1480.
22. Muhammad Asad, *The Message of the Qur'ān* (Gibraltar: Dar al-Andalus, 1980), p.92.
23. Al-Bukhārī, vol. 2, "*Kitāb al-Jihād*," hadith nos.2788–2789; Muslim, vol.7, "*Kitāb al-Imārah*," hadith no.4911.
24. Ibn al-Athīr, op. cit., vol.5, p.435.
25. Ibn al-Athīr, op. cit., vol.1, p.453.
26. Al-Nawawī, vol.7, p.59.
27. Ibn Ḥajar, *Fatḥ al-Bārī*, vol.11, "*Kitāb al-Isti'dhān*," p.93.
28. Ibid.
29. Ibid.
30. Ibid.
31. Salmā bint ʿAmr ibn Zayd ibn Labīd ibn Kharrāsh ibn ʿĀmir ibn Ghanam ibn ʿUday ibn Najjār; Umm Ḥarām bint Milḥān ibn Khālid ibn Zayd ibn Ḥarām ibn Jundub ibn ʿĀmir ibn Ghanam ibn ʿUday ibn Najjār.
32. Ibid.
33. Ibn ʿAbd al-Barr, Yūsuf ibn ʿAbd Allah, *Al-Istīʿāb fī Maʿrifat al-Aṣḥāb* (Beirut: Dār al-Kutub al-ʿIlmiyyah, 1995), vol.1, p.134.
34. Ibid., p.199.
35. Ibid., vol.4, p.494.
36. Ibid.
37. Ibn al-Athīr, *Usd al-Ghābah*, vol.5, p.456.
38. Abū Ṭalḥah died in 51 AH at the age of 70. It means he was only 21 at the time of his marriage to Umm Sulaym. See for the detail: Ibn al-Athīr, vol.5, pp.19–20.
39. Ibn Ḥajar, *Fatḥ al-Bārī*, vol.11, "*Kitāb al-Isti'dhān*," pp.93–94.
40. The Qur'an, 33:50 declares that the only the Prophet was allowed to marry as many women as he wished; it was not allowed for his followers. There are several tradition making it clear that certain things were only for the Prophet. For example, the Prophet's property was not for distribution among his legal heirs but it belonged to the entire Ummah. See for this, Muslim, vol.6, "*Kitāb al-Jihād*," hadith no.4552.
41. Muslim, vol.7, "*Kitāb al-Imārah*," hadith nos.4811–4812.
42. Muslim, vol.9, "*Kitāb al-Tawbah*," hadith nos.6898–6899.
43. Al-Bukhārī, vol.4, "*Kitāb al-Ḥudūd*," hadith no.6830.
44. Abrogation in the Qur'an is a controversial issue. For a detailed and comprehensive understanding of abrogation in the Qur'an, please see: Khan, Israr Ahmad, *Theory of Abrogation: A Critical*

Evaluation, Research Management Centre, International Islamic University Malaysia, Kuala Lumpur, 2006.) Also see, Dr. Taha J. Alalwani, *Naḥwa Mawqif Qur'ānī min al-Naskh* [Towards a Qur'anic Position on Abrogation] (Egypt: Maktabah al-Shorouk al-Dawliyyah, 2007), in which he rejects the concept of abrogation entirely.

45. Ibn Ḥajar, *Fatḥ al-Bārī*, vol.12, "*Kitāb al-Ḥudūd*," p.192.
46. Mālik ibn Anas, *Al-Muwaṭṭa'* (Beirut: Dār Iḥyā' al-Turāth al-ʿArabī, 1985) vol.2, "*Kitab al-Ḥudūd*," hadith no.10; Al-Nasā'ī, Aḥmad ibn Shuʿayb, *Al-Sunan al-Kubrā* (Beirut: Dār al-Kutub al-ʿIlmiyyah, 1991), vol.4, "*Kitāb al-Rajm*," hadith no.7156.
47. Islahi, vol.5, pp.366–367.
48. Ibid., p.367.
49. Ibn Kathīr, *Tafsīr al-Qur'ān al-ʿAẓīm* (Beirut: Dār Iḥyā' al-Turāth al-ʿArabī, 2000), vol.4, pp.329–330.
50. Al-Bukhārī, vol.1, "*Kitāb al-Ḥayḍ*," hadith no.304; Muslim, vol.1, "*Kitāb al-Īmān*," hadith no.238.
51. Al-Nawawī, vol.1, "*Kitāb al-Īmān*," p.255.
52. Ibn al-Athīr, *Al-Kāmil fī al-Tārīkh*, vol.1, p.586.
53. Muhammad Asad, p.63.
54. Al-Nasā'ī, Aḥmad ibn Shuʿayb, *Sunan* (Beirut: Dār al-Kutub al-ʿIlmīyyah, 1991), vol.5, "*Kitāb ʿIshrat al-Nisā'*," hadith no.8888.
55. Al-Bukhārī, vol.3, "*Kitāb al-Nikāḥ*," hadith no.5069.
56. Muslim, "*Kitāb al-Ṭalāq*," tradition no.3663; al-Bukhārī, vol.3, "*Kitāb al-Ṭalāq*," tradition no.5267.
57. Muslim, "*Kitāb al-Ṭalāq*," tradition no.3664; al-Bukhārī, vol.3, "*Kitāb al-Aṭʿimah*," tradition no.5431.
58. Al-Nawawī, vol.5, pp.317–318.
59. Al-ʿAynī, vol.19, p.358.
60. Islahi, vol.8, pp.457–458.
61. Muslim, "*Kitāb al-Salām*," tradition no.2241 (148–150).

CHAPTER 6

1. *The Holy Bible*, op.cit., Genesis 19:29–38.
2. The Qur'an, 21:74–75.
3. Al-Bukhārī, vol.1, "*Kitāb al-Zakāh*," hadith no.1420.
4. Ibn Saʿd, *Al-Ṭabaqāt al-Kubrā* (Beirut: Dār Iḥyā' al-Turāth al-ʿArabī, 1996), vol.4, part 8, p.269. Ibn al-Athīr says that Sawdah died towards the end of ʿUmar's Caliphate i.e. 23 AH (See, *Usd al-Ghābah*, vol.5, p.319). Whether Sawdah died in 23 AH or in 54 AH, it is clear that she dies after the death of Zaynab bint Jaḥsh.
5. Ibn al-Athīr, *Usd al-Ghābah*, vol.5, p.296.
6. Muslim, vol.8, "*Kitāb Faḍā'il al-Ṣaḥābah*," hadith no.6266.
7. Ibn Ḥajar, *Fatḥ al-Bārī*, vol.3, p.364.

8. Al-Nawawī, vol.8, p.227.
9. Al-Bukhārī, vol.1, "*Kitāb al-Janā'iz*," hadith no.1280.
10. Muslim, vol.5, "*Kitāb al-Ṭalāq*," hadith no.3709.
11. Ibn Ḥajar, *Fatḥ al-Bārī*, vol.3, "*Kitāb al-Janā'iz*," p. 188.
12. Al-Bukhārī, vol.3, "*Kitāb al-Maghāzī*," hadith no.4086.
13. Ibn Hishām, Abū Muḥammad ʿAbd al-Mālik, *Al-Sīrah al-Nabawiyyah* (Beirut: Dār Iḥyā' al-Turāth al-ʿArabī, 1997), vol.2, pp.289–321; Ibn Saʿd, vol.2, part 3, See the list of Muslim combatants on pp.509–515; Ibn Kathīr, *Al-Bidāyah wa al-Nihāyah* (Beirut: Dār al-Maʿrifah, 1997), vol.2, pp.334–345.
14. Ibn Hishām, vol.2, p.322.
15. Ibn Ḥajar, *Fatḥ al-Bārī*, vol.7, "*Kitāb al-Maghazī*," p.477.
16. Al-Bukhārī, vol.2, "*Kitāb al-Buyūʿ*," hadith no.2122.
17. Ibn Ḥajar, *Fatḥ al-Bārī*, vol.4, "*Kitāb al-Buyūʿ*," pp.431–432.
18. Ibid., p.432.
19. Al-Bukhārī, vol.3, "*Kitāb Faḍā'il al-Ṣaḥābah*," hadith no.3696.
20. Muslim, vol.6, "*Kitāb al-Ḥudūd*," hadith no.4432.
21. Al-Bukhārī, vol.3, "*Kitāb Faḍā'il al-Ṣaḥābah*," hadith no.3872.
22. Ibn Ḥajar, *Fatḥ al-Bārī*, vol.7, p.73.
23. Muslim, vol.8, "*Kitāb al-Faḍā'il*," hadith no.6055.
24. Ibid., hadith nos.6049–6052.
25. Al-Nawawī, vol.8, p.102.
26. Ibn Saʿd, vol.2, part 2, p.404.
27. Muslim, vol.8, "*Kitāb al-Faḍā'il*," hadith no.6053.
28. Ibid., hadith no.6050.
29. Ibn ʿAbd al-Barr, vol.1, p.143, 147.
30. Al-Bukhārī, vol.2, "*Kitāb Aḥādīth al-Anbiyā'*," hadith no.3366; Muslim, vol.3, "*Kitāb al-Masājid*," hadith nos.1161–1162.
31. The Qur'an, 22:25–26.
32. Ibn al-Athīr, *Al-Kāmil fī al-Tārīkh*, vol.1, pp.157–158.
33. The Qur'an, 11:71; 12:4–6.
34. The Qur'an, 12:54–56
35. The story of Moses is spread over many chapters of the Qur'an: 2, 7, 10, 17, 20 etc.
36. The Qur'an, 2:251.
37. The Qur'an, 38:30
38. Ibn Ḥajar, *Fatḥal-Bārī*, vol.6, "*Kitāb Aḥādīth al-Anbiyā'*," p.494.
39. Al-Qurṭubī, vol.2, part 4, pp.88–89.
40. Ibn Ḥajar, *Fatḥ al-Bārī*, vol.6, p.495.
41. The Qur'an, 22:26.
42. Al-Nasā'ī, vol.1, "*Kitāb al-Masājid*," hadith no.772.
43. Muslim, vol.8, "*Kitāb al-Faḍā'il*," hadith no.6359.
44. Ibn Hishām, vol.4, pp.50–52; Ibn al-Athīr, *Al-Kāmil fī al-Tārīkh*, vol.1, pp.611–613.
45. *ʿUlamā'* and *Fuqahā'* are all unanimous over the validity of marriage solemnized in a situation where both bride and groom are at different places, even thousands of kilometers away from each other. It was

Negus who solemnized the marriage of Umm Ḥabībah with the Prophet after he received the proposal plus consent of the Prophet from Madinah. Remember, the Negus had accepted Islam.

46. Ibn ʿAbd al-Barr, vol.4, p.484; Ibn al-Athīr, *Al-Kāmil fī al-Tārīkh*, vol.1, pp.582–586.
47. Ibn Hishām, vol.4, p.44.
48. Al-Nawawī, vol.8, p.279.
49. Ibid., p.280.
50. Ibid.
51. Ibid., pp.280–281.
52. Al-Bukhārī, vol.3, "*Kitāb al-Nikāḥ*," hadith no.5114 (al-Bukhārī has not mentioned the name of Maymūnah); Muslim, vol.5, "*Kitāb al-Nikāḥ*," hadith nos.3437–3438.
53. Muslim, vol.5, "*Kitāb al-Nikāḥ*," hadith no.3439.
54. Ibn Ḥajar, *Fatḥ al-Bārī*, vol.9, p.207.
55. Al-Nawawī, vol.5, p.197.
56. Ibid.
57. Muslim, vol.5, "*Kitāb al-Nikāḥ*," hadith nos.3432–3436.
58. Ibn Ḥajar, *Fatḥ al-Bārī*, vol.9, p.207.

CHAPTER 7

1. Ibn al-Jawzī, "*Kitāb al-Mawḍūʿāt*" (Beirut: Dār al-Kutub al-ʿIlmiyyah, 1995), vol.2, pp.63–64.
2. Ibid., pp.65–66. Editor's note: Some of the scholars are of the opinion that when so many of the narrators of a hadith are not reliable, having multiple chains of narrators may grant some degree of authority to render it acceptable.
3. Ibid., pp.39–40.
4. Ibn al-Qayyim, *Al-Manār al-Munīf fī al-Ṣaḥīḥ wa al-Ḍaʿīf*, p.44.
5. Ibid. p.45.
6. Ibn al-Jawzī, "*Kitāb al-Mawḍūʿāt*," vol.1, p.190.
7. Ibid., vol.2, p.350.
8. Ibid.
9. Ibid.
10. Ibid.
11. Ibid., p.347.
12. Ibid., pp.330–331.
13. Ibid., p.330.
14. Ibn al-Qayyim, pp.50–51.
15. Ibn al-Jawzī, "*Kitāb al-Mawḍūʿāt*," vol.2, p.326.
16. Ibid.
17. Ibid.
18. Ibid., vol.1, p.205.
19. Ibid.
20. Ibid., pp.352–353.
21. Ibid., p.353.
22. Ibid., p.354.
23. Ibn al-Qayyim, p.117.
24. Ibn al-Jawzī, "*Kitāb al-Mawḍūʿāt*," vol.1, p.353.
25. Ibid., p.339.
26. Ibid., p.341.
27. Ibid., p.178.
28. Ibid., pp.179–180.
29. Ibid., p.181.
30. Ibid., p.183.
31. Ibid., p.185.
32. Ibid., p.359
33. Ibid., p.357.
34. Ibid., p.374.

CHAPTER 8

1. Ibn Ḥajar, *Hadiyy al-Sārī* (Riyadh: Dār al-Salām, n.d.), pp.12–14.
2. Al-Farāhīdī, Al-Khalīl ibn Aḥmad, *Kitāb al-ʿAyn* (Beirut: Dār Iḥya' al-Turāth al-ʿArabī, 2001), p.772.
3. Al-Aṣfahānī, (Beirut: Dār al-Maʿrifah, 1998), p.395.
4. Al-Fayrūzābādī, Muḥammad ibn Yaʿqūb, *Al-Qāmūs al-Muḥīṭ* (Beiryt: Dār Iḥyā' al-Turāth al-ʿArabī, 1997), vol.1, p.641.
5. Ibn Ḥajar, *Fatḥ al-Bārī* (Riyadh: Maktabah Dār al-Salām, 2000), vol.11, p.582.
6. Ibid.
7. Al-Qasṭalānī, Aḥmad ibn Muḥammad, *Irshād al-Sārī li Sharḥ Ṣaḥīḥ al-Bukhārī* (Beirut: Dār al-Fikr, 1305 AH), vol.9, p.343.
8. Hamzah Muhammad Qasim, *Manār al-Qārī* (Damascus: Maktabah Dār al-Bayān, 1990), part 5, p.307.
9. Ibid.
10. Ibid.
11. Ibn Ḥajar, *Fatḥ al-Bārī*, vol.11, p.582.
12. Al-Bukhārī, *Ṣaḥīḥ Bukhārī*, vol.4, Book 55, hadith no.549.
13. Ibn Ḥajar, *Taqrīb al-Tahdhīb* (Beirut: Dār al-Maʿrifah, 1997), vol.2, p.325 (Hishām); vol.1, p.338 (Shuʿbah), p.319 (Sulaymān), and p.270 (Zayd).
14. Please, visit http://www.nlm. nih. gov/medlineplus/ency/article/ 002398.htm. The title of the article is "Medline Plus Encyclopedia: Fetal Development."
15. Keith L. Moore, "A Scientist's Interpretation of References to Embryology in the Qur'an," in *The Journal of Islamic Medical Association*, vol. 18, Jan–June 1986, pp.15–16; Khan, Israr Ahmad, *Qur'anic Studies: An Introduction* (Zaman Islam Media, 2000), p.22.
16. Ibn Ḥajar, *Taqrīb al-Tahdhīb*, p.385.
17. Ibn Ḥajar, *Tahdhīb al-Tahdhīb*, vol.2, p.254.
18. Al-Dhahbī, Muḥammad ibn Aḥmad, *Mizān al-Iʿtidāl fī Naqd al-Rijāl* (Beirut: Dār al-Maʿrifah, n.d.), vol.2, p.107.
19. Ibn Ḥajar, *Taqrīb al-Tahdhīb*, p.270.
20. Muslim ibn al-Ḥajjāj, *Ṣaḥīḥ* (Beirut: with al-Nawawī's commentary, Dār al-Maʿrifah, 1997), vol.8, "*Kitāb al-Qadar*," p.409, hadith no.6668.
21. Ibn Ḥajar, *Fatḥ al-Bārī*, vol.11, p.588.
22. Al-Bukhārī, *Ṣaḥīḥ*, vol.2, "*Kitāb Bad'u al-Khalq*," p.424, hadith no.3208.
23. Ibid., vol.4, "*Kitāb al-Tawḥīd*," pp.395–396, hadith no.7454.
24. Al-ʿAynī, Badr al-Dīn, *ʿUmdat al-Qārī Sharḥ Ṣaḥīḥ al-Bukhārī* (Beirut: Dār al-Kutub al-ʿIlmiyyah, 2001), vol.23, p.225.
25. Hamzah Muhammad Qasim, *Manār al-Qārī*, part 5, p.307.
26. Ibn Ḥajar, *Fatḥ al-Bārī*, vol.11, p.583.

27. See for detailed information: Al-Khair Abadi, *ʿUlūm al-Ḥadīth: Aṣīluhā wa Muʿāṣiruhā* (Malaysia: Dār al-Shākir, 2003), pp.119–120.
28. Al-Bukhārī, *Ṣaḥīḥ*, vol.2, "*Kitāb Bad'u al-Khalq*," p.424, hadith no.3208; "*Kitāb Aḥādīth al-Anbiyā'*," p.451, hadith no.3332; vol.4, "*Kitāb al-Qadar*," p.208; "*Kitāb al-Tawḥīd*," pp.395-396, hadith no.7454. These reports are recorded on the authority of ʿAbd Allah ibn Masʿūd. And for the reports on the authority of Anas ibn Mālik, vol.1, "*Kitāb al-Ḥayḍ*," p.119, hadith no.318; vol.2, "*Kitāb Aḥādīth al-Anbiyā'*," p.451, hadith no.3333; vol.4, "*Kitāb al-Qadar*," p.208, hadith no.6595.
29. Muslim, vol.8, "*Kitāb al-Qadar*," pp.407–411. Reports of Ibn Masʿūd are under hadith nos.6665–6666; those of Ḥudhayfah ibn Asīd are under hadith nos.6667–6671; and that of Anas ibn Mālik, is under hadith no.6672.
30. Aḥmad ibn Ḥanbal, *Musnad* (Beirut: Dār Iḥyā' al-Turāth al-ʿArabī, 1994), vol.4, p.561, hadith no.15649.
31. Al-Tirmidhī, *Al-Jāmiʿ al-Ṣaḥīḥ* (Beirut: Dār Iḥyā' al-Turāth al-ʿArabī, 1995), vol.4, p.448, hadith no.2144.
32. Al-Bukhārī, *Ṣaḥīḥ*, vol.4, "*Kitāb al-Daʿwāt*," p.161, hadith no.6344.
33. Abū Dāwūd, vol.1, "*Kitāb al-Ṣalāh*," hadith no.1551.
34. Al-Fayrūzābādī, vol.2, p.1705.
35. Abū Dāwūd, vol.3, "*Kitāb al-Adab*," p.336, hadith no.5116.
36. Al-Bukhārī, *Ṣaḥīḥ*, vol.4, "*Kitab al-Qadar*," p.208, hadith no.6595.
37. Al-Bukhārī, *Ṣaḥīḥ*, vol.4, "*Kitāb al-Qadar*," p.208.
38. Ibid., vol.3, "*Kitāb al-Nikāḥ*," p.357, hadith no.5076.
39. Ibid. p.375, hadith no.5149.
40. Ibid. p.356, hadith nos.5071, 5073–5075.
41. Ibn Ḥajar, *Fatḥ al-Bārī*, vol.11, p.598.
42. ʿAbdullah Yūsuf ʿAlī, *English Translation of the Qur'ān* (Madinah: King Fahd Complex for the Printing of the Qur'an, 1413 AH), p.1226.
43. Ibid., p.1664.
44. Al-Bukhārī, *Ṣaḥīḥ*, vol.4, "*Kitāb al-Qadar*," p.208, hadith no.6596.
45. Ibn Ḥajar, *Fatḥ al-Bārī*, vol.11, p.599.
46. Muslim, vol.8, "*Kitāb al-Qadar*," pp.414–415, hadith no.6681.
47. Al-Bukhārī, *Ṣaḥīḥ*, vol.4, "*Kitāb al-Qadar*," p.209, hadith no.6599.
48. Ibid., vol.1, "*Kitāb al-Janā'iz*," pp.416–417, hadith nos.1358 & 1359 and p.424, hadith no.1385.
49. Ibid., hadith no.6601.
50. Ibid., vol.2, "*Kitāb al-Buyūʿ*," p.100, hadith no.2140; "*Kitāb al-Shurūṭ*," p.76, hadith no.2723; vol.3, "*Kitāb al-Nikāḥ*," p.373,

hadith no.5144; pp.375–376, hadith no.5152.

51. Ibid. vol.1, "*Kitāb al-Janā'iz,*" p.396, hadith no.1284; vol.4, "*Kitāb al-Marḍā,*" p.26, hadith no.5655; vol.4, "*Kitāb al-Aymān wa al-Nudhūr,*" p.220, hadith no.6655; vol.4, "*Kitāb al-Tawḥīd,*" p.379, hadith no.7377; vol.4, "*Kitāb al-Tawḥīd,*" p.394, hadith no.7448.
52. Ibid., "*Kitāb al-Qadar,*" p.210, hadith no.6604.
53. Ibn Ḥajar, *Tahdhīb al-Tahdhīb*, vol.5, p.562.
54. Ibid., pp.561–562.
55. Al-Bukhārī, *Ṣaḥīḥ*, vol.2, "*Kitāb Bad'u al-Khalq,*" p.418, hadith no.3192.
56. Ibid., vol.4, "*Kitāb al-Qadar,*" p.210, hadith no.6605.
57. Ibid., vol.1, "*Kitāb al-Janā'iz,*" p.418, hadith no.1362; vol.3, "*Kitāb Tafsīr al-Qur'ān,*" p.324, hadith no.4945; p.325, hadith no.4946; p.325, hadith no.4947; pp.325–326, hadith no.4948; p.326, hadith no.4949; vol.4, "*Kitāb al-Adab,*" p.131–132, hadith no.6217; "*Kitāb al-Tawḥīd,*" p.417, hadith no.7552.
58. Ibid., "*Kitāb al-Qadar,*" p.210, hadith no.6606.
59. Ibid., "*Kitāb al-Maghāzī,*" p.136, hadith no.4203.
60. Ibid., vol.4, "*Kitāb al-Qadar,*" p.210, hadith no.6607.
61. Ibid., hadith no.6608.
62. Ibid., vol.4, "*Kitāb al-Aymān wa al-Nudhūr,*" pp.227–228, hadith no.6693.
63. Ibid., "*Kitāb al-Qadar,*" p.211, hadith no.6609.
64. Ibid., hadith no.6610.
65. Ibn Ḥajar, *Tahdhīb al-Tahdhīb*, vol.2, pp.77–78.
66. Al-Bukhārī, *Ṣaḥīḥ*, vol.2, "*Kitāb al-Jihād wa al-Siyar,*" p.356, hadith no.2992; vol.3, "*Kitāb al-Maghāzī,*" p.136, hadith no.4205; vol.4, "*Kitāb al-Daʿwāt,*" p.168, hadith no.6384; p.174, hadith no.6409; "*Kitāb al-Tawḥīd,*" p.381, hadith no.7386.
67. Ibid., vol.4, "*Kitāb al-Qadar,*" p.211, hadith no.6611.
68. Ibid., "*Kitāb al-Aḥkām,*" p.342, hadith no.7198.
69. Ibid., vol.4, "*Kitāb al-Qadar,*" pp.211–212, hadith no.6612.
70. Ibn Ḥajar, *Fatḥ al-Bārī*, vol.11, p.613.
71. Al-ʿAynī, *ʿUmdat al-Qārī*, vol.23, pp.241–242.
72. Ibn Ḥajar, *Fatḥ al-Bārī*, vol.11, p.614.
73. Al-Bukhārī, *Ṣaḥīḥ*, vol.4, "*Kitāb al-Qadar,*" p.212, hadith no.6613.
74. Ibn Ḥajar, *Fatḥ al-Bārī*, vol.11, pp.614–615.
75. Al-Bukhārī, *Ṣaḥīḥ*, vol.4, "*Kitāb al-Qadar,*" p.212, hadith no.6614.
76. Ibid., vol.2, "*Kitāb Aḥādīth al-Anbiyā',*" p.478–479, hadith no.3409; vol.3, "*Kitāb Tafsīr al-Qur'ān,*" p.260, hadith nos.4736 & 4738; vol.4, "*Kitāb al-Tawḥīd,*" p.407, hadith no.7515.
77. Ibn Ḥajar, *Fatḥ al-Bārī*, vol.11, p.622.

78. Ibid., p.621.
79. Ibid., p.623.
80. Al-Bukhārī, *Ṣaḥīḥ*, vol.4, "*Kitāb al-Qadar*," p.212, hadith no.6615.
81. Ibn Ḥajar, *Tahdhīb al-Tahdhīb*, vol.4, pp.488–489.
82. Al-Bukhārāī, *Ṣaḥīḥ*, vol.1, "*Kitāb Mawāqīt al-Ṣalāh*," p.271, hadith no.844; vol 4, "*Kitāb al-Daʿwāt*," p.159, hadith no.6330; vol.4, "*Kitāb al-Tamannī*," p.362, hadith no.7292.
83. Al-ʿAynī, *ʿUmdat al-Qārī*, vol.23, p.247.
84. Al-Bukhārī, *Ṣaḥīḥ*, vol.4, "*Kitāb al-Qadar*," p.212, hadith no.6616.
85. Ibid., "*Kitāb al-Daʿwāt*," p.162, hadith no.6347.
86. Ibid., p.213, hadith no.6617.
87. Ibid., "*Kitāb al-Aymān wa al-Nudhūr*," p.215, hadith no.6628; "*Kitāb al-Tawḥīd*," p.382, hadith no.7391.
88. Ibn Ḥajar, *Fatḥ al-Bārī*, vol.11, p.640.
89. Ibid., vol.4, "*Kitāb al-Qadar*," p.213, hadith no.6619.
90. Ibid, vol.2, "*Kitāb al-Anbiyā'*," pp.498–499, hadith no.3474; vol.4, "*Kitāb al-Ṭibb*," p.42, hadith no.5734.
91. Ibid., vol.4, "*Kitāb al-Qadar*," p.213, hadith no.6620.
92. Ibid., vol.2, "*Kitāb al-Jihād wa al-Siyar*," p.316, hadith no.2837; p.367, hadith no.3034; vol.3, "*Kitāb al-Maghāzī*," p.116, hadith no.4104; vol.4, "*Kitāb al-Tamannī*," p.351, hadith no.7236.

BIBLIOGRAPHY

Abū Dāwūd, Sulaymān ibn al-Ashʿath, *Sunan* (Beirut: Dār al-Kutub al-ʿIlmiyyah, 1996).

Abu Shahbah, Muhammad, *Al-Isrā'iliyyāt wa al-Mawḍūʿāt fī al-Tafsīr* (Cairo: Majmaʿ al-Buḥūth al-Islāmiyyah, 1973).

Abu Zahw, Muhammad, *Al-Ḥadīth wa al-Muḥaddithūn*, 1st edn.(Cairo: 1958).

ʿAlī, ʿAbdullah Yūsuf, *English Translation of the Qur'ān* (Madinah: King Fahd Complex for the Printing of the Qur'an, 1413 AH).

Al-Ālūsī, al-Sayyid Maḥmūd, *Rūḥ al-Maʿānī* (Beirut: Dār Iḥyā' al-Turāth al-ʿArabī, 1999).

Amin, Ahmad, *Fajr al-Islām*, 5th edn.(Cairo: Compilation, Translation, and Publication Committee Press, 1930).

Asad, Muhammad, *The Message of the Qur'ān* (Gibraltar: Dar al-Andalus, 1980).

Al-Aṣfahānī, al-Rāghib, *Al-Mufradāt fī Gharīb al-Qur'ān* (Beirut: Dār al-Ma ʿrifah, 1998).

Al-ʿAsqalānī, Ibn Ḥajar, Aḥmad ibn ʿAlī, *Hadiyy al-Sārī* (Riyadh: Dār al-Salām, n.d.).

AlʿAynī, Badr al-Dīn, *ʿUmdat al-Qārī: Sharḥ Ṣaḥīḥ al-Bukhārī* (Beirut: Dār al-Kutub al-ʿIlmīyyah, 2001).

Al-Bukhārī, Muḥammad ibn Ismāʿīl, *Ṣaḥīḥ* (Beirut: Dār Iḥyā' al-Turāth al-ʿArabī, 1400 AH).

Al-Dhahbī, Muḥammad ibn Aḥmad, *Mizān al-Iʿtidāl fī Naqd al-Rijāl* (Beirut: Dār al-Maʿrifah, n.d.).

Al-Dumayni, Misfir Ghuram Allah, *Maqāyīs Naqd Mutūn al-Sunnah* (Riyadh: self published by the author, 1403 AH).

Fallatah, Umar ibn Hasan Uthman, *Al-Waḍʿ fī al-Ḥadīth* (Damascus: Maktabah al-Ghazāly, 1981).

Al-Farāhīdī, al-Khalīl ibn Aḥamd, *Kitāb al-ʿAyn* (Beirut: Dār Iḥya' al-Turāth al-ʿArabī, 2001).

Al-Fayrūzābādī, Muḥammad ibn Yaʿqūb, *Al-Qāmūs al-Muḥīṭ* (Beiryt: Dār Iḥyā' al-Turāth al-ʿArabī, 1997).

Hamzah Muhammad Qasim, *Manār al-Qārī* (Damascus: Maktabah Dār al-Bayān, 1990).

The Holy Bible (Authorized King James Version, The Gideons International, 1978).

Ibn al-ʿArabī, Abū Bakr, *Aḥkām al-Qur'ān* (Beirut: Dār al-Kutub al-ʿIlmiyyah, 1996).

Ibn al-Athīr, ʿIz al-Dīn, *Al-Kāmil fī al-Tārīkh* (Beirut: Dār Iḥyā' al-Turāth al-ʿArabī, 1989).

________, *Al-Kāmil fī al-Tārīkh* (Beirut: Dār Iḥyā' al-Turāth al-ʿArabī, 1994).

________, *Usd al-Ghābah* (Beirut: Dār al-Ma ʿrifah, 1997).

Ibn ʿAbd al-Barr, Yūsuf ibn ʿAbd Allah, *Al-Istīʿāb fī Maʿrifat al-Aṣḥāb* (Beirut: Dār al-Kutub al-ʿIlmiyyah, 1995).

Ibn Anas, Mālik, *Al-Muwaṭṭa'* (Beirut: Dār Iḥyā' al-Turāth al-ʿArabī, 1985).

Ibn Ḥajar, *Fatḥ al-Bārī* (Riyadh: Maktabah Dār al-Salām, 2000).

________, *Taqrīb al-Tahdhīb* (Beirut: Dār al-Maʿrifah, 1997).

________, *Hadiyy al-Sārī* (Riyadh: Dār al-Salām, n.d.).

Ibn Ḥanbal, Aḥmad, *Musnad* (Beirut: Dār Iḥyā' al-Turāth al-ʿArabī, 1994).

Ibn Hishām, Abū Muḥammad ʿAbd al-Mālik, *Al-Sīrah al-Nabawiyyah* (Beirut: Dār Iḥyā' al-Turāth al-ʿArabī, 1997).

Ibn al-Jawzī, ʿAbd al-Raḥmān ibn ʿAlī, "*Kitāb al-Mawḍūʿāt*" (Beirut: Dār al-Kutub al-ʿIlmiyyah, 1995).

________, *Zād al-Masīr fī ʿIlm al-Tafsīr* (Beirut: Dār al-Kutub al-ʿIlmiyyah, 2002).

Ibn Kathīr, Abū al-Fidā Ismāʿīl, *Al-Bāʿith al-Ḥathīth*, 4th edn. Ahmad Muhammad Shakir, ed. (Beirut: Dār al-Kutub al-ʿIlmiyyah, 1994).

________, *Al-Bidāyah wa al-Nihāyah* (Beirut: Dār al-Maʿrifah, 1997).

________, *Tafsīr al-Qur'ān al-ʿAẓīm* (Beirut: Dār Iḥyā' al-Turāth al-ʿArabī, 2000).

Ibn Mājah, Muḥammad ibn Yazīd al-Qazwīnī, *Sunan* (Beirut: Dār al-Maʿrifah, 1997: along with the commentary of al-Sindī).

Ibn al-Qayyim, Muḥammad ibn Abū Bakr, *Al-Manār al-Munīf fī al-Ṣaḥīḥ wa al-Ḍaʿīf*. Abd al-Fattah Abu Ghuddah, ed. (Ḥalab: Maktab al-Maṭbūʿāt al-Islāmiyyah, 1982).

Ibn Saʿd, *Al-Ṭabaqāt al-Kubrā* (Beirut: Dār Iḥyā' al-Turāth al-ʿArabī, 1996)

Ibn Shuʿayb, Aḥmad, *Al-Sunan al-Kubrā* (Beirut: Dār al-Kutub al-ʿIlmiyyah, 1991).

Islahi, Amin Ahsan, *Tadabbur-i-Qur'ān* (Delhi: Taj Company, 1997).

Kamil Muhammad, Muhammad Uwaydah, *Aʿlām al-Fuqahā' wa al-Muḥaddithīn: Al-Imām al-Bukhārī* (Beirut: Dār al-Kutub al-ʿIlmiyyah, 1992).

Kamil Muhammad, *Aʿlām al-Fuqahā' wa al-Muḥaddithīn: Muslim ibn al-Ḥajjāj* (Beirut: Dār al-Kutub al-ʿIlmiyyah, 1995).

Al-Khair Abadi, Muhammad Abul Laith, *Takhrīj al-Ḥadīth: Nash'atuhu wa Manhajuhu* (Kuala Lumpur: Dār al-Shākir, 1999).

________, *ʿUlūm al-Ḥadīth: Aṣīluhā wa Muʿāṣiruhā* (Malaysia: Dār al-Shākir, 2003).

Khan, Israr Ahmad, *Qur'anic Studies: An Introduction* (Zaman Islam Media, 2000).

Mawdūdī, Sayyid Abul A'lā, *Tafhīm al-Qur'ān* (Lahore: Idara Tarjuman al-Qur'ān, 1997).

Moore, Keith L., "A Scientist's Interpretation of References to Embryology in the Qur'an," in *The Journal of Islamic Medical Association.*

Al-Muʿjam al-Wasīṭ. Ibrahim Mustafa and others, eds. (Istanbul: Al-Maktabah al-Islāmiyyah, n.d.).

Muslim, ibn al-Ḥajjāj al-Qushayrī, *Ṣaḥīḥ* (Beirut: Dār Iḥyā' al-Turāth al-ʿArabī, 2000).

________, *Ṣaḥīḥ* (Beirut: with al-Nawawī's commentary, Dār al-Maʿrifah, 1997).

Al-Nasa'ī, Ahmad ibn Shuʿayb, *Sunan* (Beirut: Dār al-Kutub al-ʿIlmīyyah, 1991)

Al-Nawawī, Muḥy al-Dīn, *Al-Minhāj: Sharḥ Ṣaḥīḥ Muslim* (Beirut: Dār al-Maʿrifah, 1997).

Al-Qasṭalānī, Aḥmad ibn Muḥammad, *Irshād al-Sārī li Sharḥ Ṣaḥīḥ al-Bukhārī* (Beirut: Dār al-Fikr, 1305 AH).

Al-Qurṭubī, Muḥammad ibn Aḥmad, *Al-Jāmiʿ li Aḥkām al-Qur'ān* (Beirut: Dār al-Kutub al-ʿIlmiyyah, 2000).

________, *Al-Jāmiʿ li Aḥkām al-Qur'ān* (Beirut: Dār al-Kutub al-ʿIlmiyyah, 2000).

Qutb, Sayyid, *Fī Ẓilāl al-Qur'ān* (Cairo: Dār al-Shurūq, 1996).

Al-Rāzī, Fakhr al-Dīn, *Mafātīḥ al-Ghayb* (Beirut: Dār Iḥyā' al-Turāth al-ʿArabī, 1997).

Al-Salih, Subhi, *ʿUlūm al-Ḥadīth wa Muṣṭalaḥuhu* (Beirut: Dār al-ʿIlm li al-Malāyīn, 1959).

Al-Suyūṭī, Jalāl al-Dīn, *Tadrīb al-Rāwī* (Beirut: Dār al-Kutub al-ʿIlmiyyah, 1989).

Tahan, Mahmud, *Taysīr Muṣṭalaḥ al-Ḥadīth* (Kuwait: Maktabah Dār al-Turāth, 1984).

Al-Tirmidhī, Muḥammad ibn ʿĪsā, *Sunan* (Beirut: Dār Iḥyā' al-Turāth al-ʿArabī, 1995).

________, *Al-Jāmiʿ al-Ṣaḥīḥ* (Beirut: Dār Iḥyā' al-Turāth al-ʿArabī, 1995).

Al-Zamakhsharī, Maḥmūd ibn ʿUmar, *Al-Kashshāf* (Beirut: Dār al-Kutub al-ʿIlmiyyah, 1995).

Al-Zarkashī, Badr al-Dīn, *Al-Ijābah*. Said al-Afghani, ed. (Beirut: al-Maktab al-Islāmī, 1980).

INDEX

Abadi, al-Khair, 33, 34, 76–77
Abbasid Dynasty, *aḥādīth* fabricated to please rulers, 20
aberrant narrations, 33–35
ablution, 73
abrogation of Hadith, 73
Abū Bakr al-Ṣiddīq
election of, 100–103, 106–107; verification of Hadith texts, 28–29
Abū Burdah, 65
Abū al-Dardā', 129
Abū Ḥanīfah, 11
examination of Hadith with Qur'anic text, 50
Abū Hurayrah, 158–59
Abu Shahbah, Muhammad, 2–3
Abū Sufyān, 119, 123–25
Abu Zahw, Muhammad, 2
Abū al-Zinād, 23, 30
Adam, 61–63, 90, 180–82
addition (*ziyādah*) in Hadith texts, 34, 42
admiration, as indication of fabrication, 135–36
adultery, stoning as punishment, 104–106
Aḥmad ibn Ḥanbal, xxi, 11, 15, 23
ʿĀ'ishah bint Abī Bakr
examination of Hadith with Qur'anic text, 48–49; fabricated reports on, 5; on evil omens, 70–71; rational examination of Hadith, 73–76; textual analysis of Hadith, 40; trick played on the Prophet, 112–16
ʿalaqah in embryonic development, 145–46
al-Albānī, Nāṣir al-Dīn, 42–43
alcohol, punishment for drinking, 121
Ali, Abdullah Yusuf, 160
ʿAlī ibn Abī Ṭālib
false attributions to, 29; fabricated reports on, 5–6; Hadith fabrication during Caliphate of, 3
Allah
as controller of hearts, 185; exclusive rights of, 182–83; seeking refuge with, 184–85
al-Ālūsī, 52, 57
Amin, Ahmad, 2
ʿAmrū ibn al-ʿĀṣ, ʿAbd Allāh, 129
ant nest, burning of, 116–17
Asad, Muhammad, 110
al-Aṣfahānī, al-Rāghib, 141

Asqalan, fabricated Hadith praising, 20
authentication of Hadith, xvi-xxi. *See also* Hadith; fabrications; Hadith reporters; textual examination of Hadith
Āyāt al-Rajm, 101, 104–106
al-ʿAynī, Badr al-Dīn, 114, 148
Ayyūb ibn Mudrik, 19

backbiting in investigations of Hadith reporters, xxi, 23
al-Balkhī, Muḥammad ibn Shujāʿ, 7
Banū Qaynuqāʿ, 120
Basra, fabricated Hadith praising, 20
bath, ritual, 73
bayān (interpretation), xiii, 47
Bilāl, *adhān* of, xvii–xviii
biographies of Hadith reporters, 25–26, 30
blastocyst in embryonic development, 145
blind adherence to Hadith, xv
breastfeeding an adult, 87–89
al-Bukhārī, Muḥammad ibn Ismāʿīl
compilation of *al-Jāmiʿ al-Ṣaḥīḥ*, 27, 31; predestination, chapter on in *al-Jāmiʿ al-Ṣaḥīḥ*, 139; role of in Hadith authentication, 34–37

camel urine, as medicine, 78–80
castration, 159
chain of narrators. *See sanad* sytem.
character, integrity of in Hadith narrators, 32–33
charity, as extending lifespan, 153
cities, fabricated *aḥādīth* praising, 20–21, 137–38
commercial propaganda as cause of Hadith fabrication, 12–14
Companions
practice of, referring to when examining Hadith, 44; use of textual examination, 39–40
condemnation of certain sects as indication of fabrication, 134–35
confusion (*iḍtirāb*) in Hadith texts, 34, 41
congregational prayer, 94–96
consensus of the Ummah, 44
continuity of the chain of narration, 32
conversion, forced, 57–59
correction of narrations, xix
creation, time take for process of, 63–64
cupping, 83
cursed tree, 179–80

al-Dārquṭnī, 37
David, 123
al-Dawliyy, Abū al-Aswad, 162–64
days of the week, 138
death
certainty of, 166–67; remaining patient during an epidemic, 185–87; wailing over the dead, 73–74
delousing of the Prophet, 96–99
destiny, predetermination of, 53–55, 139–40. *See* also *al-Qadar*
differentiation of the embryo, 145
disapprobation as indication of fabrication, 135
divorce, 166
duʿā’ (supplications), 187
al-Dumayni, Misfir Gurm Allah, 39

embryo, gestation of, 145
epidemics, 185–87

eunuchs, 93–94
evaluation of Hadith. *See* textual evaluation of Hadith
Eve, 66–69
evil omens, 69–71

fabrication
commercial propaganda as cause of, 12–14; compilations of fabricated Hadith, 27; disapprobation as indication of, 135; excessive admiration as indication of, 135–36; excessive reward and punishment as indications of, 132–34, 136–37; historical background, 2–3; inimical missions against Islam as cause of, 6–9; jurisprudential rivalry as cause of, 11–12; naming forgers of Hadith, 24–25; overenthusiasm to serve Islam as cause of, 17–19; pleasing rulers as cause of, 19–21; political movements as causes of, 3–6; probability of, xx; rich, denunciation of as indication of, 134; sects, condemnation of indication of, 134–35; of storytellers, 14–17; terms defined, 1–2; theological schools of thought as reason for, 9–11; (*See also* textual examination of Hadith; Hadith; Hadith reporters)
faith, seeing as from Allah, 187–88
al-Farāhīdī, 141
fate, resigning oneself to, 170. *See also al-Qadar*; predestination; destiny
fathers, criticism from son, 181–82
Fāṭimah, residence of, 120
al-Fayrūzābādī, 141, 154
fiṭrah (natural innocence), 164–65
food, putrefaction of, 66–67
forced conversions, 57–59
foster relationship, establishing through breast feeding, 87–89
free-mixing, damaging effects of, 165–66
Friday Sermon of ʿUmar ibn al-Khaṭṭāb, 100–103

genetic engineering, 145
good deeds, as extending lifespan, 153
guidance, seeing as the will of Allah, 187–88

Hadith
aberrant narrations, 33–35; authentication from a textual perspective, 37–44; authenticity of, xvi–xxi; commercial propaganda as cause of fabrication of, 12–14; compilations of genuine traditions, 26–27; components of, 28; contemporary approaches to, xiv–xvi; contemporary relevance, xix–xx; contradictions, resolving, 77ff; correction of, xix; evaluation of the chain and text, 31–35 (*See also sanad* system); as explaining the Qur'an, xiii–xiv; fabricated reports (*See* fabrication); historical analysis of, 118; historical background of fabrication of, 2–3 (*See also* fabrication); inimical missions against Islam as cause of fabrication of, 6–9; interpretation of, 140–41; jurisprudential rivalry as cause of fabrication of, 11–12;

narrator reliability, xix (*See also* Hadith reporters); over-enthusiasm to serve Islam as cause of fabrication of, 17–19; pleasing rulers as cause of fabrication of, 19–21; political movements as causes of fabrication of, 3–6; position of Qur'an in relation to, 46–48; probability of fabrication, xx; reliability of sources, 22–23; *sanad* system, development of, 21–22; sanctity of, xxi; textual conflict, xviii (*See also* textual examination of Hadith); theological differences as reason for fabrication of, 9–11

Hadith reporters
biographies of, 25–26; controversy over position of, xvii; integrity of character, 32–33; investigation into characters of, xxi; investigation of, 23–25; precision of reporting, 33; reliability of, xix; terms used to describe fabricators, 1

Hadith scholars
al-Bukhārī, 35–37; Muslim ibn al-Ḥajjāj, 37; use of textual examination, 39–40

Ḥafṣah bint ʿUmar, 112–13
hands, raising in salah, 11–12
Hārūn al-Rashīd, 19
Ḥassān ibn Thābit, 84
hearts, as under the disposal of Allah, 185
Hell, place reserved in, 168–71
heretical groups and fabrication of Hadith, 6–9 (*see also* fabrication)
historical analysis of Hadith, 118
honey, 112–16
horses, bad luck in, 69–71
houses, bad luck in, 69–71
hypocrisy, 172–73

Ibn ʿAbbās, ʿAbd Allāh
on the 'cursed tree', 179–80; examination of Hadith with Qur'anic text, 50; on reliable sources, 22, 29; on women as best in Ummah, 112

Ibn ʿAbd al-Barr, 62–63
Ibn Abī ʿArūbah, Saʿīd, 30
Ibn Abī al-ʿArjā', ʿAbd al-Karīm, 7
Ibn ʿAdīs, as first fabricator of Hadith, 2
Ibn ʿAqīl, 52
Ibn al-ʿArabī, Qāḍī Abū Bakr, 52, 125
Ibn al-Ashʿath, Sulaymān, 27
Ibn Baṭṭāl, 56, 178
Ibn Ḥajar, 58, 114, 123, 161
Ibn Ḥazm, 124
Ibn Isḥāq, 122
Ibn al-Jawzī, 19, 38, 52
Ibn Kathīr, 31, 41
Ibn Khuzaymah, 60
Ibn Maʿīn, Yaḥyā, 15–16
Ibn al-Qayyim
classification of Hadith as fabrications on the basis of their content, 135; examination of Hadith with Qur'anic text, 51; textual analysis of Hadith, 38–39

Ibn Saʿīd, Mughīrah, 7
Ibn Saʿīd, Muḥammad, 8–9
Ibn Saba', as fabricator of Hadith, 2–3, 7
Ibn al-Ṣalāḥ, 124
Ibn Sīrīn, Muḥammad, 22, 29
Ibn Taymiyyah, 141–42

Ibn Umm Maktūm, ʿAbd Allāh, *adhān* of, xvii–xviii
Ibrāhīm (Prophet), 51–53
Ibrāhīm ibn Jurayj, 14
ʿ*illah* (deficiency) in Hadith, 33
immutability of destiny, question of, 160
ʿImrān ibn Ḥuṣayn, 162–64
infidelity, 67–69
innocence, natural, 164–65
insertion (*idrāj*) in Hadith texts, 34, 41
intellectual deficiency in women, 108–12
intercession of the Prophet, 89–92
inversion in Hadith texts, 34, 41
Isḥāq ibn Rāhwahy, 36
Islahi, Amin Ahsan, 52, 105, 115
Islam
  excessive zeal in and Hadith fabrication, 17–19; forced conversions, 57–59
Isrā'iliyyāt, 60

Jabarite sect, 10, 152
Jeddah, fabricated Hadith praising, 20
Jerusalem, 122–23
Jesus, 91
jizyah tax, 58
Judeo-Christian traditions, 60
jurisprudence
  rivalry in as cause of Hadith fabrication, 11–12; use of textual examination, 43–44
al-Jurjānī, 23

Kaʿbah, building of, 122–23
al-Khaṭṭābī, 69
khilāfah, and freedom of thought, 149–50
Khubayb ibn ʿAdī, 119–20
Khurasan, fabricated Hadith praising, 21
khuṭbah of ʿUmar ibn al-Khattab, 100–103
al-Kirmānī, 57, 141, 160
Kitāb al-Qadar, 139–40. *See also al-Qadar*; predestination.

lifespan
  extending with charity and good deeds, 153; praying for extension of, 77–78
logical analogy, use of in examining Hadith, 44
Lot, 118

Maʿbūr, 93–94
major sins, 100
Makkah
  building of the Kaʿbah, 122–23; migration from, 121–22
Mālik ibn Anas, 11, 27
mardūd (rejected) reports, 1
Māriyyah, 93–94
marriage, 159, 165–66
al-Masjid al-Aqṣā, 122–23
matn (text) of Hadith, 28
Mawdudi, 53
Maymūnah, 125–26
al-Māzarī, 62
medicine, *aḥādīth* fabricated to promote, 13
Messengers, sent as guides, 163–64
minor pilgrimage, 75
minor sins, 177–78
mispronunciation (*taṣḥīf*) in Hadith texts, 34, 42
moderation
  prophetic approach to, 128–30; Qur'anic stance on, 127–28

Moor, Keith, 146
moral responsibility, 143
Moses, 59–63, 91–93, 180–82
Muʿāwiyah ibn Abī Sufyān, fabricated reports on, 4–5
muḍghah in embryonic development, 145–46
Muqawqis, 93–94
Murji'ite sect, Hadith fabrication and, 10
Mūsā ibn Masʿūd, 167–68
Muslim ibn al-Ḥajjāj, 27, 31
  role of in Hadith authentication, 37
Muʿtazilite school, 57
al-Muwaṭṭa', 27

al-Nahdī, Bayān ibn Samʿān, 7
narrators. *See* Hadith reporters
al-Nasā'ī, Aḥmad ibn Shuʿayb, 27
Naṣībayn, fabricated Hadith praising, 20
natural destiny, 149–50
natural innocence, 164–65
al-Nawawī, 61, 66
Noah, 90–91
nuṭfah in embryonic development, 145–46

oaths, in court cases, 76–77
omens, 69–71
omniscience of Allah, 150

Paradise
  entry into, 56–57; place reserved in, 168–71
parent-child relationship, 181
patience at time of death, 166–67
perfume, using while in pilgrim's dress, 74–75
plagues, 185–87
poetry, apparent condemnation of, 83–84
political movements as causes of Hadith fabrication, 3–6
prayer
  raising hands in, 11–12; supererogatory, 132
precision of report, maintaining, xvii–xviii
predetermination of destiny, 53–55, 139–40. *See also al-Qadar*
Prophet Muhammad
  age of, 121; mission of, xii
protection of Allah, 176–77
punishment, excessive, as indication of fabrication, 132–34
putrefaction of food, 66–67

al-Qadar
  definitions of, 141–43; determination of lifespan, sustenance and final position in womb, 148–49; exclusive rights of Allah, 182–83; human destiny, 156–57; immutability of destiny, question of, 160; natural destiny, 149–50; predetermined end result, 168–71; prefixing of destiny in the mother's womb, 144; preordainment, 158–60; role of man, predestination of, 161–64; seeing one's guidance as the Will of Allah, 187–88; sexual liaisons, predetermination of, 177–79; snatching others' rights, prohibition of, 165–66; suicide, 171–73
Qadarite sect, 10, 152
Qasim, Hamzah Muhammad, 141
al-Qāsim ibn ʿUbayd Allah, 22

Qur'an
excessive rewards for reading found in fabricated Hadith, 136–37; moderation, 127–28; position of in relation to Hadith, xiii–xiv, 46–48
al-Qurṭubī, 52
Qutb, Sayyid, 53

al-Rabīᶜ ibn Ṣabīḥ, 30
al-Rajm, Āyāt, 101, 104–106
al-Rāzī, al-Fakhr, 53
refuge, seeking with Allah, 184–85
rejected (*mardūd*) reports, 1
rejecters of Hadith, xiv–xv
religious deficiency in women, 108–12
remembrance of Allah, 176
reward, excessive, as indication of fabrication, 132–34, 136–37
rich, denunciation of as indication of fabrication, 134
role of man, predestination of, 161–64

Saᶜd ibn Ibrāhīm, 23
Saᶜd ibn ᶜUbādah, 106–107
saᶜīd (felicitous), alternative meanings of the term, 154–55
Ṣafīyyah, 113
Sahlah bint Suhayl, 87–89
salah, raising hands in, 11–12
ṣalāh al-tasbīḥ, 130–32
al-Salih, Subhi, 3
Sālim, 87–89
Salmān al-Fārsī, 129
al-Samᶜānī, 58
sanad system
development of, 21–22, 28–31; evaluation of the chain and text, 31–35; reliability of sources, 22–23; *sanad* and *matn*, defined, 28; terms used to describe fabricators, 1
sermon of ᶜUmar ibn al-Khaṭṭāb, 100–103
sexual liaisons, predetermination of, 177–79
al-Shafāᶜah (intercession), Hadith of, 89–92
al-Shāfiᶜī, Muḥammad ibn Idrīs, 11, 50–51
shaqiyy (damned), alternative meanings of term, 154–55
Shuᶜbah ibn al-Ḥajjāj, 23
shudhūdh (abberant) Hadith narrations, 33–35
ṣiddīq (paragon of truth), 51
sins
avoiding, 99–100; transference of, 64–65
slandering one's slave, indictment for, 80–82
slaves, indictment for slandering, 80–82
soft-heartedness, 166–67
solemn vows, 174–75
sons, criticising fathers, 181–82
stoning to death, 101, 104–106
storytellers and Hadith fabrication, 14–17
suicide, 171–73
Sulaymān, 123
supererogatory prayers, 132
al-Suyūṭī, 41

al-Ṭalkānī, Muḥammad ibn al-Qāsim, 10
al-tasbīḥ, ṣalāh, 130–32
Ṭāus ibn Kaysān, 23, 30
terminology describing fabricated reports, 1–2

textual conflict between Hadith, xviii
textual examination of Hadith
al-Dumayni's research, 39; among Hadith scholars, 40–43; among jurists, 43–44; among the Companions, 39–40; Ibn al-Jawzī's contribution to, 38; Ibn al-Qayyim's contribution to, 38–39
al-Thaqafī, al-Mukhtār, 6
theology, differences in as cause of Hadith fabrication, 9–11
al-Ṭībī, 63
al-Tirmidhī, Muḥammad ibn ʿĪsā, 27
towns, unnecessary praise for in fabricated Hadith, 137–38

ʿUmar ibn ʿAbd al-ʿAzīz, 65
ʿUmar ibn al-Khaṭṭāb
examination of Hadith with Qur'anic text, 50; Friday sermon of, 100–103; on Abū Bakr's election, 103–104; stoning the adulterer, 104–106; verification of Hadith texts, 29
Umm Ḥabībah, 123–25
Umm Salamah, 109–10
al-Umri, Akram Diya, 2
urine of camels, as medicine, 78–80
ʿUthmān ibn ʿAffān
assassination of, 3–4; fabrication of Hadith in Caliphate of, 2

vows, solemn, 174–75

wailing over the dead, 73–74
al-Walīd ibn ʿUqbah, 121
war, Islam not spread by, 57–59
wine, punishment for drinking, 121
witnesses, taking oaths from, 76–77
Witr salah, 75
womb, inscription of destiny in, 156–57
women, apparent intellectual and religious deficiency in, 108–12
women, bad luck in, 69–71
Yazīd ibn Muʿāwiyah, 135
Zaqqūm, tree of, 179–80
Zaynab bint Jaḥsh, 119
zygote in embryonic development, 145